UNDERSTANDING AND USING ENGLISH GRAMMAR

BETTY SCHRAMPFER AZAR

PRENTICE-HALL, INC.
Englewood Cliffs, New Jersey   07632

Library of Congress Cataloging in Publication Data

Azar, Betty Schrampfer, (date)
   Understanding and using English grammar.

   Includes index.
   1. English language—Text books for foreigners.
I. Title.
PE1128.A97   428.2'4   80-16749
ISBN 0-13-936492-7

Printed in the United States of America

10 9 8 7 6 5

Editorial/production supervision
    and interior design by Barbara Alexander
Cover design by Saiki Design Inc.
Manufacturing buyer: Harry P. Baisley

PRENTICE-HALL INTERNATIONAL, INC., *London*
PRENTICE-HALL OF AUSTRALIA PTY. LIMITED, *Sydney*
PRENTICE-HALL OF CANADA, LTD., *Toronto*
PRENTICE-HALL OF INDIA PRIVATE LIMITED, *New Delhi*
PRENTICE-HALL OF JAPAN, INC., *Tokyo*
PRENTICE-HALL OF SOUTHEAST ASIA PTE. LTD., *Singapore*
WHITEHALL BOOKS LIMITED, *Wellington, New Zealand*

To my mother,
FRANCES NIES SCHRAMPFER
and my father,
WILLIAM H. SCHRAMPFER

Contents

3

Verb Tenses   62

The Passive   123

Modal Auxiliaries—I   144

Modal Auxiliaries—II   164

Gerunds and Infinitives–I   182

Adjective Clauses   209

PART II Reduction of Adjective Clauses
to Adjective Phrases **226**

Noun Clauses 232

Conjunctions 257

Adverb Clauses and Related Structures—I:
Time and Cause and Effect 277

PART I Adverb Clauses **277**

Adverb Clauses and Related Structures—II: Opposition and Condition   301

Comparisons   319

Conditional Sentences   343

Gerunds and Infinitives—II   364

APPENDIX

Basic Grammar Terminology   382

APPENDIX 2

Preposition Combinations 387

APPENDIX 3

Guide for Correcting Compositions 392

Index 395

Preface

Understanding and Using English Grammar is a developmental skills text for intermediate through advanced students of English as a second language. It presents, in terms easily accessible to students, the forms, meanings, and usage levels (colloquial through very formal) of basic structures in English grammar. The presentations are accompanied by oral and written exercises of many types and purposes: the exercises range from simple manipulation to situational and idiomatic usage, from controlled response to open communicative interaction. The contexts in the exercises are at times directed toward university students but are, for the most part, of interest to any adult.

ACKNOWLEDGMENTS

I wish to express my gratitude to Barbara Matthies for her detailed examination of early versions of the manuscript. Her contributions to the quality of the text have been myriad. My gratitude also goes to Donald A. Azar for the support and encouragement he provided both personally and professionally during the several years it took to complete this project. Finally, I wish to express my great appreciation to my students through the years. This text has been written for them, because of them, and with their help.

Notes to the Teacher

1. In general, each chapter is organized around one area of structure, building from basic structures to related structures and usages. The text is designed to be taught in the order in which it is presented; however, the integration of material is not so extensive as to preclude your rearranging the order of presentation to suit your purposes and the needs of the class.

2. For the most part, charts consisting of examples accompanied by explanations precede exercises. The amount of preparation a class needs prior to doing an exercise depends upon the level of the class. With intermediate students, it is usually desirable for you to discuss the grammar charts in class as well as to bring your own examples to class. With an advanced group, you may wish to assign the charts for out-of-class use and to proceed directly to the exercises in class, answering questions and discussing pertinent points as they arise.

3. Some of the exercises are designated ORAL (BOOKS CLOSED). It is important that the students not look at their texts during these exercises, no matter how much they might want to. Even intermediate students should soon learn to concentrate on what you are saying and respond quickly. ("Mind-writing" should be discouraged; instead, the students should be encouraged to open their mouths and see what happens. A mistake is not of earthshaking importance.) Be flexible in the responses you accept. The main criterion is whether or not the student has understood what you said and is producing the target structure competently and communicatively. Minor changes in wording are not important. Use the ORAL (BOOKS CLOSED) exercises freely. In many of these exercises, the entries are not intended

to be "read as is," but rather are intended to prompt your mind as you engage your students (individually, not chorally) in short exchanges. Put entries into particular contexts where possible, as though you were initiating a conversation; pursue interesting responses, grammar aside; add entries that are directly relevant to your class and the here-and-now classroom context; delete irrelevant entries; encourage the students to use the exercises for out-of-class practice; use part of an exercise one day and part another day if you wish; return to the exercises from previously covered chapters for quick reviews at the beginning of a class period.

The symbol(. . .) indicates that you are to supply the name of a class member. Place and time expressions are often in parentheses, indicating that you are to supply an expression relevant to the people in your class.

The exercises designated ORAL are to be done with books open but require no writing and no preparation.

4. In many of the exercises there is often more than one possible response. Differences between two (or more) viable responses are opportunities for discussion. At times an exercise entry may involve a difference in meaning: *In her lifetime she has never seen snow.* versus *In her lifetime she never saw snow.* At other times the difference lies in usage level: *He's taller than I.* versus *He's taller than me.* Sometimes the difference may involve comparing a strictly grammatically correct response with an idiomatic or situationally appropriate response: *What do you call yourself?* versus *What is your name?*

5. Some of the exercises are designated WRITTEN. The intention is for the students to use their own paper and submit these exercises to you. Some of the WRITTEN exercises require sentence completion, but for the most part they are designed to produce short informal compositions. Generally the topics or tasks concern aspects of the students' own lives in order to encourage free and relatively effortless communication as the students practice their writing skills. While a course in English rhetoric is beyond the scope of this text, many of the elements of such are included and may be developed and emphasized according to your purposes.

APPENDIX 3 presents a system for marking errors so that students may make their own corrections and so that you may mark papers quickly and efficiently.

6. One of the intentions of the text has been to intersperse topics of interest throughout the exercises to stimulate short discussions. When possible, take time in class to pursue these topics: animal ecology, UFO's, male and female roles, dating customs, table manners, and so on.

7. The students' attention should be directed to APPENDIX 1, BASIC GRAMMAR TERMINOLOGY, at the beginning of the term.

8. APPENDIX 2 contains lists of the preposition combinations used in the exercises at the end of most of the chapters. However, the students should be encouraged to use their ears when completing the exercises rather than to consult a list. If you have time in class, play around with the preposition combinations,

especially the two-word verbs, so that the students have the opportunity to become comfortable with them and to use them creatively.

9. There is no separate unit on articles, but article usage is incorporated into various exercises. In addition, the intention is that you work on article usage daily in the students' oral and written productions, with a minimum of explanation (if any at all). The ORAL (BOOKS CLOSED) exercises provide especially good opportunities for dealing with problems of article usage.

10. An answer key is available. It contains the expected and/or possible responses to the exercises plus a few comments and suggestions.

Understanding and Using English Grammar is intended to be practical, useful, and fun—for both student and teacher. I hope you enjoy using it, and I would enjoy hearing from you.

BETTY S. AZAR

1

Questions

EXERCISE 1: Ask another member of the class a question about the given topic. With the rest of the class, discuss how this question might best be asked idiomatically (i.e., the way in which a native speaker might normally ask for this information in this situation).

> *Example:* age
> *Response:* How old are you?

1. name
2. spelling of name
3. date of birth
4. marital status
5. country of origin
6. capital city
7. location of country
8. population
9. government
10. weather
11. size of family
12. native language
13. other languages
14. length of time in (this city or country), both past and future
15. reason for coming here
16. field of study
17. residence at present
18. length of time at this residence
19. distance of residence from school
20. transportation to school
21. number of classes this term (semester, quarter, session, etc.)
22. names of courses
23. length of time spent in class each day
24. spare-time activities and interests
25. general well-being and adjustment to living here

EXERCISE 2:   Interview another student in the class. Take notes during the interview and then introduce this student to the rest of the class. (*Question for discussion:* Is it appropriate for you to ask another student for his/her date of birth?)

1-1   FORMS OF YES/NO AND INFORMATION QUESTIONS

A yes/no question = a question that may be answered by *yes* or *no*.
Question: Does he live in Chicago? *Answer:* Yes, he does. OR: No, he doesn't.

An information question = a question that asks for information by using a question word. *Question:* Where does he live? *Answer:* In Chicago.

	QUESTION WORD	AUXILIARY VERB	SUBJECT	MAIN VERB*		
(a) **She lives** there.		**Does**	she	live	there?	If the verb is in the simple present, use *does* (with *he, she, it*) or *do* (with *I, you, we, they*) in the question. If the verb is simple past, use *did*.
	Where	**does**	she	live?		
(b) **They live** there.		**Do**	they	live	there?	
	Where	**do**	they	live?		
(c) **He lived** there.		**Did**	he	live	there?	Notice: The main verb in the question is in its simple form; there is no final *-s* or *-ed*.
	Where	**did**	he	live?		
(d) **He is living** there.		**Is**	he	living	there?	If the verb has an auxiliary (a helping verb), the same auxiliary is used in the question. There is no change in the form of the main verb.
	Where	**is**	he	living?		
(e) **They have lived** there.		**Have**	they	lived	there?	
	Where	**have**	they	lived?		
(f) **Mary can live** there.		**Can**	Mary	live	there?	
	Where	**can**	Mary	live?		
(g) **He will be living** there.		**Will**	he	be living	there?	If the verb has more than one auxiliary, only the first auxiliary precedes the subject.
	Where	**will**	he	be living?		
(h) **John lives** there.		—	—	**Who**	lives	there?	If the question word is the subject, do not change the verb. Do not use *does, do,* or *did*.
(i) **Mary came.**		—	—	**Who**	came?	
(j) **They are** there.		**Are**	they		there?	*Be* in the simple present (*am, is, are*) and simple past (*was, were*) precedes the subject when *be* is the main verb.
	Where	**are**	they?			
(k) **Jim was** there.		**Was**	Jim		there?	
	Where	**was**	Jim?			

*See Appendix 1 for basic grammar terminology (*subject, verb,* etc.)

EXERCISE 3: For each of the following, make a yes/no question, then an information question using *where*.

    Example: They can stay there.
    Response: Can they stay there? Where can they stay?

1. She stays there. ————————————————————————
2. She is staying there. ————————————————————
3. She will stay there. —————————————————————
4. She is going to stay there. ——————————————————
5. They stayed there. ——————————————————————
6. They will be staying there. ——————————————————
7. They should stay there. ————————————————————
8. He has stayed there. —————————————————————
9. He has been staying there. ——————————————————
10. John is there. ————————————————————————
11. John will be there. ——————————————————————
12. John has been there.———————————————————————

    *(Repeat the exercise using **who**.)*

EXERCISE 4: Make questions for the given answers.

1.	Does he live in Chicago?	Yes, he lives in Chicago.
2.	Do you live in Chicago?	Yes, I live in Chicago.
3.	————————————	Yes, she took the bus.
4.	————————————	Yes, he wants to come with us.
5.	————————————	Yes, I am living in the dorm.
6.	————————————	Yes, Jack and Steve went home.
7.	————————————	Yes, her husband can speak English.
8.	————————————	Yes, they were invited to the party.
9.	————————————	Yes, I have met his wife.

10. _____   Yes, I have a bilingual dictionary.*

11. _____   Yes, he has a cold.

12. _____   Yes, he has seen that movie.

13. _____   Yes, there is a sharp knife in that drawer.†

14. _____   Yes, there are many problems.

15. _____   Yes, there will be another test.

EXERCISE 5—ORAL (BOOKS CLOSED): Make yes/no questions.

Example: He lives in Chicago.
Response: Does he live in Chicago?

Example: I studied last night.
Response: Did you study last night?

1. It rained last night.
2. (. . .) is sitting in the front row.
3. (. . .) has a mustache/beard.
4. (. . .) took the bus to school.
5. I drove to school.
6. There is going to be a quiz tomorrow.
7. I heard the news broadcast.
8. I have read today's paper.
9. (. . .) has bought his/her textbooks.
10. He/she bought them at the bookstore.
11. (. . .) has a briefcase.
12. (. . .) has curly hair.

13. I have written my parents a letter.
14. (. . .) speaks English.
15. I am going to study tonight.
16. (. . .) can speak English.
17. I would like to go on a picnic.
18. (. . .) will be in class tomorrow.
19. The students have been studying hard.
20. Mr. Smith taught this class last semester.
21. There will be another meeting tomorrow.
22. (. . .) did his/her homework.
23. (. . .) has a lot of friends.

---

*

(a) **Do** you **have** a car? (b) **Have** you a car? (*primarily British*)	In American English, a form of *do* is usually used in a question when the main verb is *have*. In British English, the use of *do* in this instance is not usual.
(c) **Have** you **heard** that story?	No form of *do* is used when *have* is an auxiliary verb. In (c), the main verb is *heard; have* is an auxiliary verb.

†In a question, *there* is in the subject position: *Is there a book on the table?*

24. (. . .) went to the library last
    night.
25. (. . .) gave the correct answer.
26. I have met (. . .).

27. Class begins at (nine) tomorrow.
28. This building has a fire escape.
29. (. . .) has brought his/her books
    to class.
30. (. . .) spoke to (. . .).

1-2 SHORT RESPONSES TO YES/NO QUESTIONS

	QUESTION	SHORT RESPONSES	
(a)	**Does** this book belong to you?	Yes, it **does.** No, it **doesn't.**	A short response has the same auxiliary that is used in the question. In (a): *does* is used in the question and *does* is used in the response.
(b)	**Did** Jack tell you the news?	Yes, he **did.** No, he **didn't.**	In a negative response (*no*), *not* is usually contracted with the verb; e.g., *does + not = doesn't.**
(c)	**Have** you finished your work?	Yes, I **have.** No, I **haven't.**	Notice: In an affirmative response (*yes*), the auxiliary is NOT contracted with the pronoun. It is NOT possible to say, "*Yes, I've.*"
(d)	**Will** Sue be here tomorrow?	Yes, she **will.** No, she **won't.**	
(e)	**Are** you a student?	Yes, I **am.** No, **I'm not.**	If *be* is used in the question, *be* is in the short response.
(f)	**Is** Bonnie at home?	Yes, she **is.** No, she **isn't.** No, she's **not.**	In (f) and (g): When *is* or *are* is used in a negative response, there are two possible contractions.
(g)	**Are** the students in class?	Yes, they **are.** No, they **aren't.** No, they're **not.**	
(h)	**Was** Alex at the party?	Yes, he **was.** - No, he **wasn't.**	

*See 3-9 for a chart of verb contractions used in English.

EXERCISE 6—ORAL (BOOKS CLOSED):   Answer the questions truthfully. Give short responses where appropriate. Otherwise, supply the information.

To the teacher: Pursue the topic briefly with Student A, then ask Student B questions about that conversation. For example:

To A: Have you ever been in
       New York City?

A: Yes, I have.

       When were you there?

A: A couple of weeks ago.

       Why did you go there?

A: My plane stopped there on the
    way to Pittsburgh.

	How long were you at the airport?	A: About four hours.
To B:	Has (. . .) ever been to New York City?	B: Yes, he/she has.
	When was he/she there?	B: Two weeks ago.
	Did he/she spend the week-end there?	B: No, he/she didn't. He/she was there for only a few hours.

1. Do you live in an apartment?
2. Did you walk to school (this morning)?
3. Is the student sitting next to you from the United States?
4. Have you ever been in (New York City)?
5. Did you eat (breakfast/lunch/dinner) before you came to class?
6. Do you have any sisters and brothers?
7. Have you seen/been to (a place or landmark in this city) yet?
8. Do you like to watch TV?
9. Have you met any new people in the past couple of days?
10. Were you at home all evening yesterday?
11. Does the student sitting in front of you have curly hair?
12. Are you hungry?
13. Will you be in class on (Saturday)?

1-3 QUESTION WORDS

	QUESTION	ANSWER	
WHEN	(a) When did they arrive? When will you come?	Yesterday. Next Monday.	*When* is used to ask questions about *time*.
WHERE	(b) Where is she? Where can I get tickets for the show?	At home. At the box office.	*Where* is used to ask questions about *place*.
WHY	(c) Why did he stay home? Why aren't you coming with us?	Because he was sick. I'm tired.	*Why* is used to ask questions about *reason*.
HOW	(d) How did you come to school? How does he drive?	By bus. Carefully.	*How* generally asks about *manner*, but it has many idiomatic uses. (See 1-6.)
	(e) How much money does it cost? How many people came to the meeting?	Ten dollars. Fifteen or sixteen.	*How* is used with *much* and *many*.

	QUESTION	ANSWER	
HOW	(f) How old are you? How cold is it? How soon can you get here? How fast were you driving?	Twelve. Ten below zero. In ten minutes. Fifty miles an hour.	*How* is also used with adjectives and adverbs.
	(g) How long have you been in this city? How often do you write home? How far is it to Miami from here?	Two years. Every week. 500 miles.	*How long* asks about *length of time.* *How often* asks about *frequency.* *How far* asks about *distance.*
WHO	(h) Who can answer that question? Who came to visit you?	I can. Jane and Eric.	*Who* is used as the subject of a question. It refers to people.
	(i) Who is coming to dinner tonight? Who wants to come with me?	Mary, Bob, and Bill. We do.	*Who* is usually followed by a singular verb even if the speaker is asking about more than one person.
WHOM	(j) Who(m) did you see? Who(m) are you visiting? (k) Who(m) should I talk to? To whom should I talk? *(formal)*	I saw George. My relatives. The secretary.	*Whom* is used as the object of a verb or preposition. In spoken English, *whom* is rarely used; *who* is used instead. *Whom* is used only in formal questions. Note: *Whom,* not *who*, is used if preceded by a preposition.
WHOSE	(l) Whose book did you borrow? Whose key is this? (Whose is this?)	David's. It's mine.	*Whose* asks questions about *possession.*
WHAT	(m) What made you angry? What went wrong?	His rudeness. Everything.	*What* is used as the subject of a question. It refers to "things".
	(n) What do you need? What did Alice buy? (o) What did she write about? About what did she write? *(formal)*	I need a pencil. A book. Her vacation.	*What* is also used as an object.
	(p) What classes are you taking? What time did she finally arrive? What countries did you visit? What programs do you like on TV?	Chemistry and English. Seven o'clock. Italy and Greece. The news specials.	*What* sometimes accompanies a noun. (See 1–5 for further uses of *what*.)

	QUESTION		ANSWER	
WHICH	(q) I have two pens.	Which pen do you want? Which one do you want? Which do you want?	The blue one.	*Which* is used instead of *what* when a question concerns choosing from a definite, known quantity or group.
	(r) Which book should I buy, this one or that one?		That one.	
	(s) Which countries did he visit on his trip? What countries did he visit on his trip?			In some cases, there is little difference in meaning between *which* and *what* when they accompany a noun, as in (s) and (t).
	(t) Which class are you in? What class are you in?			

1-4 USING QUESTION WORDS WITH *BE* AS THE MAIN VERB

	QUESTION WORD	+ BE +	SUBJECT	
(a) **That man is** John Smith.	Who	is	that man?	When *be* is the main verb (in the simple present and simple past), it precedes the subject. Notice the subject-verb agreement in the examples.*
(b) **They are** my friends.	Who	are	they?	
(c) **Mary was** at the library.	Where	was	Mary?	
(d) **The girls were** at the park.	Where	were	the girls?	
(e) **Her dress is** blue.	What color	is	her dress?	
(f) **His eyes are** brown.	What color	are	his eyes?	

*Compare: *Be* used as an auxiliary verb: *Who is coming to the party?*   (*Who* is the subject of the question.)
          Be used as the main verb: *Who is he?*   (*He* is the subject of the question.)
                                      Who are they?   (*They* is the subject of the question.)

EXERCISE 7:   Make questions from the following sentences. The italicized words in the sentence should be the answer to your question.

     Example: I need *five dollars.*

     Response: How much money do you need?

1. He was born in *Panama.*

2. I go out to eat *at least once at week.*

3. I am waiting for *Marie.*

4. *My sister* answered the phone.

5. I called *Benjamin.*

6. *Benjamin* called.

7. I have *a baseball* in my pocket.

8

8. He has been here *for two hours.*
9. "Deceitful" means *"dishonest."*
10. An abyss is *a bottomless hole.*
11. He went *this* way, *not that* way.
12. These are *Jim's* books and papers.
13. They have *four* children.
14. It is *two hundred miles* to New Orleans.
15. Mexico is *eight hundred miles* from here.
16. Bob can't go *because he is sick.* *
17. She bought *twelve gallons of* gas.
18. The doctor can see you *at three on Friday.*

19. Her roomate is *Jane Peters.*
20. Her roommates are *Jane Peters and Sue Lee.*
21. They have lived here *for three years.*
22. This is *Alice's* book.
23. I didn't answer the phone *because I didn't hear it ring.*
24. *The soap bubbles* made her sneeze.
25. I don't understand *the chart on page 50.*
26. *Fred and Jack* are coming over for dinner.

EXERCISE 8—ORAL (BOOKS CLOSED):

(To the teacher: Present the questions in normal contracted speech and have the students tell you what you said.)

1. What did you do last night?
2. How did you do on the test?
3. Why did you stay home?
4. How often do you go to the library?
5. What do you want?
6. Why do you always sit in the back?
7. What is your name?
8. Where is the post office?
9. Who is that woman?†
10. Who are those people?

11. What are they doing?
12. When will I see you again?
13. How long will you be gone?
14. Where did you go over vactation?
15. How do you pronounce your last name?
16. Where are your books?
17. Who is sitting in front of you?
18. Who will be in class tomorrow?
19. Who do you live with?
20. What did you buy at the book-store?

---

*Usual form of a negative question: *Why **didn't** he stay?*
  Also possible, but very formal; not often used in everday speech: *Why **did** he **not** stay?*

†COMPARE: **who's** = who is **whose** = possessive

EXERCISE 9—ORAL (BOOKS CLOSED): Make questions. Use question words.

Example: I bought a book.
Response: What did you buy?

1. It is fifty-five miles to (Springfield).
2. Fall semester begins on September 10th.
3. I bought the red pen, not the green one.
4. The secretary typed those letters.
5. I took four courses last semester.
6. "Rapid" means "fast."
7. (. . .) went to the library.
8. (. . .) telephoned me.
9. The post office is on Seventh Avenue.
10. It is three blocks to the post office.
11. I slept eight hours last night.
12. (. . .) gave a speech.
13. He/she talked about his/her country.
14. He/she talked about his/her family.
15. I need twenty-five dollars.
16. He lives on the fifth floor, not the fourth.
17. I will be in the United States for four years.
18. This is (. . .)'s pen.
19. I go to the library every day.
20. The next test is on Tuesday.
21. I have been studying English for ten years.
22. I laughed because he made a funny face.
23. (. . .) dropped his/her pen.
24. You should give that book to (. . .).
25. I didn't come to class yesterday because I wasn't feeling well.

EXERCISE 10—ORAL (BOOKS CLOSED): Make questions. Use question words.

1. I had a sandwich for lunch.
2. These are (. . .)'s books.
3. We are supposed to read Chapter Five, not Chapter Six.
4. I talked to (. . .).
5. I talked to (. . .) about the story in this morning's newspaper.
6. I fell asleep in class because I had only two hours of sleep last night.
7. That book belongs to (. . .).
8. "Request" means "ask."
9. It is 325 miles to (Chicago).
10. I can speak three languages.
11. (. . .) opened the window.
12. I didn't go to the party because I had to study.
13. I live in this house, not that one.
14. I hung my coat in the closet.
15. The letter is addressed to (. . .).
16. It took me three hours to finish my assignments.
17. Mr. Smith taught English in Japan.
18. You should be here at two o'clock.
19. I found (. . .)'s keys.
20. I visit my aunt and uncle twice a year.

EXERCISE 11—WRITTEN: Write original dialogues in which the following are the answers to questions. Write both the question and the answer.

Example: Once a week.

A: How often do you go grocery shopping?

B: Once a week.

1. Bob's.
2. Blue.
3. Alice and Betty.
4. Two years.
5. Six dollars.
6. This one, not that one.
7. Two million.
8. Chemistry.
9. 1959.
10. Five blocks.

11. Because I wanted to.
12. Every day.
13. My brother.
14. Next month.
15. Saudi Arabia.
    In the Middle East.
    Over eight million.
    Islam.
    Oil.
    Riyadh. (*capital city*)

1-5 FURTHER USES OF *WHAT*

QUESTION	ANSWER	
(a) **What** did you **do** last night? (b) **What** is Mary **doing**? (c) **What** do you want **to do** this afternoon?	I studied. Reading a book. I want to go to the park.	*What + a form of do* is used to ask questions about activities.
(d) **What** does she **do for a living**? (e) **What** does your uncle **do**?	She works at a bank. He's an electrician.	The questions in (d) and (e) ask for information about a person's occupation.
(f) **What kind of books** do you like to read? (g) **What kind of camera** do you have? (h) **What kind of soup** is that?	Novels. A Kodak.* It's chicken soup.	*What kind of* is used when the speaker wants to know the particular variety or type of something.
(i) **What is** the weather **like** in Hawaii? (j) I've never met her. **What is** she **like**? (k) I've never been to their apartment. **What is** it **like**?	It's warm and sunny. She's friendly and kind. It's small, but very nice.	*What is someone/something like* is used to ask for a general description of qualities.
(l) I've never met him. **What does** he **look like**? (m) **What does** their house **look like**?	He's about six feet tall, has curly brown hair, and weighs about 175 pounds. It's a two-story, red brick house.	*What does someone/something look like* is used to ask for a physical description.

*Kodak is a brand name.

QUESTION	ANSWER	
(n) **What** do you need to borrow money **for?** I thought you had plenty of money.	I'm broke. I spent all of my money.	**What . . . for** means **why, for what purpose.** It is used to ask questions about a purpose the speaker does not understand.
(o) A: I should go to the grocery store. B: **What for?** We have enough food in the apartment.	A: But we're out of bread and milk.	

EXERCISE 12: Complete the dialogues by making questions with **what.**

Example: A: _____ What did you do _____ last night?

B: I studied.

1. A: _____ right now?
   B: I'm doing an exercise.

2. A: Do you know Alice Jones?
   B: The name sounds familiar. Who is she?
   A: She's a student in our class.

   B: Really? _____
   A: She's about medium height. Has long brown hair. Wears glasses.*

3. A: Have you ever met Dick Barth?
   B: No, I haven't, but I've heard of him. Have you met him?
   A: He lives down the hall from me in the dorm.

   B: _____
   A: He's a nice guy. Very bright. And has a great sense of humor.*

4. A: Where are you going?
   B: The library.

   A: _____ You just got back from the library!
   B: I left my umbrella there.

5. A: I don't know very much about your country. _____
   B: It's a democratic republic.

6. A: _____ after class today?
   B: Not much. I'm going to go back to my room and maybe take a nap, then study a bit, I suppose.

7. A: I've never met her husband. _____
   B: He's a civil engineer. He works for a railroad company.

8. A: What history class are you going to take this semester?
   B: Asian History 231.

A: Who'll be your professor?

B: Dr. Anderson.

A: That's the same prof I had when I took 231 last year.

B: Really? _____

A: She's very good. Gives interesting lectures.* But I'd better warn you about her tests. They're murder!

9. A: Oh, I see you've been shopping. What did you buy?

B: Some shoes.

A: _____

B: Sandals.

10. A: I can't find my book. Would you help me look for it?

B: Sure. _____

A: *Readings in Psychology.*

B: _____

A: It's a thick paperback with a blue cover.

11. A: The waitress is coming over to take our order.

B: Good. I'm hungry.

A: _____

B: A sandwich.

A: _____

B: Grilled cheese.

12. A: Why aren't you at your math class now?

B: I dropped it.

A: Oh? _____ I thought you liked that course.

B: It was okay, but I couldn't keep up with the work in that class and all my other classes at the same time.

13. A: _____

B: He told me to go to bed and rest and drink plenty of fluids. He also told me to take these pills every four hours.

14. A: Thanks for letting me borrow your car.

B: That's okay. I'm glad to do it. But you'll have to get some gas. The gas gauge is almost on empty.

A: _____

B: Unleaded.

---

*These incomplete sentences are representative of spoken, not written, English.

1-6 FURTHER USES OF *HOW*

QUESTION	ANSWER

(a) How are you getting along?
(b) How's everything going?
(c) How's it going?
(d) How are you doing?
 	
(e) How do you feel?
(f) How are you feeling?
	Great.
	Fine.
	Okay.
	So-so.
	Not so well. Not so good.
	Terrible.
	     (Note: (e) and (f) ask about a person's
	     physical well-being.)

(g) How do you do?	How do you do? (***How do you do** is used when two people are first introduced to each other.*)
(h) How do you spell "sitting"? (i) How do you say (pronounce) this word? (j) How do you say "hello" in French?	With two *t*'s. S-I-T-T-I-N-G. ———— *Bonjour.*
(k) How do you take (like) your coffee? (l) How would you like your egg? (m) How would you like your steak?	Black. With cream and sugar. Fried. Over easy. Sunny-side up. Scrambled. Soft-boiled. Hard-boiled. Rare. Medium-rare. Medium. Medium-well. Well done.
(n) How did you sleep last night?	Very well. Like a log.
(o) How did you do on the test? (p) How did the team do?	I got a B. They won.
(q) How did you meet your wife?	My sister introduced us.
(r) How does the story end? (s) How did the argument start (begin)?	Everyone lives happily ever after. I said that he was wrong, and he got angry.
(t) How did you find out? (u) How do you know?	Someone told me. I asked her and she said it was true.
(v) How come John isn't here today?	He's sick. (***How come** means **why**. Notice: The subject is in front of the verb. Question word order is not used.*)

EXERCISE 13:   Complete the following dialogues by making questions with *how*.

Example: A: _____ How far is it to Los Angeles? _____

B: 300 miles.

1. A: Have you been at this university very long?

   B: No. This is my first semester.

   A: _____

   B: Okay. I still have some problems with my English, but otherwise I'm getting along fine.

2. A: What's the matter?

   B: I have a cold.

   A: _____

   B: Terrible. I think I'll go home and go to bed.

3. A: _____

   B: With a double *r*. O-C-C-U-R-R-E-D.

4. A: Could I get you a cup of coffee?

   B: Thanks. That sounds good.

   A: _____

   B: Black.

5. A: _____

   B: Pretty good. I got a B+.

6. A: How long have you and your wife been married?

   B: Five years.

   A: _____

   B: My cousin Jim introduced us.

7. A: I started reading that book once, but I never finished it. _____

   _____

   B: The boy and girl get married and live happily ever after.

8. A: We don't have class this afternoon. It's been cancelled.

   B: Are you sure? _____

   A: The teacher in my morning class made that announcement.

9. A: _____

   B: Because I had a dentist's appointment. But I'll be in class tomorrow.

10. A: I was late for work this morning.

    B: _____

    A: I missed my bus.

EXERCISE 14—ORAL (BOOKS CLOSED): You will be given the answer to a question. Ask a question with *how* that would produce that answer.

(To the teacher: Prompt with the verbs in parentheses if necessary.)

    Example: Ten dollars.

    Possible response: How much does that book cost?

1. Three blocks.   *(be)*
2. With cream and sugar.   *(take, like)*
3. Everything is going fine.   *(go)*
4. Two years.   *(—)*
5. I slept very well, thank you.   *(sleep)*
6. Scrambled.   *(would like, want)*
7. Every day.   *(—)*
8. She's almost six feet tall.   *(be)*
9. I'm getting along okay, I guess.   *(get)*
10. Because I was tired.   *(go to bed early, not come to the party)*
11. By taxi.   *(get)*
12. How do you do?   *(do)*
13. Terrible. I have a headache and a stomachache.   *(feel)*
14. Because I missed my bus.   *(be)*
15. I got an A on the test.   *(do)*
16. I think his mother-in-law poisoned him.   *(die, kill)*
17. Rare or medium-rare.   *(like)*
18. I don't know, but I can look it up for you in my dictionary.   *(spell, say)*

EXERCISE 15: Make questions from the following sentences. The italicized words should be the answer to your question. Use any appropriate question words.

1. I take my coffee *black*.
2. I have an *English-English* dictionary.

3. You should address the letter to *the Director of Admissions.*

4. He *runs a grocery store* for a living.

5. *Only ten* people showed up for the meeting.

6. *Due to heavy fog,* none of the planes could take off.

7. She was talking about *her experiences as a rural doctor.*

8. I was driving *sixty-five miles per hour* when the policeman stopped me.

9. I like *hot and spicy Mexican* food best.

10. *The* apartment *at the end of the hall* is mine.

11. He is *friendly, generous, and kindhearted.*

12. He is *tall and thin and has short black hair.*

13. *Ann's* dictionary fell to the floor.

14. She isn't here *because she has a doctor's appointment.*

15. All of the students in the class will be informed of their final grades *on Friday.*

16. I did *very well* on the test.

17. Of those three books, I preferred *the one by Tolstoy.*

18. I like *rock* music.

19. The weather is *hot and humid* in July.

20. The driver of the stalled car lit a flare *in order to warn oncoming cars.*

21. I want *the felt-tip* pen, *not the ballpoint.*

22. The plane is expected to be *an hour* late.

23. I'm taking *four* courses.

EXERCISE 16—ORAL (BOOKS CLOSED):   Make questions. Use question words.

Example: He lives in Chicago.
Response: Where does he live?

1. I am majoring in business administration.

2. My major is engineering.

3. I am taking four courses this (semester).

4. The population of (St. Louis) is (two million).

5. I know three languages.

6. I grew up in Florida.

7. I have three brothers and sisters.

8. I am in class for five hours every day.

9. It takes five hours to get to (Kansas City).

10. I like to read historical novels.

11. I'm planning to stay here and sleep over (spring break).

12. I will be (in the United States) for two more years.

13. The test will cover Chapters Two and Three.
14. He quit school because he wanted to travel around the world.
15. She has been sick for three days.
16. Her eyes are gray.
17. Her hair is black.
18. She's going to invite twenty people to her party.
19. She's talking to Bob Smith.
20. You should buy this camera, not that one.
21. Columbus discovered the New World.
22. Alice and John are going to get married in August.
23. Our team won, not their team.
24. We're going to have chicken for dinner.
25. Everything is going just fine!

1-7   USING *HOW ABOUT* AND *WHAT ABOUT*

(a) A: We need one more player.
   B: **How about (what about) Jack?** Let's ask him if he wants to play.
(b) A: What time should we meet?
   B: **How about (what about) three o'clock?**
	How about and *what about* have the same meaning and usage. They are used to make suggestions.
	How about and *what about* are followed by a noun (or pronoun) or the *-ing* form of a verb.

(c) A: What should we do this afternoon?
   B: **How about going** to the zoo?
(d) A: **What about asking** Sally over for dinner next Sunday?
   B: Okay. Good idea.
	Note: *How about* and *what about* are used in informal spoken English frequently, but are usually not used in writing.

(e) A: I'm tired. **How about you?**
   B: Yes, I'm tired too.
(f) A: Are you hungry?
   B: No. **What about you?**
   A: I'm a little hungry.
	How about you? and *What about you?* are used to ask a question which refers to the information or question that immediately preceded. In (e): *How about you? = Are you tired?* In (f): *What about you? = Are you hungry?*

EXERCISE 17—ORAL (BOOKS CLOSED): Respond by using *how about* or *what about*.

> *Example:*   I'm looking for a good book to read. Do you have any suggestions?
>
> *Response:*   How about (What about) *Tom Sawyer* by Mark Twain? That's a good book.

1. You and I are having dinner together this evening, (. . .). What time should we get together?
2. I can't figure out what to give my sister for her birthday.
3. I'm hungry, but I'm not sure what I want to eat.
4. We have a whole week of vacation. Where should we go?
5. What time should I call you?
6. Where should we go for dinner tonight?
7. I've already asked (. . .) and (. . .) to my party. Who else should I ask?
8. Some friends are coming to visit me this weekend. They said they wanted to see some of the interesting places in the city. I'm wondering where I should take them.

EXERCISE 18: Complete the dialogues by using *how about you* or *what about you* and an appropriate response.

Example: A: What are you going to do over vaction?

B: I'm staying here. ____What about (How about) you?____

A: ____I'm going to Texas to visit my sister.____

1. A: Did you like the movie?

   B: It was okay, I guess. _____

   A: _____

2. A: Are you going to summer school?

   B: I haven't decided yet. _____

   A: _____

3. A: Do you like living in the dorm?

   B: Sort of. _____

   A: _____

4. A: What are you going to have?

   B: Well, I'm not really hungry. I think I might have just a salad. _____

   _____

   A: _____

5. A: Where are you planning to go to school next year?

   B: I've been accepted by the state university. _____

   A: _____

6. A: Are you married?

B: _____

A: _____

EXERCISE 19—ORAL: Pair up with another member of the class. One of you will be Student A and the other will be Student B. During your conversation, find out as much information as you can about each other on the given topics.

STUDENT A: The following questions are conversation openers. Glance at a question quickly, then look up—directly into the eyes of Student B—and initiate the conversation. After the two of you have explored the topic, go on to the next question (or make up one of your own).

STUDENT B: Do not look at your text. Answer Student A's questions. Then ask *How about you?* or *What about you?* to continue the conversation.

1. How long have you been living in (this city or country)?
2. How do you like living here?
3. Where are you staying?
4. What are you going to do after class today?
5. What are your plans for this evening?
6. What are you going to do this weekend?
7. What are you planning to do at the end of this term/semester?
8. Do you come from a large family?
9. What kind of sports do you enjoy?
10. Do you speak a lot of English outside of class?

EXERCISE 20: Review of questions. Complete the dialogues by supplying appropriate questions.

1. A: _____

B: Physics 201, History 110, English 207, and Biology 22.

2. A: _____

B: I'll take this one. You can have the other one.

3. A: _____

B: He's a salesman for a computer corporation.

4. A: _____

    B: One hour by plane or five hours by car.

5. A: _____

    B: It's turkey soup.

    A: Oh really? I thought it was chicken.

6. A: _____

    B: Yes, we do. We accept Master Card, Visa, and American Express.

7. A: _____

    B: She's very nice. Very friendly and open.

8. A: _____

    B: She's tall and thin, with long brown hair and dark eyes. She also has dimples when she smiles.

9. A: Good news! Judy finally had her baby!

    B: That's great! _____

    A: A girl.

    B: _____

    A: Seven and a half pounds.

    B: _____

    A: Emily.

    B: _____

    A: Fine.

10. A: Alan and I are planning to go to Denver, Colorado over spring break.

    B: _____

    A: Next Saturday.

    B: _____

    A: By car.

    B: _____

    A: Probably two days, but we might decide to drive straight through.

    B: _____

    A: At my uncle's house.

    B: _____

    A: We'll be there for five days.

1-8 NEGATIVE QUESTIONS

(a) Doesn't she live in the dormitory? (b) Does she not live in the dormitory? (*very formal*)	In a yes/no question in which the verb is negative, usually a contraction (e.g., ***does + not = doesn't***) is used, as in (a). Example (b) is very formal and is usually not used in everyday speech. Negative questions are used to indicate the speaker's idea (i.e., what he/she believes is or is not true) or attitude (e.g., surprise, shock, annoyance, anger).
(c) Bob returns to his dorm room after his nine o'clock class. Dick, his roommate, is there. Bob is surprised. Bob says: "*What are you doing here? **Aren't you supposed to be in class now?***"	In (c): Bob believes that Dick is supposed to be in class now. *Expected answer:* **Yes.***
(d) Alice and Mary are at home. Mary is about to leave on a trip and Alice is going to take her to the airport. Alice says: "*It's already two o'clock. We'd better leave for the airport. **Doesn't your plane leave at three?***"	In (d): Alice believes that Mary's plane leaves at three. She is asking the negative question to make sure that her information is correct. *Expected answer:* **Yes.**
(e) The teacher is talking to Jim about a test he failed. The teacher is surprised that Jim failed the test because he usually does very well. The teacher says: "*What happened? **Didn't you study?***"	In (e): The teacher believes that Jim did not study. *Expected answer:* **No.**
(f) Barb and Don are riding in a car. Don is driving. He comes to a corner where there is a stop sign, but he does not stop the car. Barb is shocked. Barb says: "*What's the matter with you? **Didn't you see that stop sign?***"	In (f): Barb believes that Don did not see stop sign. *Expected answer:* **No.**

*When the expected answer to a negative question is *yes,* the answer may be either *yes* or *no.* When the expected answer is *no,* only *no* is possible. (Even native speakers sometimes find this situation confusing.)

EXERCISE 21: Notice in the examples in 1–8: sometimes the expected answer to a negative question is *yes* and sometimes *no.* In the following dialogues, make negative questions from the words in parentheses and determine the expected response.

> *Example:* A: Why didn't you come to lunch with us? <u>Weren't you hungry?</u>
> (*be hungry*)
>
> B: <u>   No.   </u> I had a late breakfast.

1. A: Did you give Linda my message when you went to class this morning?

   B: No. I didn't see her.

   A: Oh? _____
      (*be in class*)

   B: _____ She didn't come today.

2. A: Do you see that woman over there, the one in the blue dress? _____
   _____

      (*be Mrs. Robbins*)

   B: _____

   A: I thought so. I wonder what she is doing here.

3. A: It's almost dinner time and you haven't eaten since breakfast. _____
   _____ (*be hungry*)

   B: _____ I'm starving. Let's go eat.

4. A: You look tired this morning. _____
   _____ (*sleep well last night.*)

   B: _____ I tossed and turned all night.

5. A: What's the matter? Everyone else at the party seems to be enjoying him-

      self, but you look bored. _____
   _____

      (*be having a good time*)

   B: _____ I'm thinking about going home pretty soon.

6. A: We'd better leave pretty soon. _____
   _____

      (*be almost seven o'clock*)

   B: _____ It's five of.

7. A: I think I'll lie down for awhile.

   B: You look pale. What's the matter? _____
   _____ (*feel good*)

   A: _____ I think I might be coming down with something.

8. A: See that man over there, the one in the green shirt?

   B: Yes. Who is he?

A: _____
   (*recognize him*)

B: _____

9. A: Did you see Mark at the meeting?
   B: No, I didn't.

   A: Really? _____
      (*be there*)

   B: _____
   A: That's funny. I've never known him to miss a meeting before.

10. A: Why didn't you come to the meeting yesterday afternoon?
    B: What meeting? I didn't know there was a meeting.

    A: _____
       (*Mary/tell you about it*)

    B: _____ No one said a word to me about it.

1-9 TAG QUESTIONS (Questions added at the end of a sentence)

	QUESTION	EXPECTED ANSWER	
(a)	Mary **is** here, **isn't** she?	Yes, she is.	*FIRST PART OF* *TAG QUESTION*
(b)	Mary **isn't** here, **is** she?	No, she isn't.	*SENTENCE*
(c)	You **like** tea, **don't** you?	Yes, I do.	affirmative → negative
(d)	You **don't like** tea, **do** you?	No, I don't.	negative → affirmative
(e)	They **have left, haven't** they?	Yes, they have.	
(f)	They **haven't left, have** they?	No, they haven't.	
(g)	He **has** brown hair, **doesn't** he?		In American English, a form of *do* is usually used when *have* is the main verb.
(h)	**That** is your book, isn't **it**?		In (h) through (k): Notice the use of pronouns.
(i)	**This** is your book, isn't **it**?		
(j)	**Those** are your books, aren't **they**?		
(k)	**These** are your books, aren't **they**?		
(l)	**There is** a party tonight, **isn't there**?		
(m)	**There were** a lot of people at the party, **weren't there**?		
(n)	**I am** supposed to be here, **am I not**? (*formal*)		In (o): Notice the use of *aren't* in the tag question after *I am.* This use of *aren't* is common in spoken English.
(o)	**I am** supposed to be here, **aren't I**? (*informal*)		

EXERCISE 22: Add tag questions to the following.*

1. They want to come, _____ don't they _____ ?

2. Elizabeth is a dentist, _____?

3. They won't be here, _____?

4. There aren't any problems, _____?

5. That is your umbrella, _____?

6. He has learned a lot, _____?

7. You have a bicycle, _____?

8. She had a cold, _____?

9. I am invited, _____?

10. She will help us later, _____?

11. Those are Fred's books, _____?

12. Joan can't come with us, _____?

13. The tape recorder isn't broken, _____?

14. Peggy would like to come with us to the party, _____?

15. This answer is correct, _____?

EXERCISE 23—ORAL (BOOKS CLOSED): Add tag questions.

Example: He is a student . . . .
Response: . . . isn't he?

1. That's (. . .)'s pen . . . .

2. (. . .) is living in the dorm . . . .

3. (. . .) lives in an apartment . . . .

4. There isn't a test tomorrow . . . .

5. (. . .) has his/her book . . . .

6. You had a good time . . . .

7. (. . .) has been invited to the party . . . .

8. You didn't forget your key . . . .

9. You've already seen that movie . . . .

10. (. . .) can't speak (Arabic) . . . .

11. We have class tomorrow . . . .

12. Your friend doesn't need any help . . . .

13. Turtles lay eggs . . . .

---

*A tag question may be spoken (1) with a rising intonation if the speaker is truly seeking information, or (2) with a falling intonation if the speaker is expressing an idea or belief with which he/she is almost certain the listener will agree. Most of the tag questions in Exercises 22 and 23 reflect situations in which a rising intonation would probably be used.

14. These keys don't belong to you . . . .

15. You used to live in New York . . . .

16. There is a better way to solve that problem . . . .

17. (. . .) is going to come to class tomorrow . . . .

18. I am right . . . .

19. You should leave for the airport by six . . . .

20. Your parents haven't arrived yet . . . .

21. (. . .) sat next to (. . .) yesterday . . . .

22. You studied the grammar . . . .

23. (. . .) doesn't have a car . . . .

24. You renewed your visa . . . .

25. Class ends at (ten) . . . .

EXERCISE 24: Pair up with another member of the class. In a conversation, find out as much as you can about each other. Then write a short composition about the other person. Do not take notes while you are talking to each other.

In this exercise, "trade" questions (for example, if the other person asks you about your country, ask him/her about his/her country).

Example: A: What country are you from?

B: Chile. You're from Korea, aren't you?

A: Yes, I am. How long have you been here?

B: About two weeks. How about you?

A: I've been here for three months.

A or B: (*Ask another question.*)

Note: If you do not know each other, be sure to introduce yourselves at the beginning of the conversation.

EXERCISE 25: Interview someone you have met recently, perhaps a new neighbor, roommate, classmate, or colleague at work. Use the information from your interview as the basis for a composition. You might want to include a short physical description of the person you interview.

EXERCISE 26: Sometimes in spoken English, the auxiliary and the subject *you* are dropped from a question. Notice the following examples.

(a) Going to bed now? = Are you going to bed now?

(b) Finish your work? = Did you finish your work?

(c) Want to go to the movie with us? = Do you want to go to the movie with us?

Find the shortened questions in the following, and then give the complete question form.

1. A: Need some help?
   B: Thanks.
2. A: Why do you keep looking out the window? Expecting someone?
   B: I'm waiting for the mailman.
3. A: You look tired.
   B: I am.
   A: Stay up late last night?
   B: Yup.
4. A: I'm looking forward to going to Colorado over spring vacation.
   B: Ever been there before?
5. A: Why are you pacing the floor? Nervous?
   B: Who me?
6. A: Want a cup of coffee?
   B: Only if it's already made.
7. A: Heard any news about your scholarship?
   B: Not yet.
8. A: Hungry?
   B: Yeah. You?

EXERCISE 27—PREPOSITIONS: Supply an appropriate preposition for each of the following expressions of time.

1. I'll meet you _____in_____ the morning.

2. I'll meet you _____ the afternoon.

3. I'll meet you _____ the evening.

4. I usually stay home _____ night.

5. I get out of class _____ noon.

6. I'll call you _____ six o'clock.

7. She arrived _____ Monday.*

8. She arrived _____ March.

9. I was born _____ 1960.

On is used for a particular day or date.   *In* is used for a month or year.

10. I was born _____ March 15th.

11. I was born _____ March 15th, 1960.

12. He played a trick on me _____ April Fool's Day.

13. I'll help you _____ a minute, just as soon as I finish this work.

14. I'll help you _____ a moment, just as soon as I finish this work.*

15. _____ the moment, I'm doing an exercise.

16. I'm living in the dorm _____ present.

17. I like to go swimming _____ the summer.

18. I like to go skiing _____ the winter.

EXERCISE 28–PREPOSITIONS: Supply an appropriate preposition. All of the following contain two-word verbs. (A list of two-word verbs may be found in Appendix 2.)

1. A: When do we have to turn _____ our assignments?
   B: They're due next Tuesday.

2. A: How does this tape recorder work?

   B: Push this button to turn it _____ and push that button to

   shut it _____ .

3. A: May I borrow your dictionary?

   B: Sure. But please be sure to put it _____ on the shelf when you're finished.

4. A: I'm going to be in your neighborhood tomorrow.

   B: Oh? If you have time, why don't you drop _____ to see us?
   A: Thanks. That sounds like a good idea. Should I call first?

5. A: Look _____ ! A car is coming!

6. A: I got very irritated at one of my dinner guests last night.
   B: Why?

   A: There was an ashtray on the table, but she put her cigarette _____

   _____ on one of my good plates!

7. A: I need to talk to Karen.

   B: Why don't you call her _____ ? She's probably at home now.

---

*__In a moment__ means *soon*. __At the moment__ means *at this time* (or *at that time*).

8. A: Oh oh. I made a mistake on the check I just wrote.

    B: Don't try to correct the mistake. Just tear _____ the check

    and throw it _____ .

9. A: Are you here to apply for a job?

    B: Yes.

    A: Here is an application form. Fill it _____ and then give it

    _____ to me when you are finished.

10. A: Look. There's Mike.

    B: Where?

    A: At the other end of the block, walking toward the administration building.

    If we run, we can catch _____ with him.

11. A: Is your roommate here?

    B: Yes. She decided to come to the party after all. Have you ever met her?

    A: No, but I'd like to.

    B: She's the one standing over there by the far window. She has a blue dress

    _____ . Come on. I'll introduce you.

12. A: Do you have a date for Saturday night?

    B: Yes. Jim Brock asked me _____ . We're going bowling.

2

Singular and Plural

EXERCISE 1—PRETEST: Choose the correct answer in parentheses.

1. The weather in the southern states (*gets, get*) very hot during the summer.
2. The results of her experiment (*was, were*) published in a scientific journal.
3. Bob and his friend (*is, are*) coming to the anniversary party tomorrow night.

4. The bag of groceries (*was, were*) too heavy for the child to carry.
5. A lot of the students (*is, are*) already here.
6. Some of the furniture in our apartment (*is, are*) secondhand.
7. Some of the desks in the classroom (*is, are*) broken.
8. At least two-thirds of that book on famous Americans (*is, are*) about people who lived in the nineteenth century.

9. The number of students in this room right now (*is, are*) twenty.
10. A number of students in the class (*speaks, speak*) English very well.
11. Every man, woman, and child (*is, are*) protected under the law.
12. Each student in the class (*has, have*) to have a book.
13. One of the (*country, countries*) I would like to visit (*is, are*) Greece.
14. Only one of the (*book, books*) (*is, are*) required for the course.
15. None of the students (*is, are*) here.
16. There (*is, are*) some interesting pictures in today's newspaper.
17. There (*is, are*) an incorrect statement in that newspaper article.
18. The news in that magazine (*is, are*) two weeks old.
19. The United States (*is, are*) located in North America.
20. Most people (*likes, like*) to go to the zoo.
21. The police (*is, are*) coming. I've already called them.
22. Ten minutes (*is, are*) more than enough time to complete this exercise.
23. Two thousand miles (*is, are*) too far for us to travel over vacation.
24. Physics (*is, are*) my favorite subject.
25. Japanese (*is, are*) very difficult for Americans to learn.
26. The Japanese (*has, have*) a long and interesting history.
27. The old in my country (*is, are*) cared for by their children and grandchildren.
28. This exercise on singular-plural agreement of subjects and verbs (*is, are*) easy.

2-1   REVIEW OF BASICS

SINGULAR VERB	PLURAL VERB	
(a) My **friend lives** in Boston.	(b) My **friends live** in Boston.	*Verb* + *-S* = singular (simple present tense) *Noun* + *-S* = plural
	(c) My **brother and sister live** in Boston.	Two (or more) subjects connected by *and* take a plural verb.
(d) That **book** on political parties **is** interesting.	(e) The **ideas** in that book **are** interesting.	A prepositional phrase that comes between a subject and a verb does not affect the verb.

2-2   USING EXPRESSIONS OF QUANTITY

(a) **Some of the book is** good.	(b) **Some of the books are** good.	The verb is determined by the noun (or pronoun) which follows an expression of quantity. Examples of expressions of quantity: *some of, most of, half of, two-thirds of, ninety percent of*, etc.
(c) **A lot of the equipment is** new.	(d) **A lot of my friends are** here.	

SINGULAR VERB	PLURAL VERB	
(e) **The number** of students in the class **is** fifteen.	(f) **A number** of students **were** late.	In (e): *The number* is the subject. In (f): *A number of* is an expression of quantity. It is followed by a plural noun and a plural verb.

2-3 USING SINGULAR WORDS

(a) **Every student has** been invited. (b) **Every man, woman, and child needs** love and understanding. (c) **Each book and magazine is** listed in the card catalog. (d) **Each of the students has** a schedule. (e) **Everyone is** here. (f) **Everybody is** here.		*Every* and *each* require singular verbs. Notice: Nouns that immediately follow *every* and *each* are singular. *Each of,* however, is followed by a plural noun. **Everyone** and **everybody** always take a singular verb.
(g) **One of my friends needs** some help.		Notice the pattern with *one of: one of + plural noun + singular verb.*
(h) **None of the boys is** here.	(i) *Informal:* **None of the boys are** here.	Subjects with *none of* are considered singular in very formal English, but plural verbs are frequently used in informal speech and writing.

2-4 USING *THERE + BE*

(a) **There is a book** on the shelf.	(b) **There are some books** on the shelf.	The subject follows *be* when *there** is used. In (a): The subject is *book*. In (b): The subject is *books*.
(c) *Informal:* **There is a pen** and a piece of paper on the desk.	(d) *Formal:* **There are a pen** and a piece of paper on the desk.	In (c): Sometimes in informal English. a singular verb is used after *there* when the first of two subjects connected by *and* is singular.

* In the structure *there + be*, *there* is called an *expletive*.

2-5 SOME IRREGULARITIES

(a) The **news is** interesting. (b) The **United States is** a big country.		*news* = singular *the United States* = singular
	(c) Those **people are** from Canada.	*people* = plural†
	(d) The **police have** been called.	*police* = plural

†The word *people* has a final *-s* (*peoples*) only when it is used to refer to nations or ethnic groups: *All the peoples of the world desire peace.*

SINGULAR VERB	PLURAL VERB	
(e) **Eight hours** of sleep **is** enough. (f) **Ten dollars is** too much to pay. (g) **Five thousand miles is** too far to travel.		Expressions of *time, money,* and *distance* are usually singular.
(h) **Mathematics is** easy for her. (i) **Statistics is** a field of study.	(j) **The statistics** in that report **are** not accurate.	Nouns ending in *-ics* take singular verbs when they refer to an area of study, e.g., *physics, economics, linguistics.* In (j): Some *-ics* nouns take plural verbs if they refer to a particular situation instead of a field of study.
(k) **Chinese is** a difficult language. (m) **French is** spoken in many countries.	(l) **The Chinese are** kind and friendly. (n) **The French are** famous for their good wines.	In (k): *Chinese = language.* In (l): *the Chinese = people.* Note: This pattern exists with nouns of nationality that end in *-ese, -ch,* or *-sh.* Other examples: *English, Japanese, Vietnamese.*
	(o) **The poor have** many problems. (p) **The rich get** richer.	Sometimes a word that is usually an adjective is used as a noun. It is preceded by *the* and refers to people who have this quality. In (o): *the poor = people who are poor* Other examples: *the old, the young, the blind, the deaf, the living, the dead.*

EXERCISE 2: Supply the correct word from the two choices given in parentheses.

Example: My alarm clock _____rings_____ at seven o'clock every morning. (*rings, ring*)

1. Many people in the world _____ not have enough to eat. (*does, do*)

2. One of my friends _____ going to meet me at the airport. (*is, are*)

3. Each penny, nickel, dime, and quarter _____ counted carefully by the bank teller. (*is, are*)

4. An orange and black bird _____ sitting in that tree. (*is, are*)

5. My driver's license _____ in my wallet. (*is, are*)

6. Half of this money _____ to you. (*belongs, belong*)

33

7. Half of the students in the class _____ from Arabic-speaking countries. (*is, are*)

8. There _____ not any letters in the mail for you today. (*is, are*)

9. Fifty minutes _____ the maximum length of time allowed for the exam. (*is, are*)

10. The taxes on our car _____ high because we live in a city. (*is, are*)

11. _____ January and February the coldest months of the year? (*Is, Are*)

12. A number of students _____ absent today. (*is, are*)

13. The number of students at the university _____ approximately ten thousand. (*is, are*)

14. Statistics _____ a branch of mathematics. (*is, are*)

15. The statistics in that report on oil production _____ incorrect. (*is, are*)

16. The English _____ more tea than Americans do. (*drinks, drink*)

17. English _____ not my native language. (*is, are*)

18. Twenty dollars _____ an unreasonable price for that necklace. (*is, are*)

19. The United States _____ a population of over 200 million. (*has, have*)

20. The blind _____ by using Braille. (*reads, read*)

21. _____ most of the students live in the dormitories? (*Does, Do*)

22. Almost two-thirds of the land in the southwestern areas of the country _____ _____ unsuitable for farming. (*is, are*)

23. Portuguese _____ somewhat similar to Spanish, _____ _____ it? (*is, are/isn't, aren't*)

24. The news about Mr. Hogan _____ surprising. (*is, are*)

25. None of the students _____ here yet. (*is, are*)

26. A lot of the students in the class _____ from the Far East. (*is, are*)

27. Massachusetts and Connecticut _____ in New England. (*is, are*)

28. Every member of the class _____ English very well.
    (*speaks, speak*)

EXERCISE 3—ORAL (BOOKS CLOSED): Respond with *is* or *are*.

Example: Some of my classmates . . .   Some of that information . . .
Response: . . . are   . . . is

1. His idea . . .
2. His ideas . . .
3. People . . .
4. Each of the students . . .
5. Most of the fruit . . .
6. Most of the students . . .
7. The United States . . .
8. The news in this morning's paper . . .
9. One of the girls . . .
10. French . . .
11. The Chinese . . .
12. Two-thirds of the food . . .
13. The number of students . . .
14. Some of the people . . .
15. Ninety-three million miles . . .
16. The story about his adventures . . .
17. A lot of the chairs . . .
18. A lot of the furniture . . .
19. Everyone in the English classes . . .
20. The clothes in that store . . .
21. Most of the information in those books . . .
22. The news from home . . .
23. Fifty percent of the people in the world . . .
24. Fifty percent of the world's population . . .
25. The clothing in those stores . . .
26. Her husband's relatives . . .
27. Over half of the books by that author . . .
28. A million dollars . . .
29. The rich . . .
30. His method of doing things . . .
31. A number of people . . .
32. Most of the stores in this city . . .
33. Mathematics . . .
34. The police . . .
35. Everybody in the whole world . . .

EXERCISE 4—ORAL: Practice pronouncing the following words.

GROUP A: Final *-s* is pronounced /s/ after voiceless sounds:

1. hats
2. hates
3. books
4. unlocks
5. sleeps
6. trips
7. sniffs
8. laughs

GROUP B: Final *-s* is pronounced /z/ after voiced sounds:

9. robs
10. robes
11. seeds
12. fills
13. miles
14. occurs

15. homes
16. wins
17. bags
18. days
19. pies
20. agrees

GROUP C: Final *-es* and *-s* are pronounced /əz/ after *-sh, -ch, -s, -z, -x*, and *-ge/dge* sounds.

21. dishes
22. washes
23. catches
24. courses
25. passes
26. quizzes
27. buzzes
28. boxes

29. relaxes
30. pages
31. judges
32. arranges
33. faces
34. pieces
35. rises

EXERCISE 5–ORAL: Practice the pronounciation of final *-s/-es* by reading the following sentences aloud.

1. The teacher encourages the students to speak freely.
2. She never changes her mind.
3. He possesses many fine qualities.
4. My wages are low, but my taxes are high.
5. The cafeteria serves good roast beef sandwiches.
6. Chickens, ducks, and turkeys lay eggs.
7. How many pages are there in this book?
8. People come in many shapes and sizes.
9. She steps on the brakes to stop the car.
10. Are there any differences between proverbs and adages?
11. She scratches her chin when it itches.
12. She bought some shirts, shoes, socks, dresses, slacks, blouses, earrings, and necklaces.
13. He practices pronunciation by reading sentences aloud.
14. Birds build nests.

15. He coughs, sneezes, and wheezes.

16. He pronounces the final sounds of words very well.

EXERCISE 6—ORAL (BOOKS CLOSED): What do the following people, animals, and things do? Respond in a complete sentence. Say the final *-s/-es* sounds loudly and clearly.

> *Example:*   bird
> *Response:*   A bird flies. (sings, builds nests, etc.)
> *Example:*   bird watcher
> *Response:*   A bird watcher watches birds.

1. baby
2. telephone
3. star
4. dog
5. duck
6. ball
7. heart
8. river
9. cat
10. door
11. restaurant
12. grocery store
13. clock
14. doctor
15. teacher
16. truck driver
17. dog catcher
18. book publisher
19. mind reader
20. psychologist

EXERCISE 7: Use the correct present tense form of the verb in parentheses.

> *Example:*   Janice and her roommate _____ are _____ at the library. (*be*)

1. The economic and cultural center of the United States _____ New York City. (*be*)

2. Physics _____ to understand the mysteries of the physical world. (*seek*)

3. Two hours of skiing _____ plenty of exercise. (*provide*)

4. Almost every professor and student at the university _____ of the choice of Dr. Brown as the new president. (*approve*)

5. In many respects, this magazine article on wild animals in North America _____ the very real danger of extinction that many species face. (*oversimplify*)

6. The extent of his knowledge on various complex subjects _____ me. (*astound*)

7. A car with poor brakes and no brake lights _____ dangerous. (*be*)

8. A number of people from the university _____ to attend the conference. (*plan*)

9. Most of the news on the front pages of both daily newspapers _____ _____ the progress of the peace conference. (*concern*)

10. The northernmost town in the forty-eight contiguous states _____ _____ Angle Inlet, Minnesota. (*be*)

11. The number of human skeletons found at the archaeological site _____ _____ seven. (*be*)

12. Almost all of the information in those texts on the Aztec Indians and their civilization _____ to be well researched. (*appear*)

13. Every day there _____ more than a dozen traffic accidents in the city. (*be*)

14. No news _____ good news. (*be*)

15. Sensitivity to other people's feelings _____ him a kind and understanding person. (*make*)

EXERCISE 8–WRITTEN: Complete the following sentences with your own words. Use only present tenses.

| *Example:* | One of my . . . . | One of my teachers knows Chinese. |
| | Some of . . . . | Some of my friends are coming to visit me. |

1. Most of my classmates . . . .
2. In my country, there . . . .
3. Everybody . . . .
4. The people in my country . . . .
5. The number of students . . . .
6. A number of students . . . .
7. All of the rooms in the dormitory . . . .
8. The United States . . . .
9. The English language . . . .
10. The English . . . .
11. English . . . .
12. One of my . . . .
13. Most of the food at the cafeteria . . . .
14. A lot of the students in my class . . . .
15. Linguistics . . . .
16. Linguists . . . .

PART II Pronoun Agreement

2-6 AGREEMENT WITH NOUNS

(a) **A student** walked into the room. **She** was looking for the teacher. (b) **A student** walked into the room. **He** was looking for the teacher. (c) **Some students** walked into the room. **They** were looking for the teacher.	A singular pronoun is used to refer to a singular noun, as in (a) and (b). A plural pronoun is used to refer to a plural noun, as in (c).
(d) **A student** should always do **his** assignments. (e) **A student** should always do **his/her** assignments. **A student** should always do **his or her** assignments.	With an "indefinite noun" (e.g., in (d): *a student = anyone who is a student*) a singular masculine pronoun has been used traditionally, but many English speakers now use both masculine and feminine pronouns, as in (e).

2-7 AGREEMENT WITH INDEFINITE PRONOUNS

(f) **Somebody** left **his** book on the desk. (g) **Everyone** has **his/her** own ideas. (h) *Informal:* Somebody left their book on the desk. Everyone has their own ideas.	The following are indefinite pronouns: *everyone someone anyone no one* *everybody somebody anybody nobody* *everything something anything nothing* Indefinite pronouns are singular; however, in informal spoken English, a plural personal pronoun is sometimes used to refer to an indefinite pronoun.

2-8 AGREEMENT WITH COLLECTIVE NOUNS

(i) **My family is** loving and supportive. **They are** always ready to help me. (j) **My family is** large. **It** is composed of nine members.	In informal usage, a collective noun usually takes a singular verb but a plural pronoun, as in (i). However, the singular pronoun *it* is used, as in (j), if the collective noun is considered a single unit instead of a collection of various individual people.

(k) **My family are** loving and supportive. **They** are always ready to help me. (l) **The faculty have** signed **their** contracts.	In formal usage, a collective noun followed by a plural pronoun takes a plural verb, especially if the pronoun and verb occur in the same sentence, as in (1). Examples of collective nouns: *audience, class, committee, couple, crowd, faculty, family, government, group, public, staff, team.**

Government and *public* are usually followed by plural verbs in British usage but by singular verbs in American usage.

EXERCISE 9: Supply pronouns for the blanks. In some of the blanks there is more than one possibility. Choose the appropriate singular or plural verb in parentheses where necessary.

1. When a student wants to study, ___he; he/she; s/he___ should try to find a quiet place.*

2. A citizen has two primary responsibilities. _____ should vote in every election, and _____ should willingly serve on a jury.

3. Each student in Biology 101 has to spend three hours per week in the laboratory, where _____ (*does, do*) various experiments by following the directions in _____ lab manual.

4. A pharmacist fills prescriptions, but _____ (*is, are*) not allowed to prescribe medicine for patients. By law, only a doctor can prescribe medicine.

5. Anyone can learn how to dance if _____ (*wants, want*) to.

6. Hmmm. Someone forgot _____ umbrella. I wonder whose it is.

7. Everyone who came to the picnic brought _____ own food.

8. A: Is that your notebook?
 B: No. It belongs to one of the other students.
 A: Look on the inside cover. Did _____ write _____ _____ name there?

9. A dog makes a good pet if _____ (*is, are*) properly trained.

---

*Notice in 1 through 4: The problem of masculine/feminine pronouns can be avoided if a plural instead of a singular "indefinite noun" is used.

10. My cat is very independent. _____ obeys me only if _____

_____ wants to.*

11. I have a wonderful family. I love _____ very much, and _____

_____ (loves, love) me.

12. The soccer team felt unhappy because _____ had lost in the closing moments of the game.

13. A basketball team is relatively small. _____ (doesn't, don't) have as many members as a baseball team.

14. The audience clapped enthusiastically. Obviously _____ had enjoyed the concert.

15. The audience filled the room to overflowing. _____ (was, were) larger than we had expected.

16. The office staff (is, are) planning to give _____ boss a gold watch when he retires.

17. The young couple (has, have) saved enough money to make a downpayment on

_____ own house.

18. The crowd became more and more excited as the Premier's motorcade approached. _____ began to shout and wave flags in the air.

2-9 USING REFLEXIVE PRONOUNS

The following are *reflexive pronouns:*

myself	*ourselves*
yourself	*yourselves*
himself, herself, itself	*themselves*

(a) He looked at **himself** in the mirror.	A reflexive pronoun usually refers to the subject of a sentence. In (a): *he* and *himself* refer to the same person.
(b) **He himself** answered the phone, not his secretary. (c) **He** answered the phone **himself**.	Sometimes reflexive pronouns are used for emphasis, as in (b) and (c).

———————

*If the sex of a particular animal is known, usually *he* or *she* is used instead of *it*.

EXERCISE 10: Complete the sentences by using a word or expression from the given list and an appropriate reflexive pronoun.

angry at	*introduced*	*promised*
enjoy	*killed*	*proud of*
entertained	*laugh at*	*talking to*
feeling sorry for	*pat*	√ *taught*

1. Karen Williams never took lessons. She _____taught herself_____ how to play the piano.

2. Did Hank have a good time at the party? Did he _____?

3. All of you did a good job. You should be _____.

4. You did a good job, Barbara. You should _____ on the back.

5. A man down the street committed suicide. We were all shocked by the news that he had _____.

6. The children played very well without adult supervision. They _____ _____ by playing school.

7. I had always wanted to meet Mr. Anderson. When I saw him at a party last night, I walked over and _____ to him.

8. Yesterday Fred's car ran out of gas. Fred had to walk two miles to a gas station. He is still _____ for forgetting to fill the tank.

9. Nothing good ever comes from self-pity. You should stop _____ _____, George, and start doing something to solve your problems.

10. Carol made several careless mistakes at work last week and her boss is getting impatient with her. Carol has _____ to do better work in the future.

11. People might think you're a little crazy, but _____ is one way to practice using English.

12. Humor can ease the trials and tribulations of life. Sometimes we have to be able to _____.

Complete the following by using an appropriate reflexive pronoun.

13. I can't help you, Bob. You'll have to solve your problem by _____ _____.

14. Jane did not join the rest of us. She sat in the back of the room by _____

_____ .

15. You may think he is telling the truth, but I _____

don't believe him.

16. You _____ have to make that decision. No one can

make it for you.

17. Now that their children are grown, Mr. and Mrs. Grayson live by _____

_____ .

18. It is important for all of us to be honest with _____.

PART III Some Singular-Plural Usages of Nouns

EXERCISE 11—PRETEST: Give the plural form of the words in italics.

1. I met *a man* (_____ some men _____) at the meeting last night.

2. He saw *a mouse* (_____) running across the floor.

3. The baby got *a new tooth* (_____).

4. I need *a match* (_____).

5. He cooked *a potato* (_____) for dinner.

6. The professor is reading *a thesis* (_____).

7. I visited *a city* (_____) in Colombia.

8. She photographed *a leaf* (_____).

9. Before she made her decision, she talked to *an attorney* (_____
_____).

10. I caught *a fish* (_____).

11. I saw *a sheep* (_____) in the farmyard.

12. She talked to *a child* (_____).

13. She introduced me to *a woman* (_____)
at the party last night.

14. The children hid behind *a bush* (_____).

15. In science class, we studied about *a species* (_____) of
fish.

16. Before they began their scientific experiment, they made *a hypothesis* (_____
_____).

17. When I was at the park yesterday, I saw *a goose* (_____)
in a pond.

18. When we spoke in the cave, we heard *an echo* (_____).

19. He packed *a box* (_____).

20. The wagon is being pulled by *an ox* (_____).

21. Every day I read in the newspaper about *a new crisis* (_____
_____) in the world.

22. I told the children a fable about *a wolf* (_____) and
a fox (_____).

23. We read a story about *an Indian chief* (_____).

24. At the meeting last night, we listened to *a speech* (_____).

25. In science class, we studied about *a phenomenon* (_____
_____) of nature.

2-10 IRREGULAR NOUN PLURALS

(a) baby — babies duty — duties landlady — landladies	In (a): The final *-y* is preceded by a consonant; to make the plural form, change the *y* to *i* and add *-es*. (Note: If *-y* is preceded by a vowel, add only *-s*: *toys, monkeys, valleys, days.*)
(b) wife — wives thief — thieves shelf — shelves	If a noun ends in *-fe* or *-f*, the ending is changed to *-ves* (except: *beliefs, chiefs, roofs, staffs*).
(c) dish — dishes church — churches class — classes box — boxes	Add *-es* to nouns ending in *-sh, -ch, -s, -z,* and *-x*. (Exceptions: *monarchs, stomachs*)
(d) tomato — tomatoes hero — heroes mosquito — mosquitoes	Add *-es* to nouns that end in *-o* (except: *pianos, zoos, radios*).
(e) child — children foot — feet goose — geese louse — lice man — men mouse — mice ox — oxen tooth — teeth woman — women	Note: The plural possessive form of the nouns in (e) is also irregular. Compare: *Singular* *Plural* (1) the girl's ideas the girls' ideas (2) the woman's ideas *the **women's** ideas*
(f) deer — deer fish — fish sheep — sheep species — species means — means series — series	The plural form is the same as the singular form for the nouns in (f): *Singular* *Plural* one fish is . . . two fish are . . . one species is . . . several species are . . .
(g) analysis — analyses basis — bases crisis — crises thesis — theses hypothesis — hypotheses parenthesis — parentheses	The final sound of the plural forms in (g) is pronounced like the word "sees."
(h) datum — data bacterium — bacteria medium — media	In (g) through (l): Some of the words that English has borrowed or adapted from other languages have foreign plurals: *-is* becomes *-es* *-um* becomes *-a* *-on* becomes *-a* *-us* becomes *-i* *-a* becomes *-ae* *-ex* and *-ix* become *-ices*

(i)	criterion — criteria phenomenon — phenomena	Words with foreign plurals are especially common in fields of science.
(j)	stimulus — stimuli nucleus — nuclei radius — radii	
(k)	formula — formulae vertebra — vertebrae vita — vitae	In (k): *formulas* is also widely used.
(l)	index — indices appendix — appendices	In (l): *indexes* and *appendixes* are also widely used.

EXERCISE 12–PRETEST: Use *a/an** or *some* in the following.

1. I saw _____a_____ bird.

2. She made _____an_____ announcement.

3. He was thirsty, so he drank _____some_____ water.

4. I had _____ accident.

5. I have _____ homework to do tonight.

6. She gave me _____ advice.

7. We are having _____ cold weather.

8. She is carrying _____ suitcase.

9. She is carrying _____ luggage.

10. I found _____ quarter on the sidewalk.

11. We bought _____ furniture.

12. I heard _____ interesting news.

13. There was _____ earthquake in California.

14. I got _____ letter from my brother.

15. I got _____ mail yesterday.

16. She has _____ new job.

17. I have _____ work to do tonight.

_____

*Note: *an* is used in front of words which begin with a vowel (*a, e, i, o, u*) or a vowel sound.
   an apple   an elephant   an interesting book
   an hour (but: *a house*)   *an uncle* (but: *a university*)   *an onion* (but: *a one-way street*)

18. We saw _____ beautiful scenery on our trip.

19. We need to buy _____ equipment for the chemistry laboratory.

20. He listened to _____ music while he was studying last night.

2-11 COUNT AND NONCOUNT NOUNS

	SINGULAR	PLURAL	
COUNT NOUN	a book one book	books some books two books several books a number of books a lot of books many books few books a few books	*A count noun:* (1) may be preceded by *a* or *an* in the singular; (2) takes a final *-s* or *-es* in the plural.
NONCOUNT NOUN	money some money a lot of money a great deal of money much money little money a little money		*A noncount noun:* (1) is not preceded by *a* or *an*; (2) has no plural form; does not take a final *-s*.

Following is a list of some common nouns which are usually or always used as noncount nouns:

advice	weather	equipment
information	water	furniture
news	rain	jewelry
evidence	snow	luggage
	wind	machinery
work*	air	money
homework		music
housework	clothing	postage

---

*__Work__ is used as a count noun when it means "a work of art"; e.g., *There are many works of art in the museum.* (Compare: *I have some work to do tonight.*)

scenery	rice	enjoyment
traffic	salt	happiness
transportation	sugar	sadness
	tea	
fruit*		courage
food	slang	honesty
bread	vocabulary	luck
butter		patience
cheese	intelligence	peace
coffee	ignorance	progress
meat	knowledge	violence
milk	significance	poverty
pepper	fun	wealth

EXERCISE 13: *A lot of* is used with both count and noncount nouns. Complete each of the following by using *a lot of* and the correct form of the noun in parentheses.

1. (*money*) He has _____ a lot of money _____.

2. (*sandwich*) They ate _____.

3. (*good idea*) That book has _____.

4. (*bad weather*) We've been having _____

   _____.

5. (*homework*) We have _____
   to do tonight.

6. (*good advice*) She gave me _____.

7. (*photograph*) She took _____.

8. (*information*) An encyclopedia contains _____

   _____.

9. (*new vocabulary*) I have learned _____.

10. (*American slang*) He knows _____.

11. (*luck*) A gambler needs _____.

---

*Many food terms are used as count nouns when they mean "a kind of"; e.g., *An orange is a fruit*. (Compare: *I had fruit for dessert*.)

12. (*traffic*)   We were late because there (*was/were*) _____

_____ .

13. (*courage*)   She has _____ .

14. (*human being*)   _____
                       (*goes/go*) to bed hungry every night.

15. (*progress*)   Our country has made _____

_____ in the last twenty
                       years.

16. (*knowledge*)   My friend has _____ .

17. (*product*)   That company makes _____

_____ .

18. (*new furniture*) They bought _____
                       for their house.

19. (*fun*)   We all had _____ at the
                       picnic.

20. (*beautiful scenery*) We saw _____
                       on our cross-country trip.

EXERCISE 14: *Many* is used with count nouns; *much* is used with noncount nouns. Complete the following sentences by using *many* or *much* and the correct form of the noun in parentheses.

1. (*money*)   I don't have _____ much money _____ .

2. (*city*)   I haven't visited _____ many cities _____
                   in the United States.

3. (*mail*)   I haven't gotten _____
                   lately.

4. (*work*)   I can't go with you because I have too _____

_____ to do.

5. (*edge*)   How _____
                   does a pentagon have?

6. (*equipment*)   How _____
                   does a skier need?

7. (*information*) I couldn't find _____
                   in that book.

8. (*homework*)   How _____
                    did the teacher assign?

9. (*people*)   I haven't met _____
                    since I came here.

10. (*postage*)   How _____
                    do I need to mail this letter?

11. (*patience*)   I don't have _____
                    with incompetence.

12. (*patient*)   The doctor has so _____
                    that she has to work at least twelve hours a day.

13. (*tooth*)   How _____
                    does the average person have?

14. (*violence*)   I think there (*is/are*) too _____

                    _____ on television.

15. (*news*)   There (*isn't/aren't*) _____

                    _____ in the paper
                    tonight.

16. (*fish*)   How _____
                    (*is/are*) there in the ocean?

17. (*traffic*)   It didn't take us long to get here because there

                    (*wasn't/weren't*) _____ .

18. (*continent*)   How _____
                    (*is/are*) there in the world?

19. (*progress*)   How _____ has your
                    country made in improving the quality of
                    medical care available to the average citizen?

20. (*great-grandchild*) How _____
                    does Mrs. Cunningham have?

EXERCISE 15—ORAL: Use *many* or *much* with the following words, changing
the word to plural if necessary.*

Examples: (a) sentence   (b) water   (c) shelf
Responses: many sentences   much water   many shelves

_____

*You may want to practice using these words in sentences. *Much* is usually not used in affirmative sentences; instead, *a lot of* or *a great deal of* is frequently used. *Much* is used primarily in
negative sentences and questions.

1. furniture	16. clothing	31. desk
2. people	17. clothes	32. traffic
3. branch	18. homework	33. kiss
4. equipment	19. foot	34. hypothesis
5. machinery	20. prize	35. mail
6. machine	21. goose	36. mistake
7. woman	22. music	37. fish
8. news	23. progress	38. sugar
9. thief	24. face	39. office
10. niece	25. knowledge	40. luggage
11. mouse	26. zoo	41. gentleman
12. advice	27. child	42. tooth
13. marriage	28. bridge	43. ax
14. wife	29. information	44. slang
15. sheep	30. luck	45. human being

2-12 USING *A FEW* AND *FEW; A LITTLE* AND *LITTLE*

COUNT	NONCOUNT	
(a) She has been here only two weeks, but she has already made **a few friends**. (Positive idea: *She had made some friends.*)	(b) I'm very pleased. I've been able to save **a little money** this month. (Positive idea: *I have saved some money instead of spending all of it.*)	*A few* and *few* are used with plural count nouns. *A little* and *little* are used with noncount nouns.
		In (a) and (b): *A few* and *a little* give a positive idea; they indicate that something exists, is present.
(c) I feel sorry for her. She has **few friends**. (Negative idea: *She does not have many friends; she has almost no friends.*)	(d) I have **little money**. I don't even have enough money to buy food for dinner. (Negative idea: *I do not have much money; I have almost no money.*)	In (c) and (d): *Few* and *little* give a negative idea; they indicate that something is largely absent. (Often *few* and *little* are preceded by *very:* *She has very few friends.* *I have very little money.*)

EXERCISE 16: In the following, use *a few*, (*very*) *few, a little*, or (*very*) *little*.

1. Do you have _____a few_____ minutes? I'd like to ask you _____

_____a few_____ questions. I need _____a little_____ more information.

2. She is very careful. She makes _____(very) few_____ mistakes in her work.

3. After Rodney tasted the soup, he added _____ salt to it.

4. I don't like a lot of salt on my food. I add _____ salt to my food.

5. The professor lectured very clearly. As a result, _____ students had questions at the end of the class period.

6. I like music. I like to listen to _____ music after dinner before I begin studying.

7. He is very unpopular. _____ people like him.

8. I have to go to the post office because I have _____ letters to mail.

9. Every day Max goes to his mailbox, but it is usually empty. He gets _____ _____ mail.

10. We're looking forward to our vacation. We're planning to spend _____ _____ days with my folks and then _____ days with my husband's folks. After that, we're going to go to a fishing resort in Canada.

11. Driving downtown to the stadium for the baseball game was easy. We got there quickly because there was _____ traffic.

12. My friend arrived in the United States _____ months ago.

13. I think you could use some help. Let me give you _____ advice.

14. Because the family is very poor, the children have _____ clothes.

15. A: Are you finished?

    B: Not yet. I need _____ more minutes.

16. A: Are you finished?

    B: Not yet. I need _____ more time.*

17. _____ days ago I met a very interesting person.

18. Into each life, _____ rain must fall. (*a saying*)

_____

*The noun *time,* like many other nouns, may be either count or noncount. Compare:
  Count: *I have visited San Francisco many times.*
  Noncount: *We have to hurry. We don't have much time.*

2-13 USING NOUNS AS MODIFIERS

(a) The soup has vegetables in it. It is **vegetable soup**. (b) The building has offices in it. It is **an office building**.	Notice: When a noun is used as a modifier, it is in its singular form.
(c) The test lasted two hours. It was **a two-hour test**. (d) Her son is five years old. She has **a five-year-old son**.	When a noun used as a modifier is combined with a number expression, the noun is singular and a hyphen (-) is used.

EXERCISE 17: Use the italicized noun or noun phrase in the first sentence as a modifier in the second sentence.

1. My garden has *flowers* in it. It is _____ a flower garden. _____

2. That handbook is for *students*. It is _____

3. Their baby is *ten months old*. They have _____

4. Our trip lasted for *three days*. We took _____

5. She is a psychologist for *children*. She is _____

6. I wrote a check for *fifty dollars*. I wrote _____

7. I will get *three credits* for that course. It is _____

8. Their house has *nine rooms*. It is _____

9. That food is for *dogs*. It is _____

10. That room is for *guests*. It is _____

11. The professor asked us to write a paper of *five pages*. She asked us to write

_____

12. I have a sister who is *ten years old* and a brother who is *twelve years old*.

I have _____

EXERCISE 18: Answer the questions, as shown in the examples.

1. What do you call someone who robs banks? _____ a bank robber _____

2. . . . someone who fights bulls? _____ a bullfighter _____ *

3. . . . someone who collects stamps? _____ a stamp collector _____ †

4. . . . someone who trains animals? _____

5. . . . someone who tells stories? _____ *

6. . . . someone who takes tickets? _____

7. . . . someone who operates a

switchboard? _____ †

8. . . . someone who loves nature? _____

9. . . . someone who tames lions? _____

10. . . . someone who keeps books? _____ *

11. . . . someone who tastes wine? _____

12. . . . someone who blows glass? _____ *

13. . . . someone who smokes

cigarettes? _____

14. . . . someone who makes trouble? _____ *

15. . . . someone who earns wages? _____

16. . . . someone who pushes dope? _____

17. . . . someone who reads minds? _____

18. . . . someone who collects taxes? _____ †

19. . . . someone who manages an

office? _____

20. . . . someone who grows lettuce? _____

21. . . . What do you call something

that is used to open cans? _____

22. . . . to light cigarettes? _____

23. . . . to hold pots? _____

24. . . . to wipe a windshield? _____

25. . . . to peel potatoes? _____

26. . . . to dry hair? _____

27. . . . to remove spots? _____

---

*Usually spelled as one word.
†Spelled with *-or* instead of *-er*.

28. . . . to kill pain?   _____

29. . . . to detect lies?   _____†

30. . . . to extinguish fires?   _____

EXERCISE 19—ORAL (BOOKS CLOSED):

1. When you enter a theater, who do you give your ticket to?
2. What is another word for an accountant—for someone who takes care of the books for a business company?
3. If you are in your car and it begins to rain, what device are you going to turn on (in order to see out of the windshield)?
4. You want to have a can of beans for dinner. What are you going to use to open the can?
5. What do you call someone who has ESP—who knows what other people are thinking?
6. If I have a headache, I might take an aspirin to get rid of the pain. What do you call a substance such as aspirin?
7. If there is a small fire in this room, what might you use to put out the fire?
8. Who is in charge of an office?
9. If you go to a beauty salon, what will the hairdresser use to dry your hair?
10. What do you call someone who gets weekly or monthly wages?

11. The tip of your pencil is dull. What are you going to use to sharpen it?
12. If you want to open a letter neatly, what are you going to use?
13. What do you call someone who paints houses for a living?
14. What do you call someone who operates an elevator?
15. When you want to shake some salt onto your food, what do you use?
16. Some people are skilled in climbing mountains. What do you call them?
17. Some people own homes. What do you call them?
18. Some people collect garbage. What do you call them?
19. What do you use if you want to grind some pepper?
20. What do you call a person or a device that washes dishes?

EXERCISE 20—ERROR ANALYSIS: The following sentences are adapted from student writing and contain typical errors. Test your skill by finding and correcting these errors.

Example: I sent two letter to one of my friend.
Correction: I sent two letters to one of my friends.

1. This book contain many different kind of story and article.
2. There is a lot of differences between United State and my country.
3. The English is one of the most important language in the world.
4. She is always willing to help her friends in every possible ways.
5. I don't have enough time to make all of my homeworks.
6. He succeeded in creating one of the best army in the world.
7. There are many equipments in the research laboratory, but undergraduates are not allowed to use them.
8. All of the guest enjoyed themself at the reception.
9. I have a five years old daughter and a three years old son.
10. I am not accustomed to a cold weather.
11. Each states in the country have a different language.
12. Most of the people in my apartment building is friendly.
13. A political leader should have the ability to adapt themselves to a changing world.
14. In my opinion, a foreign student should live in a dormitory because they will meet many people and can practice their English every day. Also, if you live in a dormitory, your food is provided for you.

2-14 FORMS OF *OTHER*

	ADJECTIVE	PRONOUN	
singular: *plural:*	another book (is) other books (are)	another (is) others (are)	Forms of *other* are used as either adjectives or pronouns. Notice: A final *-s* is used only for a plural pronoun (*others*).
singular: *plural:*	the other book (is) the other books (are)	the other (is) the others (are)	
(a)	The students in the class come from many countries. One of the students is from Mexico. **Another student is** from Iraq. **Another is** from Japan. **Other students are** from Brazil. **Others are** from Algeria.		The meaning of ***another***: *one more in addition to the one(s) already mentioned.* The meaning of ***other/others*** (without ***the***): *several more in addition to the one(s) already mentioned.*
(b) (c)	I have three books. Two are mine. **The other book is** yours. (**The other is** yours.) I have three books. One is mine. **The other books are** yours. (**The others are** yours.)		The meaning of ***the other(s)***: *all that remains from a given number; the rest of a specific group.*

(d) We write to **each other** every week. (e) We write to **one another** every week.	*Each other* and *one another* indicate a reciprocal relationship. In (d) and (e): I write to him every week, and he writes to me every week.
(f) Please write on **every other** line. (g) I see her **every other** week.	*Every other* gives the idea of "alternate." In (f): Write on the first line. Do not write on the second line. Write on the third line. Do not write on the fourth line. (etc.)
(h) I will be here for **another three years.** (i) I need **another five dollars.** (j) We drove **another ten miles.**	*Another* is used with expressions of time, money, and distance, even if these expressions contain plural nouns.

EXERCISE 21: Supply a form of *other* in the following.

1. Look at your hand. There is a total of five fingers. One is your thumb. _____ is your index finger. _____ one is your middle finger. _____ finger is your ring finger. And _____ _____ finger (the last of the five) is your little finger.

2. Look at your hands. One is your right hand. _____ is your left hand.

3. I got three letters. One was from my father. _____ one was from my sister. _____ letter was from my girlfriend.

4. I invited five people to my party. Out of those five people, only John and Mary can come. _____ can't come.

5. I invited five people to my party. Out of those five people, only John and Mary can come. _____ people can't come.

6. I would like some more books on this subject. Do you have any _____ _____ that you could lend me?

7. I would like to read more about this subject. Do you have any _____ _____ books that you could lend me?

8. There are many means of transportation. The airplane is one means of transportation. The train is _____ .

9. There are many means of transportation. The airplane is one. _____

    _____ are the train, the automobile, and the horse.

10. There are two women standing on the corner. One is Helen Jansen and _____

    _____ is Pat Hendricks.

11. Alice reads *The New York Times* every day. She doesn't read any _____

    _____ newspapers.

12. Some people prefer classical music, but _____ prefer rock music.

13. Mr. and Mrs. Cunningham are a happily married couple. They love _____

    _____ . They support _____ . They like _____

    _____ .

14. He will graduate in _____ two years.

15. I'm almost finished. I just need _____ five minutes.

EXERCISE 22:   Same as the preceding exercise.

1. One common English abbreviation is *lb.* _____ common one is

    oz. _____ are *ft., hr.,* and *p.*

2. Two countries border on the United States. One is Canada. _____
    is Mexico.

3. One of the countries I would like to visit is Sweden. _____ is

    Mexico. Of course, besides these two countries, there are many _____

    _____ places I would like to see.

4. They have three children. One has graduated from college and has a job.

    _____ is in school at the University of Arkansas. _____

    _____ is still living at home.

5. Thank you for inviting me to go on the picnic. I'd like to go with you, but I've

    already made _____ plans.

6. Most of the guests have already arrived, and I'm sure that all of _____

    _____ will be here soon.

7. Some people are tall; _____ are short. Some people are fat;

    _____ are thin. Some people are nearsighted; _____

    _____ people are farsighted.

8. That country has two basic problems. One is inflation, and _____ is the instability of the government.

9. I have been in only three cities since I came to the United States. One is New York, and _____ are Washington, D.C., and Chicago.

10. When his alarm went off this morning, he shut it off, rolled over, and slept for _____ twenty minutes.

11. Louis and I have been friends for a long time. We've known _____ _____ since we were children.

12. Individual differences in children must be recognized. Whereas one child might have a strong interest in mathematics and science, _____ child might tend more toward artistic endeavors.

13. It's a long trip. I'm getting tired of riding in the car, but we still have _____ _____ two hundred miles to go.

14. In just _____ three weeks, he will be a married man.

15. Prices continually rise. Next year a new car will cost _____ three or four hundred dollars.

EXERCISE 23—ORAL (BOOKS CLOSED): Complete the sentence, using an appropriate form of *other*.

    Example: There are two books on the desk. One is . . . .
    Response: (One is . . .) mine and the other is yours.
                  (One is . . .) red. The other is blue.

1. I speak two languages. One is . . . .
2. I speak three languages. One is . . . .
3. I lost my textbook, so I had to buy . . . .
4. Some people have straight hair, but . . . .
5. I'm still thirsty. I'd like . . . .
6. George Washington is one American hero. Abraham Lincoln . . . .
7. I have two books. One is . . . .
8. Some TV programs are excellent, but . . . .
9. Some people need at least eight hours of sleep each night, but . . . .
10. Only two of the students failed the quiz. All of . . . .
11. Mary and John are in love. They love . . . .
12. There are three colors that I especially like. One is . . . .
13. I have two candy bars. I want only one of them. Would you like . . . .

14. I'm still hungry. I'd like . . .
15. There are three places in particular that I would like to visit while I am in the United States. One is . . .

EXERCISE 24—WRITTEN: Write a paragraph on each of the following topics. *Write as quickly as you can.* Write whatever comes into your mind.*

1. food
2. English
3. this room
4. animals

EXERCISE 25—PREPOSITIONS: Supply an appropriate preposition. Each of the following contains a two-word verb. (A reference list of two-word verbs may be found in Appendix 2.)

1. A: Where did you grow _____?
   B: In Seattle, Washington.

2. A: I'm trying to find yesterday's newspaper. Have you seen it?
   B: I'm afraid I threw it _____. I thought you had finished reading it.

3. A: Don't forget to turn the lights _____ before you go to bed.
   B: I won't.

4. A: I have a car, so I can drive us to the festival.
   B: Good.

   A: What time should I pick you _____?
   B: Anytime after five would be fine.

5. A: We couldn't see the show at the outside theater last night.
   B: Why not?

   A: It was called _____ on account of rain.
   B: Did you get a raincheck?

6. A: Thomas looks sad.

   B: I think he misses his girlfriend. Let's try to cheer him _____.

7. A: I would like to check this book _____. What am I supposed to do?
   B: Take the book to the circulation desk and give the librarian your student I.D.

---

*Suggested time limit: ten to fifteen minutes for each topic. Each paragraph should be approximately 100 words.

8. A: What brought _____ your decision to quit your present job?

   B: I was offered a better job.

9. A: How many people showed _____ for the meeting yesterday?

   B: About twenty.

10. A: How was your vacation?

    B: I had a great time.

    A: When did you get _____ in town?

    B: A couple of days ago. I had planned to stay a little longer, but I

       ran _____ _____ money.

Verb Tenses

PART 1 Preliminary Review: Irregular Verbs and Spelling of **-ing** and **-ed** Forms

EXERCISE 1—ORAL (BOOKS CLOSED): In order to practice using irregular verbs, answer each question with "yes."

Example: Did you speak to the teacher?
Response: Yes, I did. I spoke to the teacher.

1. Did you drink some coffee before class?
2. Did you bring your books to class?
3. Did you forget your briefcase?
4. Did you shake your head?
5. Did you catch the bus this morning?
6. Did you drive to school?
7. Did you lose your book?
8. Did you find your book?
9. Did you wind your watch this morning?
10. Did you understand what I said?
11. Did you tell your friend the news?
12. Did you spread the news?
13. Did you fall on the ice?
14. Did you hurt yourself when you fell?
15. Did you fly to (this city)?
16. Did you wear a coat to class?
17. Did you hang your coat on a hook?
18. Did you eat lunch?

19. Did you take chemistry in high school?
20. Did you ride the bus to school?
21. Did you swear to tell the truth?
22. I made a mistake. Did you forgive me?
23. Did you write a letter to your family?
24. Did you bite the dog???

EXERCISE 2–ORAL (BOOKS CLOSED): Answer, "No, I didn't. Someone else . . . ."

> *Example:* Did you shut the door?
> *Response:* No, I didn't. Someone else shut the door.

1. Did you make a mistake?
2. Did you break that window?
3. Did you steal my wallet?
4. Did you take my piece of paper?
5. Did you draw that picture?
6. Did you sweep the floor this morning?
7. Did you teach class yesterday?
8. Did you dig that hole in the ground?
9. Did you feed the cat?
10. Did you hide my book from me?
11. Did you blow that whistle?
12. Did you throw a piece of chalk out the window?
13. Did you tear that piece of paper?
14. Did you build that house?

EXERCISE 3–ORAL (BOOKS CLOSED): Answer with "yes."

> *Example:* Did you sit down?
> *Response:* Yes, I did. I sat down.

1. Did you give me some money?
2. Did you stand at the bus stop?
3. Did you choose the blue pen?
4. Did you run to class this (morning)?
5. Did you sleep well last night?
6. Did you hear that noise outside the window?
7. Did you withdraw some money from the bank?
8. Did you wake up at seven this morning?
9. Did you swim in the ocean?
10. Did you go home after class yesterday?
11. Did you bend your elbow?
12. Did you send a letter?
13. Did you sing a song?
14. Did you stick your hand in your pocket?
15. Did you grind the pepper?
16. Did you strike the desk with your hand?
17. Did you light a cigarette?
18. Did you mean what you said?
19. Did you hold your hand up?
20. Did you speak to (. . .)?

EXERCISE 4–ORAL (BOOKS CLOSED):   Answer with "yes."

Example: Did the students come to class?
Response: Yes, they did. They came to class.

1. Did class begin at (nine)?
2. Did the sun rise at six this morning?
3. Did you cut your finger?
4. Did it bleed when you cut it?
5. Did the grass grow after the rain?
6. Did a bee sting you?
7. Did the telephone ring?
8. Did the water freeze?
9. Did your friend quit school?
10. Did the soldiers fight?
11. Did the thief creep into the room?
12. Did the policeman shoot at the thief?
13. Did the thief flee?
14. Did your team win the game yesterday?
15. Did your car slide on the ice?
16. Did the door swing open?
17. Did the children blow up some balloons?
18. Did the balloons burst?
19. Did the radio station broadcast the news?
20. Did you know all of the irregular verbs?

3-1   IRREGULAR VERBS

SIMPLE FORM	SIMPLE PAST	PAST PARTICIPLE	*(To the student: Cover the left side of the page and test yourself. Be very careful about spelling.)*		
arise	arose	arisen	arise	_____	_____
be	was, were	been	be	_____	_____
beat	beat	beaten (beat)	beat	_____	_____
become	became	become	become	_____	_____
begin	began	begun	begin	_____	_____
bend	bent	bent	bend	_____	_____
bet	bet	bet	bet	_____	_____
bite	bit	bitten	bite	_____	_____
bleed	bled	bled	bleed	_____	_____
blow	blew	blown	blow	_____	_____
break	broke	broken	break	_____	_____
breed	bred	bred	breed	_____	_____

SIMPLE FORM	SIMPLE PAST	PAST PARTICIPLE			
bring	brought	brought	bring	_____	_____
broadcast	broadcast	broadcast	broadcast	_____	_____
burst	burst	burst	burst	_____	_____
buy	bought	bought	buy	_____	_____
catch	caught	caught	catch	_____	_____
choose	chose	chosen	choose	_____	_____
cling	clung	clung	cling	_____	_____
come	came	come	come	_____	_____
cost	cost	cost	cost	_____	_____
creep	crept	crept	creep	_____	_____
cut	cut	cut	cut	_____	_____
deal	dealt	dealt	deal	_____	_____
dig	dug	dug	dig	_____	_____
do	did	done	do	_____	_____
draw	drew	drawn	draw	_____	_____
drink	drank	drunk	drink	_____	_____
drive	drove	driven	drive	_____	_____
eat	ate	eaten	eat	_____	_____
fall	fell	fallen	fall	_____	_____
feed	fed	fed	feed	_____	_____
feel	felt	felt	feel	_____	_____
fight	fought	fought	fight	_____	_____
find	found	found	find	_____	_____
flee	fled	fled	flee	_____	_____
fly	flew	flown	fly	_____	_____
forbid	forbade	forbidden	forbid	_____	_____
forget	forgot	forgotten (forgot)	forget	_____	_____

SIMPLE FORM	*SIMPLE PAST*	*PAST PARTICIPLE*			
forgive	forgave	forgiven	forgive	_____	_____
freeze	froze	frozen	freeze	_____	_____
get	got	gotten (got)	get	_____	_____
give	gave	given	give	_____	_____
go	went	gone	go	_____	_____
grind	ground	ground	grind	_____	_____
grow	grew	grown	grow	_____	_____
hang	hung	hung	hang	_____	_____
have	had	had	have	_____	_____
hear	heard	heard	hear	_____	_____
hide	hid	hidden	hide	_____	_____
hit	hit	hit	hit	_____	_____
hold	held	held	hold	_____	_____
hurt	hurt	hurt	hurt	_____	_____
keep	kept	kept	keep	_____	_____
know	knew	known	know	_____	_____
lay	laid	laid	lay	_____	_____
lead	led	led	lead	_____	_____
let	let	let	let	_____	_____
lie	lay	lain	lie	_____	_____
light	lit (lighted)	lit (lighted)	light	_____	_____
lose	lost	lost	lose	_____	_____
make	made	made	make	_____	_____
mean	meant	meant	mean	_____	_____
meet	met	met	meet	_____	_____
pay	paid	paid	pay	_____	_____
put	put	put	put	_____	_____

SIMPLE FORM	SIMPLE PAST	PAST PARTICIPLE			
quit	quit	quit	quit	_____	_____
read	read	read	read	_____	_____
ride	rode	ridden	ride	_____	_____
ring	rang	rung	ring	_____	_____
rise	rose	risen	rise	_____	_____
run	ran	run	run	_____	_____
say	said	said	say	_____	_____
see	saw	seen	see	_____	_____
seek	sought	sought	seek	_____	_____
sell	sold	sold	sell	_____	_____
send	sent	sent	send	_____	_____
set	set	set	set	_____	_____
shake	shook	shaken	shake	_____	_____
shine	shone	shone	shine	_____	_____
shoot	shot	shot	shoot	_____	_____
show	showed	shown (showed)	show	_____	_____
shrink	shrank (shrunk)	shrunk	shrink	_____	_____
shut	shut	shut	shut	_____	_____
sing	sang	sung	sing	_____	_____
sit	sat	sat	sit	_____	_____
sleep	slept	slept	sleep	_____	_____
slide	slid	slid	slide	_____	_____
slit	slit	slit	slit	_____	_____
speak	spoke	spoken	speak	_____	_____
spend	spent	spent	spend	_____	_____
split	split	split	split	_____	_____

SIMPLE FORM	SIMPLE PAST	PAST PARTICIPLE			
spread	spread	spread	spread	_____	_____
stand	stood	stood	stand	_____	_____
steal	stole	stolen	steal	_____	_____
stick	stuck	stuck	stick	_____	_____
sting	stung	stung	sting	_____	_____
stink	stank	stunk	stink	_____	_____
strike	struck	struck	strike	_____	_____
swear	swore	sworn	swear	_____	_____
sweep	swept	swept	sweep	_____	_____
swim	swam	swum	swim	_____	_____
swing	swung	swung	swing	_____	_____
take	took	taken	take	_____	_____
teach	taught	taught	teach	_____	_____
tear	tore	torn	tear	_____	_____
tell	told	told	tell	_____	_____
think	thought	thought	think	_____	_____
throw	threw	thrown	throw	_____	_____
understand	understood	understood	understand	_____	_____
upset	upset	upset	upset	_____	_____
wake	woke	waked (woken)	wake	_____	_____
wear	wore	worn	wear	_____	_____
weave	wove	woven	weave	_____	_____
weep	wept	wept	weep	_____	_____
win	won	won	win	_____	_____
wind	wound	wound	wind	_____	_____
withdraw	withdrew	withdrawn	withdraw	_____	_____
write	wrote	written	write	_____	_____

3-2 TROUBLESOME VERBS*

TRANSITIVE (followed by an object)	INTRANSITIVE (not followed by an object)
(a) **raise, raised, raised** The farmer raises vegetables.	(b) **rise, rose, risen** The sun rises in the east.
(c) **set, set, set** I will set the book on the desk.	(d) **sit, sat, sat** I sit in the front row.
(e) **lay, laid, laid** I am laying the book on the desk.	(f) **lie†, lay, lain** He is lying on his bed.
(g) **shine, shined, shined** I shined my shoes.	(h) **shine, shone, shone** The sun shone through the window.
(i) **hang, hung, hung** I hung my clothes in the closet. (j) **hang, hanged, hanged** They hanged the criminal by the neck until he was dead.	

*Many native speakers find some of these verbs troublesome, too, especially *lay* and *lie.*
† *Lie* is a regular verb (*lie, lied*) when it means "not tell the truth": *He lied to me about his age.*

EXERCISE 5: Choose the correct word in parentheses.

1. The student (raised, rose) his hand in class.
2. Hot air (raises, rises).
3. She (set, sat) in a chair because she was tired.
4. I (set, sat) your dictionary on the table a few minutes ago.
5. Hens (lay, lie) eggs.
6. He is (laying, lying) on the grass in the park right now.
7. She (laid, lay) the comb on top of the dresser a few minutes ago.
8. If you are tired, you should (lay, lie) down and take a nap.
9. San Francisco (lays, lies) to the north of Los Angeles.
10. The sun (shined, shone).
11. We (hanged, hung) the picture on the wall.
12. She (hanged, hung) up the telephone.

EXERCISE 6–ORAL: Practice pronouncing the following.

GROUP A: Final *-ed* is pronounced /t/ after voiceless sounds:

1. looked
2. asked
3. helped
4. laughed

5. pushed
6. watched
7. dressed
8. boxed

GROUP B: Final *-ed* is pronounced /d/ after voiced sounds:

9. sobbed
10. believed
11. filled
12. poured

13. roamed
14. judged
15. enjoyed
16. dried

GROUP C: Final *-ed* is pronounced /əd/ after *d* and *t:*

17. needed
18. defended
19. added
20. loaded

21. waited
22. rested
23. counted
24. halted

Practice the following sentences.

25. My friend jumped up and down and shouted when she heard the news.
26. The concert lasted for two hours.
27. With the coming of spring, the river flooded and inundated several villages.
28. She tapped the top of her desk.
29. He described his house.
30. They demanded to know the answer.
31. The airplane departed at six and landed at eight.
32. Alice pushed and I pulled.
33. He handed me his dictionary.
34. Jack tooted his horn.
35. They asked us to help them.

EXERCISE 7–PRETEST (BOOKS CLOSED): On another piece of paper, write the words that your teacher says. This is a spelling test.

Example: Cried. I cried because I was unhappy. Cried.

Written response: cried

1. (hope + -*ed*)	11. (enjoy + -*ed*)
2. (dine + -*ing*)	12. (play + -*ing*)
3. (stop + -*ed*)	13. (study + -*ing*)
4. (plan + -*ing*)	14. (worry + -*ed*)
5. (rain + -*ed*)	15. (die + -*ed*)
6. (wait + -*ing*)	16. (lie + -*ing*)
7. (listen + -*ing*)	17. (start + -*ing*)
8. (happen + -*ed*)	18. (harm + -*ed*)
9. (begin + -*ing*)	
10. (occur + -*ed*)	

3–3 SPELLING OF -*ING* AND -*ED* FORMS

1. VERBS THAT END IN -*E*	(a)	hope date injure	hoping dating injuring	hoped dated injured	-*ING FORM:* If the word ends in -*e*, drop the -*e* and add -*ing*. -*ED FORM:* If the word ends in -*e*, just add -*d*.
2. VERBS THAT END IN A VOWEL AND A CONSONANT		**ONE-SYLLABLE VERBS**			
	(b)	stop rob beg	stopping robbing begging	stopped robbed begged	*1* vowel → *2* consonants
	(c)	rain fool dream	raining fooling dreaming	rained fooled dreamed	*2* vowels → *1* consonant
		TWO-SYLLABLE VERBS			
	(d)	listen offer open	listening offering opening	listened offered opened	*1st* syllable stressed → *1* consonant
	(e)	begin prefer control	beginning preferring controlling	(began) preferred controlled	*2nd* syllable stressed → *2* consonants
3. VERBS THAT END IN -*Y*	(f)	enjoy pray buy	enjoying praying buying	enjoyed prayed (bought)	If -*y* is preceded by a vowel, keep the -*y*.
	(g)	study try reply	studying trying replying	studied tried replied	If -*y* is preceded by a consonant: -*ING FORM:* keep the -*y*, add -*ing*. -*ED FORM:* change -*y* to -*i*, add -*ed*.

4. VERBS THAT END IN *-IE*	(h)	die lie tie	dying lying tying	died lied tied	*-ING FORM:* Change *-ie* to *-y*, add *-ing*. *-ED FORM:* Add *-d*.
5. VERBS THAT END IN TWO CONSONANTS	(i)	start fold demand	starting folding demanding	started folded demanded	If the word ends in two consonants, just add the ending.

EXERCISE 8: Give the correct *-ing* form for the following.

1. hold   _____holding_____
2. hide   _____
3. run   _____
4. ruin   _____
5. sit   _____
6. write   _____
7. eat   _____
8. pat   _____

9. act   _____
10. come   _____
11. open   _____
12. begin   _____
13. die   _____
14. fry   _____
15. earn   _____

EXERCISE 9: Give the correct *-ing* and *-ed* forms for the following.

1. boil   _____boiling_____   _____boiled_____
2. try   _____   _____
3. stay   _____   _____
4. tape   _____   _____
5. tap   _____   _____
6. offer   _____   _____
7. prefer   _____   _____
8. gain   _____   _____
9. plan   _____   _____
10. tie   _____   _____
11. help   _____   _____

12. study   _____   _____

13. admit   _____   _____

14. visit   _____   _____

15. hug   _____   _____

EXERCISE 10:   Give the correct *-ed* form for the following.

1. bore   _____

6. loot   _____

2. jar   _____

7. sob   _____

3. jeer   _____

8. ripen   _____

4. dry   _____

9. refer   _____

5. guide   _____

10. intensify   _____

EXERCISE 11:   Give the correct *-ing* form for the following.

1. raid   _____

6. lie   _____

2. ride   _____

7. tame   _____

3. bid   _____

8. teem   _____

4. succeed   _____

9. trim   _____

5. bury   _____

10. argue   _____

PART II An Overview of English Verb Tenses

This diagram will be used in the tense descriptions:

3-4 THE SIMPLE TENSES

TENSE	EXAMPLES	MEANING
SIMPLE PRESENT	(a) It **snows** in Alaska. (b) I **watch** television every day.	In general, the simple present expresses events or situations that *exist always, usually, habitually;* they exist now, have existed in the past, and probably will exist in the future.
SIMPLE PAST	(c) It **snowed** yesterday. (d) I **watched** television last night.	*At one particular time in the past,* this happened. It began and ended in the past.
SIMPLE FUTURE	(e) It **will snow** tomorrow. (f) I **will watch** television tonight.	*At one particular time in the future,* this will happen.

3-5 THE PROGRESSIVE TENSES*

Form:	**be + -ing** (present participle)	
Meaning:	The progressive tenses give the idea that an action is *in progress* during a particular time. The tenses say that an action *begins before, is in progress during,* and *continues after* another time or action.	

PRESENT PROGRESSIVE		
(diagram: 10:00, 11:00)	(a) He **is sleeping** right now.	He went to sleep at 10:00 tonight. It is now 11:00 and he is still asleep. His sleep began in the past, *is in progress at the present time,* and probably will continue.
PAST PROGRESSIVE		
(diagram: 10:00, 11:00)	(b) He **was sleeping** when I arrived.	He went to sleep at 10:00 last night. I arrived at 11:00. He was still asleep. His sleep began before and *was in progress at a particular time in the past.* It probably continued.
FUTURE PROGRESSIVE		
(diagram: 10:00, 11:00)	(c) He **will be sleeping** when we arrive.	He will go to sleep at 10:00 tomorrow night. We will arrive at 11:00. The action of sleeping will begin before we arrive and it *will be in progress at a particular time in the future.* Probably his sleep will continue.

*The progressive tenses are also called the continuous tenses: *present continuous, past continuous,* and *future continuous.*

3-6 THE PERFECT TENSES

Form:	*have + -ed* (past participle)	
Meaning:	The perfect tenses all give the idea that one thing *happens before* another time or event.	

PRESENT PERFECT eat — now X — X (time ?)	(a) **I have** already **eaten**.	I *finished* eating sometime *before now*. The exact time is not important.
PAST PERFECT eat — arrive X — X	(b) **I had** already **eaten** when they arrived.	First I finished eating. Later they arrived. My eating was completely *finished before another time in the past*.
FUTURE PERFECT eat — arrive X — X	(c) **I will** already **have eaten** when they arrive.	First I will finish eating. Later they will arrive. My eating will be completely *finished before another time in the future*.

3-7 THE PERFECT PROGRESSIVE TENSES

Form:	*have + been + -ing*	
Meaning:	The perfect progressive tenses give the idea that one event is *in progress immediately before, up to, until another time or event.* The tenses are used to express the *duration* of the first event.	

PRESENT PERFECT PROGRESSIVE	(a) **I have been studying** for two hours.	Event in progress: studying. When? *Before now, up to now.* How long? For two hours.
2 hrs.		
PAST PERFECT PROGRESSIVE	(b) **I had been studying** for two hours before my friend came.	Event in progress: studying. When? *Before another event in the past.* How long? For two hours.
2 hrs.		
FUTURE PERFECT PROGRESSIVE	(c) **I will have been studying** for two hours by the time you arrive.	Event in progress: studying. When? *Before another event in the future.* How long? For two hours.
2 hrs.		

3-8 SUMMARY CHART OF VERB TENSES

SIMPLE PRESENT	PRESENT PROGRESSIVE
The world **is** round. I **study** every day.	I **am studying** right now.
SIMPLE PAST	PAST PROGRESSIVE
I **studied** last night.	I **was studying** when they came.
SIMPLE FUTURE	FUTURE PROGRESSIVE
I **will study** tomorrow.	I **will be studying** when you come.

PRESENT PERFECT	**PRESENT PERFECT PROGRESSIVE**
I **have** already **studied** Chapter One.	I **have been studying** for two hours.
PAST PERFECT	**PAST PERFECT PROGRESSIVE**
I **had** already **studied** Chapter One before I began to study Chapter Two.	I **had been studying** for two hours before my friends came.
FUTURE PERFECT	**FUTURE PERFECT PROGRESSIVE**
I **will** already **have studied** Chapter Four before I study Chapter Five.	I **will have been studying** for two hours by the time you arrive.

3-9 CONTRACTIONS

	WITH PRONOUNS (usually spoken; usually written)*	WITH NOUNS (usually spoken; *not* ordinarily written)	WITH *NOT*
am	*I'm* reading a book.	————	————†
is	*She's* studying. *It's* going to rain.	"My *book's* on the table."	*isn't*
are	*You're* coming. *They're* waiting for us.	"My *books're* on the table."	*aren't*
has	*She's* been here for a year. *It's* been cold lately.	"*Mary's* never met him" "The *weather's* been cold."	*hasn't*
have	*I've* finished my work. *They've* never met you.	"The *students've* finished their work."	*haven't*
had	*He'd* been waiting for us. *We'd* forgotten.	"*Mary'd* never met him before."	*hadn't*
will	*I'll* come later. *She'll* help us.	"*John'll* be coming soon." "I hope the *weather'll* be nice tomorrow."	*won't*

*Contractions with pronouns are not used in very formal writing.

† Sometimes in spoken English you will hear "ain't." It means *am not, isn't,* or *aren't.* "Ain't" is not considered good English, but many people use "ain't" regularly and it is also frequently used for humor.

PART III Using Verb Tenses

3-10 SIMPLE PRESENT

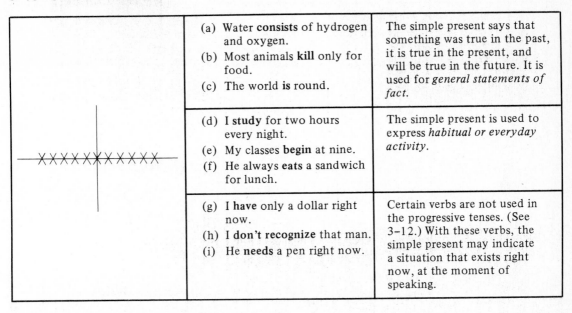

	(a) Water **consists** of hydrogen and oxygen. (b) Most animals **kill** only for food. (c) The world **is** round.	The simple present says that something was true in the past, it is true in the present, and will be true in the future. It is used for *general statements of fact.*
	(d) I **study** for two hours every night. (e) My classes **begin** at nine. (f) He always **eats** a sandwich for lunch.	The simple present is used to express *habitual or everyday activity.*
	(g) I **have** only a dollar right now. (h) I **don't recognize** that man. (i) He **needs** a pen right now.	Certain verbs are not used in the progressive tenses. (See 3-12.) With these verbs, the simple present may indicate a situation that exists right now, at the moment of speaking.

3-11 PRESENT PROGRESSIVE

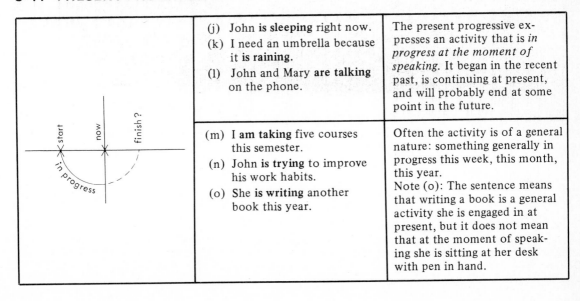

	(j) John **is sleeping** right now. (k) I need an umbrella because it **is raining**. (l) John and Mary **are talking** on the phone.	The present progressive expresses an activity that is *in progress at the moment of speaking.* It began in the recent past, is continuing at present, and will probably end at some point in the future.
	(m) I **am taking** five courses this semester. (n) John **is trying** to improve his work habits. (o) She **is writing** another book this year.	Often the activity is of a general nature: something generally in progress this week, this month, this year. Note (o): The sentence means that writing a book is a general activity she is engaged in at present, but it does not mean that at the moment of speaking she is sitting at her desk with pen in hand.

3-12 VERBS USUALLY NOT USED IN ANY OF THE PROGRESSIVE TENSES

VERB	EXAMPLE	OTHER USES OF THIS VERB
be	(a) I **am** hungry.	
SENSES		
hear	(b) I **hear** a noise.	You *will be hearing* from me. (meaning: I will write or phone you.)
taste	(c) This food **tastes** good.	
smell	(d) I **smell** gas.	
see	(e) I **see** a butterfly.	The doctor *is seeing* a patient. (meaning: meeting with)
MENTAL ACTIVITY		
know	(f) I **know** his phone number.	
believe	(g) I **believe** his story.	
think	(h) I **think** he is a kind man. (meaning: believe)	I *am thinking* about this grammar. (meaning: Certain thoughts are going through my mind right now.)
understand	(i) I **understand** your problem now.	
recognize	(j) I **don't recognize** him.	
remember	(k) I **remember** my first teacher.	
	(l) I **forget** his name.	
mean	(m) I **mean** this book, not that one.	I *have been meaning* to call you. (meaning: intending)
POSSESSION		
possess	(n) He **possesses** many fine qualities.	
own	(o) She **owns** a house.	
have	(p) He **has** a car. (meaning: possesses)	I *am having* trouble. He *is having* a good time. (meaning: experiencing)
belong	(q) That **belongs** to me.	
ATTITUDES		
want	(r) I **want** to leave now.	
prefer	(s) He **prefers** to stay here.	
need	(t) I **need** some help.	
appreciate	(u) I **appreciate** your help.	
love	(v) I **love** my family.	
like	(w) I **like** this book.	
hate	(x) She **hates** dishonesty.	
dislike	(y) I **dislike** this book.	
seem	(z) He **seems** to be a nice person.	

VERB	EXAMPLE	OTHER USES OF THIS VERB
ATTITUDES look *appear*	(aa) She **looks** cold. (meaning: seems to be) (bb) He **appears** to be asleep. (meaning: seems to be)	I *am looking* out the window. (meaning: using my eyes to see) The actor *is appearing* on the stage.

EXERCISE 12: Use either the *simple present* or the *present progressive* of the verbs in parentheses.

1. Kathy (*sit, usually**) _____ in the front row during class, but today she (*sit*) _____ in the last row.

2. Diane can't come to the phone because she (*wash*) _____ _____ her hair.

3. Diane (*wash*) _____ her hair every other day or so.

4. Please be quiet. I (*try*) _____ to concentrate.

5. (*Lock, you, always*) _____ the door to your apartment when you leave?

6. Look! It (*snow*) _____ .

7. Mike (*go, not*) _____ to school right now because it is summer. He (*attend*) _____ college from September to May every year, but in the summers he (*have, usually*) _____ _____ a job at the post office. In fact, he (*work*) _____ there this summer.

8. Right now I (*look*) _____ around the classroom. Ahmed (*write*) _____ in his book. Carlos (*bite*) _____

_____

*Frequency adverbs (e.g., *always, usually, often, never*) have usual positions:
   (1) In front of simple present and simple past verbs, except **be:**
     (a) He *always comes* on time.   BUT: (c) He *is always* on time.
     (b) He *always came* on time.   (d) He *was always* on time.
   (2) Between an auxiliary and a main verb:
     (e) He *has always come* on time.
Note: Most other midsentence adverbs have the same usual positions as frequency adverbs.

_____ his pencil. Wan-Ning (*scratch*) _____

_____ his head. Reza (*stare*) _____

_____ out the window. He (*seem*) _____

_____ to be daydreaming, but perhaps he (*think*)

_____ hard about verb tenses.

EXERCISE 13: Same as the preceding exercise.

1. After three days of rain, I'm glad that the sun (*shine*) _____

   _____ again.

2. I wrote to my friend last week. She hasn't answered my letter yet. I (*wait, still*)

   _____ for a reply.

3. Barbara (*tutor, often*) _____ other students in her

   math class. This afternoon she (*help*) _____ Steve with

   his math assignment because he (*understand, not*) _____

   the material they (*work*) _____ on in their class this
   week.

4. Look. It (*begin*) _____ to rain. Unfortunately, I (*have,
   not*) _____ my umbrella with me.

5. A: Where (*be*) _____ Pete and Janice?

   B: They (*be*) _____ out of town. They (*visit*) _____

      _____ some friends in Chicago.

6. A: Who is that woman who (*stand*) _____ next to the
      window?

   B: Which woman? (*Talk, you*) _____ about the

      women who (*wear*) _____ the blue and gold dress?

   A: No. I (*talk, not*) _____ about her. I (*mean*) _____

      _____ the woman who (*wear*) _____

      _____ the green suit.

   B: Oh. I (*know, not*) _____ . I (*recognize, not*) _____

      _____ her.

EXERCISE 14—ORAL: On a piece of paper, write one direction that you want a classmate to follow. Examples: *Stand up. Smile. Open the door. Sneeze.*

(To the teacher: Collect and then redistribute the directions. Ask each student in turn to perform the required action and have another student use the present progressive to describe this action.)

EXERCISE 15: An expression of place sometimes comes between the auxiliary *be* and the *-ing* main verb when the present progressive tense is used.

> *Example:* (a) She **is visiting** her sister *in California.*
>
> (b) She **is** *in California* **visiting** her sister.

In the following, change the position of the expression of place.

1. She is listening to music in her room.
2. He is taking a nap in the bedroom.
3. She is attending a conference in England.
4. He is playing pool at the student union.

Complete the following:

5. A: Where's Joan?

   B: She's at the library _____ studying for a test _____.

6. A: Is Mark here?

   B: Yes. He's upstairs _____.

7. A: Have you seen Professor Marx?

   B: Yes. She's in her office _____.

8. A: Where's your mother, Jimmy?

   B: She's in the kitchen _____.

9. A: Is Frank out of town?

   B: Yes, he's in New York _____.

EXERCISE 16—WRITTEN: Go to a place where there are many people (or imagine yourself to be in such a place). Describe the activities you observe. Let your reader see what you see; draw a "picture" by using words.

Use present tenses. Begin your writing with a description of your own immediate activities; e.g., *I am at the zoo sitting on a bench.*

3-13 SIMPLE PAST

(image)	(a) **I walked** to school yesterday. (b) He **lived** in Paris for ten years, but now he is living in Rome. (c) **I bought** a new car three days ago.	The simple past indicates that an activity or situation *began and ended at a particular time in the past.*
	(d) **I stood** under a tree when it **began** to rain. (e) When she **heard** a strange noise, she **got** up to investigate. (f) When **I dropped** my cup, the coffee **spilled** on my lap.	If a sentence contains *when* and has the simple past in both clauses, the action in the *"when clause"* happens first. In (d): 1st: The rain began. 2nd: I stood under a tree.

3-14 PAST PROGRESSIVE

(image)	(i) **I was walking** down the street when it began to rain. (j) While **I was walking** down the street, it began to rain. (k) **I was standing** under a tree when it began to rain. (l) At eight o'clock last night, **I was studying.** (m) Last year at this time, I **was attending** school.	In (i): 1st: I was walking down the street. 2nd: It began to rain. In other words, both actions occurred at the *same* time, but *one action began earlier and was in progress when the other action occurred.* In (l): My studying began before 8:00, was in progress at that time, and probably continued.
	(n) Last January, while you **were trudging** through snow in Iowa, **I was lying** on the beach in Florida. (o) While **I was studying** in one room of our apartment, my roomate **was having** a party in the other room.	Sometimes the past progressive is used in both parts of a sentence when two actions are in progress simultaneously.
	(p) **It rained** this morning. (q) **It was raining** this morning.	In some cases, the simple past and the past progressive give almost the same meaning, as in (o) and (p).

EXERCISE 17: Change the italicized sentences to the past. Notice the relationship between the present progressive and the past progressive.

1. *I am sitting in class right now.* | <u>I was sitting in class</u> at this time yesterday.

2. *I don't want to go to the zoo because it is raining.* | Yesterday _____

_____

3. *The boys aren't at home. They are playing soccer in the park.* | _____

_____

4. *Today is a beautiful day. The sun is shining. A cool breeze is blowing. The*

   birds are singing. | Yesterday _____

_____

EXERCISE 18: Use the *simple past* or the *past progressive* in the following.

1. I (*read*) _____ only two chapters last week.

2. I (*read*) _____ a book last night when you called.

3. I (*call*) _____ John at nine last night, but he (*be, not*)

   _____ at home. He (*study*) _____

   _____ at the library.

4. I (*hear, not*) _____ the thunder during the storm last

   night because I (*sleep*) _____ .

5. My brother and sister (*argue*) _____ about something

   when I (*walk*) _____ into the room.

6. When I (*open*) _____ the package, I (*find*) _____

   _____ a surprise.

7. He (*climb*) _____ the stairs when he (*trip*) _____

   _____ and (*fall*) _____ . Luck-

   ily, he (*hurt, not*) _____ himself.

8. While I (*read*) _____ the little boy a story, he (*fall*)

   _____ asleep, so I (*close*) _____

   the book and quietly (*tiptoe*) _____ out of the room.

EXERCISE 19: Same as the preceding exercise.

1. I (*have, almost*) _____ a car accident last night. I
(*drive*) _____ down Washington Avenue when suddenly I (*see*) _____ a car in my lane. It (*come*) _____
_____ right at my car. I (*step*) _____
_____ on the brakes and (*swerve*) _____
_____ to the right. The other car (*miss, just*) _____
_____ my car by about an inch.

2. Ten years ago, the government (*decide*) _____ to begin
a food program. At that time, many people in the rural areas of the country
(*starve*) _____ due to several years of drought.

3. It was my first day of class. I (*find, finally*) _____ the
right room. The room (*be, already*) _____ full of
students. On one side of the room, students (*talk, busily*) _____
_____ to each other in Spanish. Other students (*speak*)
_____ Japanese, and some (*converse*) _____
_____ in Arabic. It sounded like the United Nations.
Some of the students, however, (*sit, just*) _____ quietly
by themselves. I (*choose*) _____ an empty seat in the
last row and (*sit*) _____ down. In a few minutes, the
teacher (*walk*) _____ into the room and all the multi-
lingual conversation (*stop*) _____ .

4. A: (*Hear, you*) _____ what she just said?
   B: No. I (*listen, not*) _____ . I (*think*) _____
   _____ about something else.

5. A: Why weren't you at the meeting?
   B: I (*wait*) _____ for an overseas call from my family.

6. A: How (*break, you*) _____ your arm?
   B: I (*slip*) _____ on the ice while I (*cross*) _____
   _____ the street in front of the dorm.

7. A: I'm sure you met Carol Jones at the party last night.

   B: I don't remember her. What (*wear, she*) _____?

8. A: What's wrong with your foot?

   B: I (*step*) _____ on a bee while I (*run*) _____

   _____ barefoot through the grass. It (*sting*) _____

   _____ me.

EXERCISE 20—WRITTEN: Describe your first day in this class. What did you see, hear, feel, think?

3-15 PRESENT PERFECT

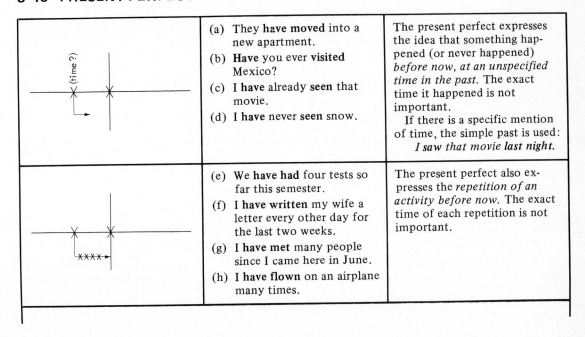

	(a) They **have moved** into a new apartment. (b) **Have** you ever **visited** Mexico? (c) I **have** already **seen** that movie. (d) I **have** never **seen** snow.	The present perfect expresses the idea that something happened (or never happened) *before now, at an unspecified time in the past.* The exact time it happened is not important. If there is a specific mention of time, the simple past is used: *I saw that movie **last night.***
	(e) We **have had** four tests so far this semester. (f) I **have written** my wife a letter every other day for the last two weeks. (g) I **have met** many people since I came here in June. (h) I **have flown** on an airplane many times.	The present perfect also expresses the *repetition of an activity before now.* The exact time of each repetition is not important.

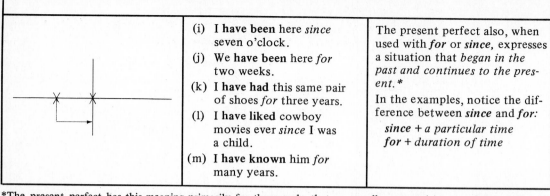

	(i) **I have been** here *since* seven o'clock.	The present perfect also, when used with *for* or *since*, expresses a situation that *began in the past and continues to the present.* *
	(j) We **have been** here *for* two weeks.	
	(k) **I have had** this same pair of shoes *for* three years.	In the examples, notice the difference between *since* and *for:*
	(l) **I have liked** cowboy movies ever *since* I was a child.	*since + a particular time* *for + duration of time*
	(m) **I have known** him *for* many years.	

*The present perfect has this meaning primarily for those verbs that are usually not used in any of the progressive tenses. (See 3-12 for a list.) This meaning is exactly the same as the meaning of the present perfect progressive tense.

Note: The expression ***have got*** is common in very informal spoken English. It has the same meaning as ***have***.

    (a) *I've got a cold.*   (b) *I have a cold.*

The meaning of ***have got*** is present. It has no past form. ***Have got*** is not present perfect.

    Compare: (c) *I have gotten three letters so far this week.* (present perfect meaning)

                 (d) *I have got a problem.* (present meaning)

See 5-8 for ***have got to*** meaning ***must***.

EXERCISE 21—ORAL (BOOKS CLOSED): Begin your response with "I have never . . ."

    Example: see that movie
    Response: I've never seen that movie.

1. drive a truck
2. buy an airplane
3. read that book
4. break a window
5. draw a picture of yourself
6. ride a horse
7. eat paper
8. teach English
9. catch a butterfly
10. make apple pie
11. win a million dollars
12. fly an airplane
13. sleep past ten o'clock
14. write a letter to the President of the United States
15. lose your wallet

16. have a car accident
17. speak to (a local personage)
18. steal anything
19. fall off a mountain
20. bring a friend to class
21. hold a snake
22. feed a lion
23. build a house

24. forget your name
25. wear a kimono
26. drink Turkish coffee
27. understand Einstein's theory of relativity
28. leave your umbrella at a restaurant

EXERCISE 22—ORAL (BOOKS CLOSED): *Student A:* Ask a question beginning with "Have you ever . . . ." *Student B:* Answer the question.

Example: break your arm

Student A: Have you ever broken your arm?

Student B: Yes, I have. OR: No, I haven't.

1. climb a mountain
2. write a book
3. be in (Japan)
4. tell a lie
5. smoke a cigar
6. ride a motorcycle
7. teach English
8. see a ghost
9. meet (. . .)
10. give a speech in English

11. eat (Thai) food
12. study biology
13. play a violin
14. go to (a particular landmark in this city)
15. walk on the moon
16. watch (a particular TV show)
17. take a course in chemistry
18. drive (a particular kind of car)
19. fall asleep during class
20. have (a particular kind of food)

EXERCISE 23—ORAL (BOOKS CLOSED): Answer the question in a complete sentence.

Example: How many tests have you taken since the beginning of the (semester)?

Response: I have taken (three, several, many) tests since the beginning of the (semester).

OR: I haven't taken any tests since the beginning of the (semester).

1. How many books have you bought since the beginning of the (semester)?
2. How many letters have you gotten so far this month/week?
3. How many letters have you written since the beginning of the month/week?

4. How many questions have I asked so far?
5. How many times have you flown in an airplane?
6. How many people have you met since you came here?
7. How many classes have you missed since the beginning of the (semester)?
8. How many cigarettes have you smoked since you got up this morning?
9. How many classes have you had so far today?
10. How many times have you eaten (your native) food/eaten at a restaurant since you came here?

EXERCISE 24: Give the correct form of the verbs in parentheses and use appropriate time expressions after *for* and *since*.

1. Today is the 14th of June. I (*buy*) _____bought_____ this book two weeks ago. I (*have*) _____have had_____ this book since _____June 1st_____. I (*have*) _____have had_____ this book for _____two weeks_____.

2. Today is October 1st. I (*come*) _____ here on September 1st. I (*be*) _____ here for _____. I (*be*) _____ _____ since _____.

3. I (*meet*) _____ John in 1978. I (*know*) _____ him for _____. I (*know*) _____ since _____ _____.

4. Today is Friday. I (*buy*) _____ this pen last Monday. I (*have*) _____ this pen since _____. I (*have*) _____ _____ this pen for _____.

EXERCISE 25—ORAL (BOOKS CLOSED): Answer the questions in complete sentences.

(*To the teacher: Following is an example of a possible exchange.*

To Student A:　*When did you come to (the United States)?*
　　　　　　　 —I came here on June 2nd.
To Student B:　*How long has (Student A) been here?*
　　　　　　　 —He/she has been here for two weeks.
　　　　　　　 Or, using **since**?
　　　　　　　 —He/she has been here since June 2nd.)

1. **A:** When did you arrive (in this city/country)? **B:** How long has (. . .) been here?

2. **A:** When did you get to class today? **B:** How long has (. . .) been in class?

3. **A:** What time did you get up this morning? **B:** How long has (. . .) been up?

4. Who owns a car/bicycle? **A:** When did you buy it? **B:** How long has (. . .) had a car/bicycle?

5. Who is wearing a watch? **A:** When did you get it? **B:** How long has (. . .) had his/her watch?

6. Who is married? **A:** When did you get married? **B:** How long has (. . .) been married?

7. **A:** Do you know (. . .)? When did you meet him/her? **B:** How long has (. . .) known (. . .)?

8. **A:** Is that your pen/notebook/pencil sharpener? When did you buy it? **B:** How long has (. . .) had his/her pen/notebook/pencil sharpener?

EXERCISE 26: Use the *simple past* or the *present perfect*. In some sentences, either tense is possible but the meaning is different.

1. I (*attend, not*)_____ any parties since I came here.

2. I (*go*) _____ to a party at Sally's apartment last Saturday night.

3. Bill (*arrive*) _____ here three days ago.

4. Bill (*be*) _____ here since the 22nd.

5. Try not to be absent from class again for the rest of the term. You (*miss, already*) _____ too many classes.

   You (*miss*) _____two classes just last week.

6. Last January, I (*see*)_____ snow for the first time in my life.

7. In her whole lifetime, she (*see, never*) _____ snow.

8. I (*know*)_____ Greg Adams for ten years.

9. So far this week, I (*have*)_____ two tests and a quiz.

10. Up to now, Professor Williams (*give*) _____ our class five tests.

EXERCISE 27: Same as the preceding exercise.

1. The science of medicine (*advance*) _____
   a great deal in the nineteenth century.

2. Since the beginning of the twentieth century, medical scientists (*make*) _____
   _____ many important discoveries.

3. I (*learn*) _____ to read and write French when I was a child, but
   now I (*forget*) _____ almost everything I learned.

4. I (*have, not*) _____ much free time since classes began.

5. Last night I (*have*) _____ some free time, so I (*go*) _____

_____ to a show.

6. A: Are you taking Chemistry 101 this semester?

B: No, I (*take, already*) _____ it. I (*take*) _____
it last semester. This semester I'm in 102.

7. A: Hi, Judy. Welcome to the party. (*Meet, you, ever*) _____
my cousin?

B: No, I _____.

A: Then let me introduce you.

8. A: Do you like lobster?

B: I don't know. I (*eat, never*) _____ it.

9. A: Do you do much traveling?

B: Yes. I like to travel.

A: What countries (*visit, you*) _____ ?

B: Well, I (*be*) _____ in India, Turkey, Afghanistan, and Nepal,
among others.

A: I (*be, never*) _____ in any of those countries. When (*be,*
you) _____ in India?

B: Two years ago. I (*visit, also*) _____ many of the countries in
Central America. I (*take*) _____ a tour of Central America
about six years ago.

A: Which countries (*visit, you*) _____ ?

B: Guatemala, El Salvador, Honduras, and Nicaragua.

EXERCISE 28: Come to class prepared to do a pantomime. While you are doing
your pantomime, the rest of the class will try to determine what you are doing and
then, when you are finished, will describe what you did, step by step.

Examples of subjects for a pantomime:
   (a) Threading a needle and sewing on a button
   (b) Washing dishes, and perhaps breaking one
   (c) Bowling
   (d) Reading a newspaper while eating breakfast

(*To the teacher: Suggested time limit for each pantomime: two minutes. In all,*
each pantomime and the oral description should take no more than four or five

minutes. The intention is that a few pantomimes be presented each day for the rest of the time spent working on verb tenses.)

EXERCISE 29—WRITTEN: In writing, describe one or more of the pantomimes which are performed by your classmates. Give a title to the pantomime and identify the pantomimist. Use a few "time words" to show the order in which the actions were performed; e.g., *first, next, then, after that, before, when, while.*

3-16 PRESENT PERFECT PROGRESSIVE

	Right now I am sitting at my desk. (a) I **have been sitting** here *since* seven o'clock. (b) I **have been sitting** here *for* two hours. (c) You **have been studying** *for* five straight hours. Why don't you take a break? (d) He **has been watching** television *since* nine o'clock this morning. (e) It **has been raining** *all day.* It is still raining right now.	This tense is used to indicate the *duration* of an activity that *began in the past and continues to the present.* When the tense has this meaning, it is used with time words such as *for, since, all morning, all day, all week.*
 (recently)	(f) I **have been thinking** about changing my major. (g) All of the students **have been studying** hard. (h) John **has been doing** a lot of work on his thesis. He should be finished by May. (i) My back hurts, so I **have been sleeping** on the floor lately. The bed is too soft.	When the tense is used without any specific mention of time, it expresses *a general activity in progress recently, lately.*
	(j) I **have lived** here since 1975. I **have been living** here since 1975. (k) He **has worked** at the same store for ten years. He **has been working** at the same store for ten years.	With certain verbs (most notably *live, work, teach*) there is little or no difference in meaning between the two tenses when *since* or *for* is used.

EXERCISE 30: Use the *present perfect progressive* in the following.

1. The boys are playing soccer right now. They (*play*) __have been playing__ for almost two hours. They must be getting tired.

2. Alex is talking on the phone. He (*talk*) _____ on the phone for over a half an hour. He should hang up soon. Long distance is expensive.

3. I'm trying to study. I (*try*) _____ to study for the last hour, but something always seems to interrupt me. I think I'd better go to the library.

Complete the following by writing two sentences. Use the present perfect progressive in the first sentence; then make another sentence that might typically follow in this situation.

4. The baby is crying. She _____ has been crying for almost ten minutes.
   _____ I wonder what's wrong. _____

5. It's raining. It _____
   _____

6. I'm studying. I _____
   _____

7. I'm waiting for my friend. I _____
   _____

8. Bob is sitting in the waiting room. He _____
   _____

EXERCISE 31: Use the *present perfect* or the *present perfect progressive*. In some sentences, either tense may be used with little or no change in meaning.

1. It (*snow*) _____ all day. I wonder when it will stop.

2. We (*have*) _____ three major snowstorms so far this winter. I wonder how many more we will have.

3. It's ten P.M. I (*study*) _____ for two hours and probably won't finish until midnight.

4. I (*write*) _____ them three times, but I still haven't received a reply.

5. I (*live*) _____ here since last March.

6. The telephone (*ring*) _____ four times in the last hour, and each time it has been for my roommate.

7. The telephone (*ring*) _____ for almost a minute. Why doesn't someone answer it?

8. The little boy is dirty from head to foot because he (*play*) _____ in the mud.

EXERCISE 32: Same as the preceding exercise.

1. A: (*Be, you*) _____ able to reach Bob on the phone yet?

   B: Not yet. I (*try*) _____ for the last twenty minutes, but the the line (*be*) _____ busy.

2. A: Hi, Jenny. I (*see, not*) _____ you for weeks. What (*do, you*) _____ lately?

   B: Studying.

3. A: What are you going to order for dinner?

   B: Well, I (*have, never*) _____ pizza, so I think I'll order that.

4. A: What's the matter? Your eyes are red and puffy. (*Cry, you*) _____ _____ ?

   B: No. I just finished peeling some onions.

5. A: Dr. Jones is a good teacher. How long (*be, he*) _____ at the university?

   B: He (*teach*) _____ here for twenty-five years.

EXERCISE 33–WRITTEN: Complete the following with your own ideas.

1. _____ since 8 o'clock this morning.

2. _____ since I came to _____ .

3. _____ since 19. . (year).

4. _____ since _____ (month).

5. _____ since _____ (day).

3-17 PAST PERFECT

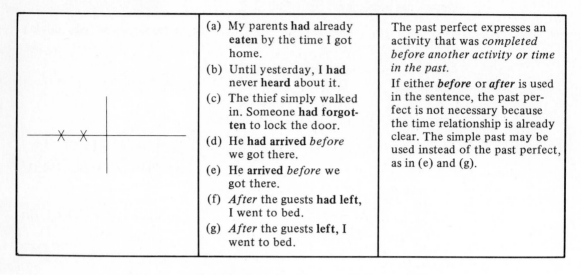

(a) My parents **had already eaten** by the time I got home. (b) Until yesterday, I **had** never **heard** about it. (c) The thief simply walked in. Someone **had forgotten** to lock the door. (d) He **had arrived** *before* we got there. (e) He **arrived** *before* we got there. (f) *After* the guests **had left,** I went to bed. (g) *After* the guests **left,** I went to bed.	The past perfect expresses an activity that was *completed before another activity or time in the past.* If either *before* or *after* is used in the sentence, the past perfect is not necessary because the time relationship is already clear. The simple past may be used instead of the past perfect, as in (e) and (g).

3-18 PAST PERFECT PROGRESSIVE

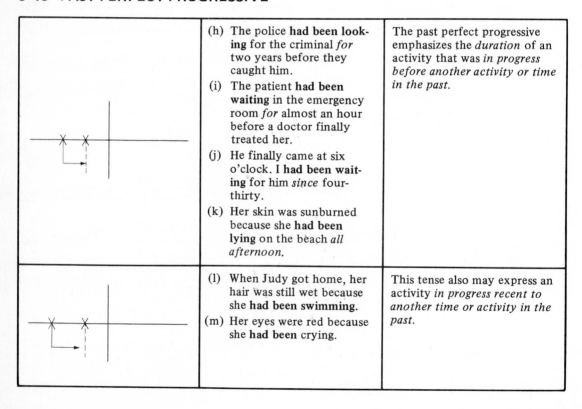

(h) The police **had been looking** for the criminal *for two years* before they caught him. (i) The patient **had been waiting** in the emergency room *for almost an hour* before a doctor finally treated her. (j) He finally came at six o'clock. I **had been waiting** for him *since four-thirty.* (k) Her skin was sunburned because she **had been lying** on the beach *all afternoon.*	The past perfect progressive emphasizes the *duration* of an activity that was *in progress before another activity or time in the past.*
(l) When Judy got home, her hair was still wet because she **had been swimming.** (m) Her eyes were red because she **had been** crying.	This tense also may express an activity *in progress recent to another time or activity in the past.*

EXERCISE 34: Use the *simple past* or the *past perfect*. Are there some blanks where either tense is possible?

1. He (*be*) _____ a newspaper reporter before he (*become*) _____

   _____ a businessman.

2. I (*feel*) _____ a little better after I (*take*) _____
   the medicine.

3. I was late. The teacher (*give, already*) _____ a quiz when I (*get*)

   _____ to class.

4. The anthropologist (*leave*) _____ the village when she (*collect*)

   _____ enough data.

5. It was raining hard, but by the time class (*be*) _____ over, the

   rain (*stop*) _____ .

EXERCISE 35: Same as the preceding.

1. Millions of years ago, dinosaurs (*roam*) _____ the earth, but they

   (*become*) _____ extinct by the time humankind first (*appear*)

   _____ .

2. Class (*begin, already*) _____ by the time I (*get*) _____

   _____ there, so I (*take, quietly*) _____
   a seat in the back.

3. I (*see, never*) _____ any of Picasso's paintings before I (*visit*)

   _____ the art museum.

4. I almost missed my plane. All of the other passengers (*board, already*) _____

   _____ by the time I (*get*) _____ there.

5. Yesterday at a restaurant, I (*see*) _____ Pam Donnelly, an old

   friend of mine. I (*see, not*) _____ her in years. At first, I (*recog-

   nize, not*) _____ her because she (*lose*) _____ at
   least fifty pounds.

EXERCISE 36: Use the *present perfect progressive* or the *past perfect progressive*.

1. It is midnight. I (*study*)_____for five straight hours.
   No wonder I'm getting tired.

2. It was midnight. I (*study*) _____ for five straight hours. No wonder I was getting tired.

3. Jack suddenly realized that the teacher was asking him a question. He couldn't answer because he (*daydream*) _____ for the last ten minutes.

4. Wake up! You (*sleep*) _____ long enough. It's time to get up.

5. At least two hundred people were waiting in line to buy tickets to the game. Some of them (*stand*) _____ in line for more than four hours. We decided not to try to get tickets for ourselves.

3-19 SIMPLE FUTURE/*BE GOING TO*

	(a) He **will finish** his work tomorrow. (b) He **is going to finish** his work tomorrow. (c) I **will wash** the dishes later. (d) I **am going to wash** the dishes later.	*Will* or *be going to* is used to express future time. *Shall* may be used with *I* or *we*, but *will/be going to* is more commonly used.* In speech, *going to* is often pronounced "gonna."

	(e) Bob will come soon. *When Bob comes*, we will see him.
	(f) Linda will leave soon. *Before she leaves*, she is going to finish her work.
	(g) I will get home at 5:30. *After I get home*, I will eat dinner.
	(h) The taxi will arrive in less than five minutes. *As soon as the taxi arrives*, we will be able to leave for the airport.
	(i) They are going to come soon. I will wait here *until they come*.
		A clause is a grammatical structure which has a subject and a verb. A "time clause" begins with such words as *when, before, after, as soon as, until.*† These words may be followed by a subject and verb:
		  When he comes, we will see him.
		  When + subject + verb = time clause
		A future tense is *not* used in a time clause. The meaning of the clause is future, but the simple present tense is used.

	(j) I will go to bed *after I finish* my work. (k) I will go to bed *after I have finished* my work.	Occasionally, the present perfect is used in a time clause, as in (k). Examples (j) and (k) have the same meaning. The present perfect stresses the completion of the act in the time clause before the other act occurs in the future.

Shall is used much more frequently in British English than in American English.
† A "time clause" is an adverb clause. See 11-2.

EXERCISE 37: Use the *simple future/be going to** or the *simple present.*

1. I'm going to leave in half an hour. I (*finish*) <u>will finish / am going to finish</u>
   all of my work before I (*leave*) <u>   leave   </u> .

2. I'm going to eat lunch at 12:30. After I (*eat*) _____ lunch, I
   (*take*) _____ a nap.

3. I'll get home around six. When I (*get*) _____ home, I (*call*)
   _____ Sharon.

4. I'm going to watch a TV program at nine. Before I (*watch*) _____
   that program at nine, I (*write*) _____ a letter to my parents.

5. Gary will come soon. I (*wait*) _____ here until he (*come*) _____
   _____ .

6. It will stop raining soon. As soon as the rain (*stop*) _____ , I
   (*walk*) _____ to the drugstore to get some film.

7. The seasons are predictable. For example, when spring (*come*) _____
   _____ the weather (*get*) _____ warmer. This
   happens every year.

8. Right now it is winter. I'm tired of cold weather, but spring (*come*) _____
   _____ soon. When spring (*come*) _____ this year,
   I (*go*) _____ to the park every day to enjoy the good weather.

9. At a dinner party in the United States, people usually sit in the living room and
   (*talk*) _____ for a while before they (*go*) _____
   into the dining room.

10. Tomorrow I'm going to give a dinner party. I have planned it very carefully.
    Before I (*ask*) _____ my guests to come to the dining room, I
    (*serve*) _____ drinks and hors d'oeuvres in the living room.

11. A: Have you mailed your application yet?

---

*Usually there is little or no difference in meaning between *will* and *be going to. Will* and *be
going to* indicate inevitability (i.e., they express a simple factual statement about a future
activity or situation), but *be going to* is used more frequently than *will* in spoken English when
the speaker is expressing a definite plan or intention.

The present progressive is also sometimes used to express a future meaning (see 3–20).
The future intention expressed by the present progressive is usually stronger than that expressed by *be going to.*

B: Not yet. I (*fill*) _____ it out later this evening. Then I (*mail*)

_____ it on my way to class tomorrow.

12. A: (*Be, Louise*) _____ at the meeting tomorrow?

B: No. She (*be, not*) _____ there.

13. Right now I am a junior. After I (*graduate*) _____ with a B.A.,

I (*intend*) _____ to enter graduate school and work for an M.A.

Perhaps I (*go*) _____ on for a Ph.D. after I (*get*) _____

_____ my Master's degree.

14. A: How long (*stay, you*) _____ in this country?

B: I (*plan*) _____ to be here for about one more year. I (*hope*)

_____ to graduate a year from this June.

A: What (*do, you*) _____ after you (*leave*) _____

_____?

B: I (*return*) _____ home and (*get*) _____ a job.

3-20 USING THE PRESENT PROGRESSIVE AND THE SIMPLE PRESENT TO EXPRESS FUTURE TIME

PRESENT PROGRESSIVE	
(a) My wife has an appointment with a doctor. She **is seeing** Dr. North *next Tuesday*.	The present progressive may be used to express future time when the idea of the sentence concerns a planned event or definite intention. (COMPARE: A verb such as *rain* is not used in the present progressive to indicate future time because rain is not a planned event.)
(b) Sam has already made his plans. He **is leaving** *at noon tomorrow*.	
(c) A: What are you going to do this afternoon? B: *After lunch* I **am meeting** a friend of mine. We **are going** shopping. Would you like to come along?	A future meaning for the present progressive tense is indicated either by future time words in the sentence or by the context.
(d) A: My car is in the garage for repairs. B: How are you going to get to work tomorrow? A: I **am taking** the bus.	
SIMPLE PRESENT	
(e) The museum **opens** *at ten tomorrow morning*.	Sometimes the simple present is used in sentences that contain future time words. The simple present is used primarily with verbs such as *open/close, begin/end, arrive/leave* and expresses an established fact.
(f) Classes **begin** *next week*.	
(g) John's plane **arrives** *at 6:05 next Monday*.	(Note: In expressing future time, the present progressive is used in a much wider range of situations than the simple present.)

EXERCISE 38: Indicate the meaning expressed by the italicized verbs by writing *in the future*, *now*, or *habitually* in the blanks.

1. I *am taking* four courses next semester.   in the future

2. I *am taking* four courses this semester.   now

3. Students usually *take* four courses every semester.   habitually

4. I'll mail this letter at the corner when I *take* Susan home. _____

5. My brother's birthday is next week. I *am giving* him a sweater. _____

6. Shhh. The broadcaster *is giving* the latest news about the crisis in England. I want to hear what she is saying. _____

7. When I *graduate*, I'm going to return home. _____

8. When students *graduate*, they receive their diplomas. _____

9. I'm tired. I *am going* to bed early tonight. _____

10. When I *am* in New York, I'm going to visit the Museum of Modern Art. _____

11. When I *am* home alone in the evening, I like to read or watch television. _____

12. A: Where *are* you *going* over vacation?   A: _____

     B: *I'm going* to Chicago.   B: _____

     A: How *are* you *getting* there?   A: _____

     B: I *'m taking* a bus.   B: _____

13. A: Are you busy?

     B: Not really.

     A: What *are* you *doing*?   A: _____

     B: I *'m writing* a letter to my folks.   B: _____

A: When you *finish* your letter,
do you want to go downtown
and do some shopping?

B: Sure.

A: _____

14. A: What *are* you *doing* after class?

A: _____

B: I*'m eating* lunch at the
cafeteria with Cindy. Do you
want to join us?

B: _____

15. Tony *will arrive* at eight
tomorrow evening.

_____

16. Tony *is going to arrive* at eight
tomorrow evening.

_____

17. Tony *is arriving* at eight tomorrow
evening.

_____

18. Tony *arrives* at eight tomorrow
evening.

_____

19. When Tony *arrives,* we'll have a
party.

_____

3-21 FUTURE PROGRESSIVE

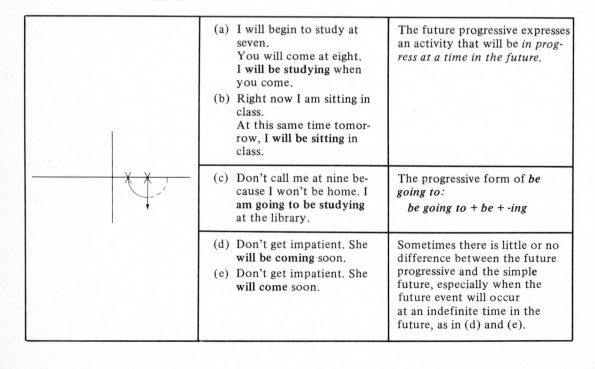

	(a) I will begin to study at seven. You will come at eight. **I will be studying** when you come. (b) Right now I am sitting in class. At this same time tomorrow, **I will be sitting** in class.	The future progressive expresses an activity that will be *in progress at a time in the future.*
	(c) Don't call me at nine because I won't be home. I **am going to be studying** at the library.	The progressive form of *be going to:* *be going to + be + -ing*
	(d) Don't get impatient. She **will be coming** soon. (e) Don't get impatient. She **will come** soon.	Sometimes there is little or no difference between the future progressive and the simple future, especially when the future event will occur at an indefinite time in the future, as in (d) and (e).

EXERCISE 39: Use the *future progressive* or the *simple present*.

1. Right now I am attending class. Yesterday at this time, I was attending class. Tomorrow at this time, I (*attend*) _____ class.

2. Tomorrow I'm going to leave for home. When I (*arrive*) _____ at the airport, my whole family (*wait*)_____ for me.

3. When I (*get*) _____ up tomorrow morning, the sun (*shine*) _____ , the birds (*sing*) _____ , and my roommate (*lie, still*) _____ in bed fast asleep.

4. A: When do you leave for Florida?

   B: Tomorrow. Just think. Two days from now I (*lie*) _____ on the beach in the sun.

   A: Have a good time. I (*think*) _____ about you.

5. A: How can I get in touch with you while you're out of town?

   B: I (*stay*) _____ at the Pilgrim Hotel. You can reach me there.

6. Next year at this time, I (*do*) _____ exactly what I am doing now. I (*attend*) _____ school and (*study*) _____ hard next year.

7. Look at those dark clouds. When class (*be*) _____ over, it (*rain, probably*) _____ .

8. A: Are you going to be in town next Saturday?

   B: No. I (*visit*) _____my aunt and uncle in Chicago.

3-22 FUTURE PERFECT

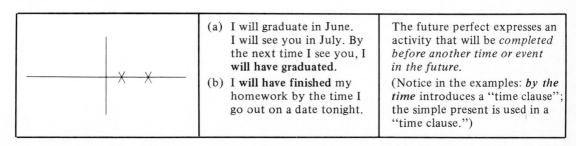

	(a) I will graduate in June. I will see you in July. By the next time I see you, I **will have graduated.** (b) I **will have finished** my homework by the time I go out on a date tonight.	The future perfect expresses an activity that will be *completed before another time or event in the future.* (Notice in the examples: *by the time* introduces a "time clause"; the simple present is used in a "time clause.")

3-23 FUTURE PERFECT PROGRESSIVE

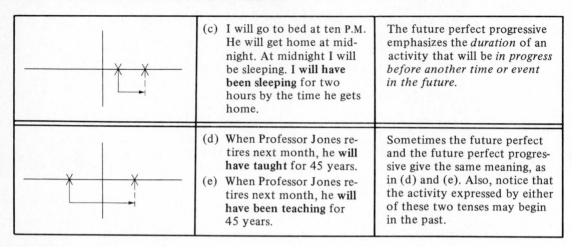

	(c) I will go to bed at ten P.M. He will get home at midnight. At midnight I will be sleeping. **I will have been sleeping** for two hours by the time he gets home.	The future perfect progressive emphasizes the *duration* of an activity that will be *in progress before another time or event in the future.*
	(d) When Professor Jones retires next month, he **will have taught** for 45 years. (e) When Professor Jones retires next month, he **will have been teaching** for 45 years.	Sometimes the future perfect and the future perfect progressive give the same meaning, as in (d) and (e). Also, notice that the activity expressed by either of these two tenses may begin in the past.

EXERCISE 40: Use any appropriate tense.

1. Ann and Andy got married on June 1st. Today is June 14th. Ann and Andy (*be*) _____ married for two weeks. By June 7th, they (*be*) _____ married for one week. By June 28th, they (*be*) _____ married for four weeks.

2. This traffic is terrible. We're going to be late. By the time we (*get*) _____ to the airport, Bob's plane (*arrive, already**) _____ , and he will be wondering where we are.

3. The traffic was very heavy. By the time we (*get*) _____ to the airport, Bob's plane (*arrive, already*) _____ .

4. This morning I came to class at 9:00. Right now it is 10:00 and I am still in class. I (*sit*) _____ at this desk for an hour. By 9:30, I (*sit*) _____ this desk for a half an hour. By 11:00, I (*sit*) _____ at my desk for two hours.

5. I'm getting tired of sitting in the car. Do you realize that by the time we arrive

---

*With the future perfect, *already* has two possible positions:
   I will already have finished.   *I will have already finished.*

in Phoenix, we (*drive*) _____ for twenty straight hours?

6. Margaret was born in 1950. By the year 2000, she (*live*) _____

_____ on this earth for 50 years.

7. Go ahead and leave on your vacation. Don't worry about this work. By the

time you (*get*) _____ back, we (*take*) _____

_____ care of everything.

8. I don't understand how those marathon runners do it! The race began over an

hour ago. By the time they reach the finish line, they (*run*) _____

_____ steadily for more than two hours. I don't think

I can run more than two minutes!

9. What? He got married again? At this rate, he (*have*) _____

a dozen wives by the time he (*die*) _____ .

10. We have been married for a long time. By our next anniversary, we (*be*) _____

_____ married for 43 years.

EXERCISE 41—ORAL: Discuss: What do you think the twenty-first century will
be like?

Suggestions for discussion topics:

1. Means of transportation?
2. Sources of energy?
3. Population growth?
4. Food sources?
5. Extinction of animal species?
6. Weapon technology?
7. Exploration of the oceans; exploration of the earth's interior?
8. Space exploration; contact with beings from outer space?
9. Role of computers in daily life?
10. Long-term solutions to today's political crises?
11. Architecture?
12. Clothing styles?
13. International language?
14. International world government?
15. International television; international communication via communication
satellites?

EXERCISE 42:   Discuss the differences (if any) in meaning in the following groups of sentences. Some of the sentences need to be completed to make their meaning clear.

1. (a) He watches television.
   (b) He is watching television.
2. (a) I am sitting in class . . . .
   (b) I was sitting in class . . . .
   (c) I will be sitting in class . . . .
3. (a) I have finished my homework.
   (b) I had finished my homework . . . .
   (c) I will have finished my homework . . . .
4. (a) The students had left before the teacher arrived.
   (b) The students left before the teacher arrived.
   (c) The students had left when the teacher arrived.
   (d) The students left when the teacher arrived.
   (e) The students were leaving when the teacher arrived.
5. (a) I have been waiting for her for two hours.
   (b) I had been waiting for her for two hours . . . .
   (c) I will have been waiting for her for two hours . . . .
6. (a) I have been studying Chapter Three.
   (b) I have studied Chapter Two.
   (c) I studied Chapter Two . . . .
7. (a) She has been doing a lot of research on that project.
   (b) She has done a lot of research on that project.
8. (a) I will study when you come.
   (b) I am going to study when you come.
   (c) I will be studying when you come.
   (d) I am going to be studying when you come.
   (e) I will have studied by the time you come.
   (f) I will have been studying for two hours by the time you come.
9. (a) He worked for that company for two years.
   (b) He has been working for that company for two years.
10. (a) The train will leave at 10:00 tomorrow morning.
    (b) The train is going to leave at 10:00 tomorrow morning.
    (c) The train leaves at 10:00 tomorrow morning.
    (d) The train is leaving at 10:00 tomorrow morning.

EXERCISE 43—ORAL (BOOKS CLOSED): Answer the questions in complete sentences.

1. What places have you visited since you came to (this city)? When?
2. What countries have you been to? When?
3. What programs have you seen on television? What did you watch last night?
4. What are you doing right now? What is (. . .) doing? What am I doing?
5. What kind of shoes is (. . .) wearing?
6. What are you wearing today?
7. What will you be doing tonight at midnight? What were you doing last night at midnight?
8. What are you going to be doing at this time tomorrow?
9. What time are you coming to class tomorrow?
10. Where will you be living three years from now?
11. How long have you been going to school?
12. What have we been doing for the last five minutes?
13. How long have you been sitting in that chair?
14. How long will you have been sitting in that chair by the time class is over?
15. Where are you living? Where were you living five years ago?
16. How long are you going to be living in (this city)? How long will you have been living here by the time you leave?
17. What have I been doing?
18. What have we been studying in class?

EXERCISE 44: Use any appropriate tense for the verbs in parentheses.

1. John is in my English class. He (*study*) _____ English this semester. He (*take, also*) _____ a couple of other classes. His classes (*begin*) _____ at 9:00 every day.

2. Yesterday John ate breakfast at 8:00. He (*eat, already*) _____ _____ breakfast when he (*leave*) _____ _____ for class at 8:45. He (*eat, always*) _____ _____ breakfast before he (*go*) _____ _____ to class. I (*eat, not, usually*) _____ _____ breakfast before I (*go*) _____

_____ to class. But I (*get, usually*) _____

_____ hungry about midmorning. Tomorrow before I

(*go*) _____ to class, I (*eat*) _____
breakfast.

3. John is in class every morning from 9:00 to 12:00. Two days ago, I (*call*)

_____ him at 11:30, but I could not reach him because

he (*attend*) _____ class at that time.

4. Don't try to call John at 11:30 tomorrow morning because he (*attend*) _____

_____ at that time.

5. Yesterday John took a nap from 1:00 to 2:00. I came at 1:45. When I (*get*)

_____ there, John (*sleep*) _____ .

He (*sleep*) _____ for 45 minutes by the time I came.

6. Right now John (*take*) _____ a nap. He (*fall*) _____

_____ asleep an hour ago. He (*sleep*) _____

_____ for an hour.

7. Three days ago, John (*start*) _____ to read *A Farewell
   to Arms*, a novel by Ernest Hemingway. It is a long novel. He (*finish, not*)

_____ reading it yet. He (*read*) _____

_____ it because his English teacher assigned it.

8. Since the beginning of the semester, John (*read*) _____

three novels. Right now he (*read*) _____ *A Farewell to

Arms*. He (*read*) _____ that novel for the past three

days. He (*intend*) _____ to finish it next week. In his

lifetime, he (*read*) _____ many novels, but this is the

first Hemingway novel he (*read, ever*) _____ .

9. Tomorrow, after he (*eat*) _____ dinner, John (*go*)

_____ to a movie. In other words, he (*eat*) _____

_____ dinner by the time he (*go*) _____

_____ to the movie.

EXERCISE 45: Use any appropriate tense for the verbs in parentheses.

1. A: There is something I have to tell you.

   B: Go ahead. I (*listen*) ————————————————— .

2. A: Hi, Ann. (*Meet, you*) ————————————————— my friend, George Smith?

   B: No, I (*have, never*) ————————————————— the pleasure.

   A: Then let me introduce you.

3. A: Stop! What (*you, do*) ————————————————— ?

   B: I (*try*) ————————————————— to get this piece of toast out of the toaster. It's stuck.

   A: Well, don't use a knife. You (*electrocute*) ————————————————— yourself!

   B: What do you suggest I do?

   A: Unplug it first.

4. A: There's Jack.

   B: Where?

   A: He (*lie*) ————————————————— on the grass under that tree over there.

   B: Oh yes. I (*see*) ————————————————— him. He (*look, certainly*)

   ————————————————— comfortable. Let's go talk to him.

5. A: (*Take, you*) —— ————————————————— Econ 120 this semester?

   B: No, I ————————————————— .

   A: (*Take, you ever*) ————————————————— it?

   B: Yes, I ————————————————— .

A: When (*take, you*) _____ it?

B: Last semester.

A: Who (*be*) _____ your professor?

B: Dr. Lee.

A: Oh, I have the same professor. What (*be, he*) _____ like?

B: He (*be*) _____ very good.

6. A: What's wrong with Chris?

B: While he (*yawn*) _____, a fly (*fly*) _____

_____ into his mouth.

A: I (*believe, not*) _____ that! You (*kid*) _____

_____!

7. A: I (*go*) _____ to a play last night.

B: (*Be, it*) _____ any good?

A: I thought so. I (*enjoy*) _____ it a lot.

B: What (*be, it*) _____?

A: *Arsenic and Old Lace.* I (*see, never*) _____ it before.

B: Oh, I (*see*) _____ that play too. I (*see*) _____

_____ it a couple of years ago. It (*be*) _____

_____ good, (*be, not*) _____ it?

8. A: I was in your hometown last month. It looked like a nice town. I (*be, never*)

_____ there before.

B: What (*do, you*) _____ in that part of the country?

A: My wife and I (*drive*) _____ to Washington to visit her folks.

9. A: May I borrow some money? My check (*be*) _____

supposed to arrive yesterday, but I still (*receive, not*) _____

_____ it. I (*need*) _____ to

buy a book for one of my classes, but I (*have, not*) _____

_____ any money.

B: Sure. I'd be happy to lend you some. How much (*need, you*) _____

_____ ?

A: Five bucks (*be*) _____ enough. Thanks. I (*pay*)

_____ you back as soon as I (*get*) _____

_____ my check.

10. A: Hello?

B: Hello. May I speak to Sue?

A: She (*be, not*) _____ in right now. May I take a message?

B: Yes. This is Art O'Brien. Would you please ask her to meet me at the library

this afternoon? I (*sit*) _____ at one of the study booths on the second floor.

EXERCISE 46: Use any appropriate tense for the verbs in parentheses.

1. My grandfather (*fly, never*) _____ in an airplane, and he has no intention of ever doing so.

2. Jane isn't here yet. I (*wait*) _____ for her since noon,

but she still (*arrive, not*) _____ .

3. In all the world, there (*be*) _____ only 14 mountains

that (*reach*) _____ above 8,000 meters (26,247 feet).

4. I have a long trip ahead of me tomorrow, so I think I'd better go to bed. But let me say good-bye now because I won't see you in the morning. I (*leave,*

already) _____ by the time you (*get*) _____

_____ up.

5. Right now we (*have*) _____ a heat wave. The tempera-

ture (*be*) _____ in the upper 90's for the last six days.

6. Last night I (*go*) _____ to a party. When I (*get*) _____

_____ there, the room was full of people. Some of

them (*dance*) _____ and others (*talk*) _____

_____ . One young woman (*stand*) _____

_____ by herself. I (*meet, never*) _____ _____

_____ her, so I (*introduce*) _____ myself to her.

7. About three yesterday afternoon, Jessica (*lie*) _____ in bed reading a book. Suddenly she (*hear*) _____ a loud noise and (*get*) _____ up to see what it was. She (*look*) _____ out the window. A truck (*back, just*) _____ into her new car!

8. Next month I have a week's vacation. I (*plan*) _____ to take a trip. First, I (*go*) _____ to Madison, Wisconsin, to visit my brother. After I (*leave*) _____ Madison, I (*go*) _____ to Chicago to see a friend who (*study*) _____ at a university there. She (*live*) _____ in Chicago for three years, so she (*know*) _____ her way around the city. She (*promise*) _____ to take me to many interesting places. I (*be, never*) _____ in Chicago, so I (*look*) _____ forward to going there.

9. Yesterday while I (*sit*) _____ in class, I (*get*) _____ the hiccups. The person who (*sit*) _____ next to me told me to hold my breath. I (*try*) _____ that, but it didn't work. The instructor (*lecture*) _____, and I didn't want to interrupt him, so I just sat there trying to hiccup quietly. Finally, after I (*hiccup*) _____ for almost five minutes, I (*raise*) _____ my hand and (*excuse*) _____ myself from the class to go get a drink of water.

10. The weather has been terrible lately. It (*rain*) _____ off and on for two days, and the temperature (*drop*) _____ at least twenty degrees. It (*be*) _____

_____ in the low 40's right now. Just three days ago, the sun (*shine*) _____ and the weather was pleasant. The weather certainly (*change*) _____ quickly here. I never know what to expect. Who knows? When I (*wake*) _____ _____ up tomorrow morning, maybe it (*snow*) _____ _____ .

EXERCISE 47:   Use any appropriate tense.

(1)   On June 20th, I returned home. I (*be*) _____

(2) away from home for two years. My family (*meet*) _____

(3) me at the airport with kisses and tears. They (*miss*) _____

(4) me as much as I had missed them. I (*be*) _____ very

(5) happy to see them again. When I (*get*) _____ the

(6) chance, I (*take*) _____ a long look at them. My little

(7) brother (*be*) _____ no longer so little. He (*grow*)

(8) _____ at least a foot. He (*be*) _____

(9) almost as tall as my father. My little sister (*wear*) _____

(10) a green dress. She (*change*) _____ quite a bit, too, but

(11) she (*be, still*) _____ mischievous and inquisitive. She

(12) (*ask*) _____ me a thousand questions a minute, or so

(13) it seemed. My father (*gain*) _____ some weight, and

(14) his hair (*turn*) _____ a little bit grayer, but otherwise

(15) he was just as I had remembered him. My mother (*look*) _____

(16) a little older, but not much. The wrinkles on her face (*be*) _____
(17) smile wrinkles.

EXERCISE 48:   Use any appropriate tenses.

(1)   On June 20th, I will return home. I (*be*) _____

(2) away from home for two years by that time. My family (*meet*)

(3) _____ me at the airport with kisses and tears. They

(4) (*miss*) _____ me as much as I have missed them. I

(5) (*be*) _____ very happy to see them again. When

(6) I (*get*) _____ a chance, I (*take*) _____

(7) a long look at them. My little brother (*be, no longer*) _____

(8) so little. He (*grow*) _____ at least a foot. He (*be*)

(9) _____ almost as tall as my father. My little sister

(10) (*wear, probably*) _____ a green dress. She (*change*)

(11) _____ quite a bit, too, but she (*be, still*)

(12) _____ mischievous and inquisitive. She (*ask, prob-*

(13) *ably*) _____ me a thousand questions a minute, or so

(14) it will seem. My father (*gain, probably*) _____ some

(15) weight, and his hair (*turn*) _____ a little grayer, but

(16) otherwise he will be just as I remember him. My mother (*look*)

(17) _____ just the same. Perhaps she (*look*)

(18) _____ a little older, but not much. The wrinkles on

(19) her face (*be*) _____ smile wrinkles.

EXERCISE 49: Use any appropriate tenses.

(1) Dear Ann,

(2)   I (*receive*) _____ your letter about two weeks

(3) ago and (*try*) _____ to find time to write you back

(4) ever since. I (*be*) _____ very busy lately. In the past

(5) two weeks, I (*have*) _____ four tests, and I have

(6) another test next week. In addition, a friend (*stay*) _____

(7) with me since last Thursday. She wanted to see the city, so we (*spend*)

(8) _____ a lot of time visiting some of the interesting

(9) places here. We (*be*) _____ to the zoo, the art

(10) museum, and the botanical gardens. Yesterday we (*go*) _____

(11) to the park and (*watch*) _____ a balloon race. Be-

(12) tween showing her the city and studying for my exams, I (*have, barely*)

(13) _____ enough time to breathe.

(14)   Right now it (*be*) _____ 3 A.M. and I (*sit*)

(15) _____ at my desk. I (*sit*) _____

(16) here five hours doing my studying. My friend's plane (*leave*) _____

(17) _____ at 6:05, so I (*decide*) _____

(18) not to go to bed. That's why I (*write*) _____ you at

(19) such an early hour in the day. I (*get*) _____ a little

(20) sleepy, but I would rather stay up. I (*take*) _____ a

(21) nap after I (*get*) _____ back from taking her to the

(22) airport.

(23)   How (*get, you*) _____ along? How (*go, your*)

(24) *classes*) _____ ? Please write soon.

Yours truly,

EXERCISE 50:   Use any appropriate tense.

    A: Hi, my name is Jose.

    B: Hi, my name is Ali.

(1) Jose: (*You, study*) _____ at this university?

(2)   Ali: Yes, I _____ . _____
you?

(3) Jose: Yes, I (*be*) _____ here since last September.
Before that I (*study*) _____ English at another
school.

(4)   Ali: What (*you, take*) _____ ?

(5) Jose: I (*take*) _____ chemistry, math, psychology,
and American history. What (*take, you*) _____ ?

(6)   Ali: I (*study*) _____ English. I (*need*)
_____ to improve my English before I (*take*)
_____ regular academic courses next semester.

(7) Jose: How long (*you, be*) _____ here?

(8)   Ali: I (*be*) _____ here since the beginning of this

semester. Actually, I (*arrive*) _____ in the
United States six months ago, but I (*study*) _____
English at this university only since January. Before that I (*live*)

_____ with my brother in Washington, D.C.

(9) Jose: You (*speak*) _____ English very well. (*You,*

study) _____ a lot of English before you

(*come*) _____ to the United States?

(10) Ali: Yes. I (*study*) _____ English for ten years in my

own country. And also, I (*spend*) _____ some

time in Canada a couple of years ago. I (*pick*) _____

up a lot of English while I (*live*) _____ there.

(11) Jose: You (*be*) _____ lucky. When I (*come*)

_____ to the United States, I (*study, never*)

_____ any English at all. So I had to spend a

whole year studying nothing but English before I (*start*) _____
school.

(12) Ali: How long (*you, plan*) _____ to be in the U.S.?

(13) Jose: I (*be, not*) _____ sure. Probably by the time I

(*return*) _____ home, I (*be*) _____
here for at least five years. How about you?

(14) Ali: I (*hope*) _____ to be finished with all my work
in two and a half years.

EXERCISE 51—ORAL: Pair up with another student in the class.

STUDENT A: (1) Use the questions in this exercise to initiate conversation with
Student B.
(2) Do not simply read the questions. Look at the text briefly,
then look directly at Student B each time you ask a question.
(3) If Student B does not answer fully or you are interested in getting more information, ask your own questions in addition to
those which are suggested.
(4) Pay special attention to verb tense usage in both the questions
and the responses.

STUDENT B: (1) Do not look at the written questions in this exercise. Only Student A should look at the text.

              (2) Answer the questions fully. Often your response will consist of more than one sentence.

              (3) Answer in complete sentences in order to practice using verb tenses.

1. What is happening in this room?
   What else is happening?

2. What was happening in this room when you walked in today?
   What else was happening?

3. What did you do yesterday?   (*Student A: Listen carefully for past tense verbs*
   What else did you do?   *in the responses.*)
   What else did you do?

4. How long have you been living in (this city)?
   How long will you have been living here by the end of (the semester/term, etc.)?

5. Where did you eat dinner last night?
   What did you have?
   How was it?
   What did you do after you had eaten?

6. What were you doing at 8 o'clock last night?
   What will you be doing at 8 o'clock tomorrow night?

7. Are you taking any classes besides English?
   How is everything going?
   What are you doing in one of your classes?

8. How long have we been talking to each other?
   What have we been talking about?

9. How do you like living here?
   Have you had any interesting experiences since you came here? Have you met any interesting people?

10. What do you think the world will be like when you are seventy years old?

EXERCISE 52—ORAL: Same as the preceding exercise.

1. What are you doing right now?
   What are you going to be doing for the next ten minutes or so?

2. What did you do last weekend?   (*Student A: Listen carefully for past tense*
   What else did you do?   *verbs in the response.*)
   What else did you do?

3. What is the teacher doing?
   How long has he/she been (doing that)?

4. What are you going to do for the rest of today?
   What will you be doing at midnight?

5. What will you have done by the time you go to bed tonight?

6. How long have you been studying English at this school?
   How long had you studied English before you came here?
   What have you been doing outside of class to improve your English?

7. What have we been doing for the past ten minutes or so?
   Why have we been (doing that)?

8. What are some of the things you have done since you came to (this city)?

9. Have you read a newspaper lately?
   What is happening in the world?

10. What countries have you visited?
    When did you visit (a particular country).
    Why did you go there?
    What did you like about that country?
    What did you dislike about that country?
    Are you planning to go back there again someday?

EXERCISE 53: Before you come to class, think of an interesting, dangerous, or amusing experience you have had. You will then tell that story to a classmate, who will report that experience in a composition.

EXERCISE 54—ORAL: In a short speech (two or three minutes) summarize an article in a recent newspaper. You may speak from notes if necessary, but your notes should contain no more than fifteen words. Use your notes only for a very brief outline of important information.

EXERCISE 55—WRITTEN: Write a letter to a friend or family member. Discuss your activities, thoughts, feelings, adventures in the present, past, and future.

The purpose of this exercise is for you to use every possible tense. Try to include all of them. Following are the verb forms you should try to use, with *I* and the verb *do* given as an example. Some "time expressions" are also suggested.

I do	*I had been doing*
I am doing	*I will do/am going to do*
I have done	*I will be doing*
I have been doing	*I will have done*
I did	*I will have been doing*
I was doing	*right now*
I had done	*already*

every day	*since*
so far this week	*soon*
after	*never*
before	*still*
when	*in my entire lifetime*
while	*next week*
by (*a particular time*)	*yet*
for (*a length of time*)	(*etc.*)

Use the verb tenses in any order you wish and as many times as necessary. Be sure to use other subjects than *I*. Try to write a natural-sounding letter.

EXERCISE 56—ERROR ANALYSIS: All of the following sentences adapted from student writing contain errors. Test your skill by seeing how many of these errors you can find correct.

> *Example:*   I happy because my friend were there to meet me.
> *Correction:* I was happy because my friend **was** (OR: friends were) there to meet me.

1. My friends will meet me when I will arrive at the airport.
2. I am living at 3371 grand avenue since last september.
3. My country have change its capital city five time.
4. The phone rung while I doing the dishes. I dry my hands and answer it. When I am hear my husband voice, I very happy.
5. I will intend to go back home when I will get my Master's degree.
6. I am in the United States for the last four months. During this time, I had done many thing and saw many place.
7. When the old man started to walk back to his cave, the sun has already hided itself behind the mountain.
8. My life in this country is changing a great deal since I arrive here six month ago.
9. When I went to the orientation meeting, I have met many of the another students.
10. While I am writing my composition last night, someone knocks on the door.

EXERCISE 57—PREPOSITIONS: Supply an appropriate preposition.

1. I am not familiar _____ that author's works.

2. He doesn't approve _____ smoking.

3. I subscribe _____ several magazines.

4. Water consists _____ oxygen and hydrogen.

5. I became uncomfortable because she was staring _____ me.

6. She hid the candy _____ the children.

7. He never argues _____ his wife.

8. I arrived _____ this country two weeks ago.

9. We arrived _____ the airport ten minutes late.

10. Has Mary recovered _____ her illness?

11. I pray _____ peace.

12. I am envious _____ people who can speak three or four languages fluently.

13. Why are you angry _____ me? Did I do something wrong?

14. They are very patient _____ their children.

15. The students responded _____ the questions.

The Passive

4-1 FORMING THE PASSIVE

ACTIVE	PASSIVE	
(a) Mary **helps** John.	John **is helped** by Mary.	Form of the passive: **be** + **-ed** (past participle)
(b) Mary **is helping** John.	John **is being helped** by Mary.	
(c) Mary **has helped** John.	John **has been helped** by Mary.	In the passive, the *object* of an active verb *becomes the subject* of the passive verb.
(d) Mary **helped** John.	John **was helped** by Mary.	
(e) Mary **was helping** John.	John **was being helped** by Mary.	
(f) Mary **had helped** John.	John **had been helped** by Mary.	
(g) Mary **will help** John.	John **will be helped** by Mary.	Only transitive verbs (verbs that are followed by an object) are used in the passive. It is not possible to use verbs such as *happen, sleep, come,* and *seem* (intransitive verbs) in the passive.
(h) Mary **is going to help** John.	John **is going to be helped** by Mary.	
(i) Mary **will have helped** John.	John **will have been helped** by Mary.*	

*The progressive forms of the present perfect, past perfect, future, and future perfect are not used in the passive.

EXERCISE 1: Change the sentences from the active to the passive.

1a. The doctor *treats* the patient.

1b. The patient _____ _____ by the doctor.
              (simple present   +   *(-ed)*
              form of be)

2a. The doctor *is treating* the patient.

2b. The patient _____ _____ by the doctor.
           (present progressive   +   *(-ed)*
             form of be)

3a. The doctor *has treated* the patient.

3b. The patient _____ _____ by the doctor.
           (present perfect   +   *(-ed)*
             form of be)

4a. The doctor *treated* the patient.

4b. The patient _____ _____ by the doctor.
           (simple past   +   *(-ed)*
             form of be)

5a. The doctor *was treating* the patient.

5b. The patient _____ _____ by the doctor.
           (past progressive   +   *(-ed)*
             form of be)

6a. The doctor *had treated* the patient.

6b. The patient _____ _____ by the doctor.
           (past perfect   +   *(-ed)*
             form of be)

7a. The doctor *will treat* the patient.

7b. The patient _____ _____ by the doctor.
           (simple future   +   *(-ed)*
             form of be)

8a. The doctor *is going to treat* the patient.

8b. The patient _____ _____ by the doctor.
           (be going to   +   *(-ed)*
             and be)

9a. The doctor *will have treated* the patient.

9b. The patient _____ _____ by the doctor.
           (future perfect   +   *(-ed)*
             form of be)

10. Shakespeare *wrote* that play. _____

11. Bob *will invite* Ann to the party. _____

12. Alex *is preparing* that report. _____

13. Waitresses and waiters *serve* customers. _____

14. The teacher *is going to explain* the lesson. _____

15. Shirley *has suggested* a new idea. _____

16. Kathy *had returned* the book to the library. _____

17. When I got back to my hotel room, a maid *was making* the bed. _____

18. By this time tomorrow, the President *will have made* the announcement. _____

_____

4-2 THE *"BY* PHRASE"

(a) That book **was written** by Mark Twain.	A passive verb is followed with a *"by* phrase" only if it is important to know who performs an action. In (a): *by Mark Twain* is important information.
(b) This house *was built* in 1890. (*by someone; by house builders*) (c) Rice **is grown** in India. (*by people; by farmers*)	Usually the *"by* phrase" is omitted from a passive sentence: the passive is most frequently used when it is not known or not important to know *exactly* who performs an action, as in (b) and (c). The *"by* phrase" is often generally understood; e.g., in (b): *by house builders.*

EXERCISE 2: The *"by* phrase" is omitted in the following sentences. Suggest an "understood *by* phrase" for each. What would be an equivalent active sentence?

1. My sweater was made in England.
2. The new highway will be completed sometime next month.
3. Language skills are taught in every school in the country.
4. His book is going to be published next year.
5. Beethoven's Seventh Symphony was performed at the concert last night.
6. A lost tribe was discovered in the Philippine rain forest.

EXERCISE 3: Change the following active sentences to passive sentences, if possible. (Some of the verbs are intransitive and cannot be changed.) Keep the same tense. Include the *"by* phrase" only if necessary.

1. People grow corn in Iowa. _____ Corn is grown in Iowa. _____

2. Peter came here two months ago. _____ (no change) _____

3. Someone made this antique table in 1734. _____

_____

4. My aunt made this rug. _____

5. An accident happened at the corner of Fifth and Main. _____

_____

6. Translators have translated that book into many languages. _____

_____

7. Someone stole my purse. _____

_____

8. The old man had acquired a great deal of wealth before he died. _____

_____

9. Professor Rivers is teaching that course this semester. _____

_____

10. Some people are going to build a new hospital next year. _____

_____

11. Hundreds of people visit the Washington Monument every day. _____

_____

12. My sister's plane will arrive at 10:35. _____

_____

13. The mail carrier had already delivered the mail by the time I left for school this morning. _____

_____

14. Jim's daughter drew that picture. _____

_____

15. The news surprised me. _____

_____

16. Did the news surprise you? _____

_____

17. When is someone going to announce the results of the contest? _____

_____

18. The judges will judge the applicants on the basis of their originality. _____

_____

19. The child's aunt and uncle are bringing him up. _____

_____

20. The officials will call off the game if it rains. _____

_____

21. Ever since I arrived here, I have been living in the dormitory because someone told me that it was cheaper to live there than in an apartment. _____

_____

22. After the concert was over, hundreds of fans mobbed the rock music star outside the theater. _____

_____

EXERCISE 4—ORAL (BOOKS CLOSED): Change active to passive.

Example: Someone built that house ten years ago.
Response: That house was built ten years ago.

1. Someone invited you to go to a party.
2. Someone wrote that book in 1980.
3. John Smith wrote that book in 1980.
4. People grow rice in many countries.
5. Columbus discovered the New World.
6. The secretary is typing the letter.
7. Teachers teach reading in the first grade.
8. Someone told you to be here at ten o'clock.
9. Someone published that book in 1981.
10. People produce coffee in Brazil.
11. The mailman delivered the mail at noon.
12. Someone made that hat in Mexico.
13. Someone will serve dinner at six.
14. Someone is going to serve dinner at six.
15. Someone will announce the news tomorrow.
16. Someone will give the examination next week.
17. Someone has paid the bill.
18. Someone has made a mistake.
19. Someone has watered the plants.
20. The teacher is giving a test in the next room right now.
21. The teacher is asking you to use the passive.

EXERCISE 5—ORAL (BOOKS CLOSED): Use the passive in your response.

Example: *Teacher to A:* Someone stole your watch.
                        A: My watch was stolen.
              Teacher to B: What happened to (. . .)'s watch?
                        B: It was stolen.

Example: *Teacher to A:* People speak Arabic in many countries.
                        A: Arabic is spoken in many countries.

Teacher to B: Is Arabic a common language?
　　　　　　B: Yes. It is spoken in many countries.

1. A: Someone stole your pen.
   B: What happened to (. . .)'s pen?

2. A: People speak Spanish in many countries.
   B: Is Spanish a common language?

3. A: People play soccer in many countries.
   B: Is soccer a popular sport?

4. A: Mark Twain wrote that book.
   B: Who is the author of that book?

5. A: You went to a movie last night, but it bored you.
   B: Why did (. . .) leave the movie before it ended?

6. A: Someone returned your letter.
   B: (. . .) sent a letter last week, but he/she put the wrong address on it. What happened to the letter?

7. A: Someone robbed the bank.
   B: What happened to the bank?

8. A: The police caught the bank robber.
   B: Did the bank robber get away?

9. A: A judge sent the bank robber to jail.
   B: What happened to the bank robber?

10. A: The government requires foreign students to have a visa.
    B: Is it necessary for foreign students to have a visa?

11. A: Someone established this school in 1900.
    B: How long has this school been in existence?

12. A: There is a party tomorrow night. Someone has invited you to go to that party.
    B: Is (. . .) going to the party?

13. A: Something confused you.
    B: Why did (. . .) ask you a question?

14. A: Someone discovered gold in California in 1848.
    B: What happened in California in 1848?

15. A: I read about a village in the newspaper. Terrorists attacked the village.
    B: What happened to the village?

16. A: People used candles for light in the seventeenth century.
    B: Was electricity used for light in the seventeenth century?

17. A: The pilot flew the hijacked plane to another country.
    B: What happened to the hijacked plane?

18. A: When you had car trouble, a passing motorist helped you.
    B: Yesterday (. . .) was driving down (Highway 40) when suddenly his/her car started to make a terrible noise. So he/she pulled over to the side of the road. Did anyone help him/her?

19. A: Someone had already made the coffee by the time you got up this morning.

B: Did (. . .) have to make the coffee when he/she got up?

20. A: Someone had already sold the chair by the time you returned to the store.

B: (. . .) went to (name of a local store) yesterday to buy a chair. He/she found a chair he/she wanted, but then discovered that he/she didn't have his/her checkbook with him/her, so he/she went home to get it. Then he/she returned to the store. Did he/she buy the chair?

EXERCISE 6: Use the words in the following list to complete the sentences. All of the sentences are passive. Use any appropriate tense.

build	*frighten*	*report*
cause	√ *invent*	*spell*
confuse	*kill*	*surprise*
divide	*offer*	*surround*
expect	*order*	*wear*

1. The electric light bulb _____was invented_____ by Thomas Edison.

2. An island _____ by water.

3. The *-ing* form of "sit" _____ with a double *t*.

4. Even though construction costs are high, a new dormitory _____ next year.

5. The class was too large, so it _____ into two sections.

6. A bracelet _____ around the wrist.

7. The Johnson's house burned down. According to the inspector, the fire _____ _____ by lightning.

8. Al got a ticket for reckless driving. When he went to traffic court, he _____ _____ to pay a fine of $100.

9. I read about a hunter who _____ by a man-eating tiger.

10. The hunter's fatal accident _____ in the newspaper yesterday.

11. I didn't expect Lisa to come to the meeting last night, but she was there. I _____ _____ to see her there.

12. Last week I _____ a job at a local bank, but I didn't accept.

13. The children _____ in the middle of the night when they heard strange noises in the house.

14. Could you try to explain this math problem to me again? Yesterday in class I

_____ by the teacher's explanation.

15. A: Is the plane going to be late?

   B: No. It _____ to be on time.

4-3   PASSIVE VERBS USED AS ADJECTIVES (STATIVE PASSIVE)

(a) The door **is old**. (b) The door **is green**. (c) The door **is locked**.	In (a) and (b): *old* and *green* are adjectives. They describe the door. In (c): *locked* is a past participle. It is used as an adjective. It describes the door.
(d) I locked the door five minutes ago. (e) The door was locked by me five minutes ago. (f) Now the door **is locked**. (g) Ann broke the window. (h) The window was broken by Ann. (i) Now the window **is broken**.	The passive form may be used to describe an existing situation, as in (f) and (i). No action is taking place. The action happened before. There is no "*by* phrase." The *-ed* verb (past participle) functions as an adjective.
(j) I don't know where I am. **I am lost**. (k) I can't find my purse. **It is gone**. (l) **I am finished** with my work. (m) **I am done** with my work.	(j) through (m) are examples of idiomatic usage of the passive form. These sentences have no equivalent active sentences.

EXERCISE 7: Supply the passive form of the given verbs. Use *simple present* or *simple past*.

1. It is hot in this room because the window (*close*) _____ .

2. Yesterday it was hot in this room because the window (*close*) _____

   _____ .

3. Sarah is wearing a blouse. It (*make*) _____ of cotton.

4. The door to this room (*shut*) _____ .

5. Jim is sitting quietly. His elbows (*bend*) _____ and his hands

   (*fold*) _____ in front of him.

6. We can leave now because class (*finish*) _____ .

7. The lights in this room (*turn*) _____ on.

8. This room (*crowd, not*) _____ .

9. We can't go any farther. The car (*stick*) _____ in the mud.

10. We couldn't go any farther. The car (*stick*) _____ in the mud.

11. My room is very neat right now. The bed (*make*) _____ , the floor (*sweep*) _____ , and the dishes (*wash*) _____ .

12. We are ready to sit down and eat dinner. The table (*set*) _____ , the meat and rice (*do*) _____ , and the candles (*light*) _____ .

13. Where's my wallet? It (*go*) _____ ! Did you take it?

14. Hmmm. My dress (*tear*) _____ . I wonder how that happened.

15. Don't look in the hall closet. Your birthday present (*hide*) _____ there.

EXERCISE 8:   Use an appropriate form of the words in the following list to complete the sentences.

bear (born)*	*exhaust*	*plug in*
block	*go*	*qualify*
confuse	*insure*	*schedule*
crowd	*locate*	*spoil*
divorce	√ *lose*	*stick*
do	*marry*	*turn off*

1. Excuse me, sir. Could you give me some directions? I _____ am lost _____

2. Let's find another restaurant. This one _____ too _____ . We would have to wait at least an hour for a table.

3. The meeting _____ for tomorrow at nine.

4. That's hard work! I _____ . I need to rest for a while.

_____

*In the passive, **born** is used as the past participle of **bear**. Active: *bear-bore-borne*

5. You told me one thing and John told me another. I don't know what to think.

 I _____ .

6. Louise is probably sleeping. The lights in her room _____ .

7. Mrs. Wentworth's jewelry _____ for $50,000.

8. I can't open the window. It _____ .

9. Carolyn and Joe were married to each other for five years, but now they _____

 _____ .

10. I thought I had left my book on this desk, but it isn't here. It _____

 _____ . I wonder where it is.

11. I'm sorry. You _____ not _____ for the job. We need someone with a degree in electrical engineering.

12. I love my wife. I _____ to a wonderful woman.

13. We can't eat this fruit. It _____ . We'll have to throw it away.

14. We'd better call a plumber. The water won't go down the drain. The drain

 _____ .

15. Vietnam _____ in Southeast Asia.

16. A: How old is Jack?

 B: He _____ in 1960.

17. A: The TV set doesn't work.

 B: Are you sure? _____ it _____ ?

18. A: Is dinner ready?

 B: Not yet. The potatoes _____ not _____ . They need another ten minutes.

EXERCISE 9: Some passive-form verbs are followed by prepositions other than *by*. Supply the correct form of the verb in parentheses and an appropriate preposition. Use the *simple present*.

1. (*interest*)   She ___is interested in___ art.

2. (*accustom*)   I _____ living here.

3. (*compose*)   Water _____ hydrogen and oxygen.

4. (*terrify*)   Our son _____ dogs.

5. (*finish*)   She _____ her composition.

6. (*oppose*)   I _____ that suggestion.

7. (*cover*)   It's winter, and the ground _____ snow.

8. (*satisfy*)   I _____ the progress I have made.

9. (*marry*)   Jack _____ Ruth.

10. (*divorce*)   Elaine _____ her husband.

11. (*acquaint*)   I _____ not _____ that author's works.

12. (*tire*)   I _____ sitting here.

13. (*relate*)   Your name is Mary Smith. _____ you _____ John Smith?

14. (*dedicate*)   Mrs. Robinson works in an orphanage. She _____ her work.

15. (*disappoint*)   He got a bad grade because he didn't study. He _____ himself.

16. (*scare*)   He is not very brave. He _____ his own shadow.

17. (*commit*)   The administration _____ improving the quality of education at the university.

18. (*devote*)   Mr. and Mrs. Miller _____ each other.

19. (*dress*)   He _____ his best suit.

20. (*do*)   We _____ this exercise.

4-4 ADJECTIVES WITH *GET;* THE PASSIVE WITH *GET*

(a) **I'm getting hungry.** Let's eat soon. (b) You shouldn't eat so much. **You'll get fat.** (c) I stopped working because **I got sleepy.**	*Get* may be followed by certain adjectives. In this instance, *get* has the meaning of **become.** *
(d) I stopped working because **I got tired.** (e) They are **getting married** next month. (f) **I got worried** because he was two hours late.	*Get* may also be followed by a past participle (*-ed*). The past participle functions as an adjective; it describes the subject.

*Some of the common adjectives that follow *get* are: *angry, anxious, bald, big, busy, chilly, cold, dark, empty, fat, full, good, heavy, hot, hungry, late, light, mad, nervous, old, rich, sick, sleepy, tall, thirsty, warm, well, wet.*

EXERCISE 10: Use any appropriate tense of *get* and an adjective from the following list to complete the sentences.

better	*hot*	*nervous*
busy	√ *hungry*	*sleepy*
dark	*late*	*well*
full	*light*	*wet*

1. What time are we going to eat? I _____ am getting hungry _____ .

2. A: I _____ .
   B: Why don't you take a nap? A couple of hours of sleep will do you good.

3. A: What time is it?
   B: Almost ten.
   A: I'd better leave soon. It _____ . I have to be at the airport by eleven.

4. I didn't have an umbrella, so I _____ while I was waiting for the bus yesterday.

5. Let's turn on the airconditioner. It _____ hot in here.

6. Everytime I have to give a speech, I _____ .

7. Would you mind turning on the light? It _____ in here.

8. A: It's a long drive from Denver to here. I'm glad you finally arrived. What time did you leave this morning?
   B: At sunrise. We left as soon as it _____ outside.

9. A: Won't you have another helping?
   B: All of the food is delicious, but I really can't eat much more. I _____

   _____ .

10. Maria's English is improving. It _____ .

11. Shake a leg! We don't have all day to finish this work! Get moving! Let's step

on it! _____ and finish your work. There's no time to
waste.

12. My friend was sick, so I sent him a card. It said, "_____
soon."

EXERCISE 11–ORAL (BOOKS CLOSED):   Answer the questions.

1. Is the weather getting warmer or colder?
2. What time does it usually get dark?
3. Do you ever get angry?
4. What is the best way to get rich quick?
5. Are you getting younger?
6. What happens when you blow up a balloon?
7. Do you ever get nervous?
8. What happens if you eat too much?
9. (. . .) was sick, but then he/she recovered. Did he/she get worse?
10. What time does it usually get light?

EXERCISE 12:   Complete the sentences by using an appropriate form for *get* and
the given verbs.*

1. (*tire*)   I think I'll stop working soon. I
    <u> am getting tired </u> .

2. (*hurt*)   It was a bad accident, but luckily nobody

    _____ .

3. (*lose*)   We didn't have a map, so we _____ .

4. (*dress*)   We can leave as soon as you _____ .

5. (*marry*)   When _____ you _____ ?

6. (*accustom*)   How long did it take you to _____
    to living here?

7. (*worry*)   Sam was supposed to be home an hour ago, but

    he still isn't here. I _____ .

———————

*The passive with *get* is common in informal English but is often not appropriate in very formal
usage.

8. (*upset*)   Just try to take it easy. Don't _____.
                      Everything will be all right.

9. (*confuse*)   Everybody gave me different advice. I

                      _____.

10. (*finish*)   We can leave as soon as I _____
                      with this work.

11. (*drink*)   Chris _____ at the party last
                      night, so I wouldn't let her drive home.

12. (*invite*)   Did you _____ to the party?

13. (*bore*)   I didn't stay for the end of the movie because

                      I _____.

14. (*pack*)   I'll be ready to leave as soon as I

                      _____.

15. (*pay*)   I'll give you the money I owe you next Friday.

                      I _____ then.

16. (*hire*)   After he graduated, he _____ by
                      an engineering firm.

17. (*fire*)   But later he _____ because he
                      didn't do his work.

18. (*do*)   Last night I didn't _____ with
                      my homework until midnight.

19. (*disgust*)   The things she was saying were ridiculous.

                      Finally I _____ and left.

20. (*engage*)   First, they _____ .

    (*marry*)   Then, they _____ .

    (*divorce*)   Later, they _____ .

    (*remarry*)   Finally, they _____ .
                      Today they are very happy.

EXERCISE 13: Use active or passive, in any appropriate tense, for the verbs in parentheses.

1. It's noon. The mail should be here soon. It (*deliver, usually*) _____

   _____ sometime between noon and one o'clock.

2. Only five of us (*work*) _____ in the laboratory yesterday when the explosion (*occur*) _____ . Luckily, no
one (*hurt*) _____ .

3. I was supposed to take a test yesterday, but I (*admit, not*) _____
_____ into the testing room because the examination
(*begin, already*) _____ .

4. According to a recent survey, out of every dollar an American spends on food,
thirty-six cents (*spend*) _____ at restaurants.

5. I'm sorry I'm late. I (*hold up*) _____ by the rush hour
traffic. It (*take*) _____ thirty minutes for me to get
here instead of fifteen.

6. Before she graduated last May, Susan (*offer, already*) _____
a position with a law firm.

7. According to many scientists, solar energy (*use*) _____
extensively in the twenty-first century.

8. I (*study*) _____ English here for the last two months. My English (*get*) _____ better, but I still find it difficult to
understand lectures.

9. Right now a student trip to the planetarium (*organize*) _____
by Mrs. Hunt. You can sign up for it at her office.

10. He is a man whose name will go down in history. He (*forget, never*) _____
_____ by his countrymen.

11. When you (*arrive*) _____ at the airport tomorrow, you
(*meet*) _____ by a friend of mine. He (*wear*) _____
_____ a red shirt and blue jeans. He (*be*) _____
_____ fairly tall and (*have*) _____
dark hair. He (*stand*) _____ near the main entrance.
I'm sure you will be able to find him.

12. A: Yesterday (*be*) _____ a terrible day.

    B: What (*happen*) _____ ?

    A: First, I (*flunk*) _____ a test, or at least I think I
    did. Then I (*drop*) _____ my books while I (*walk*)

_____ across campus and they (*fall*) _____

_____ into a mud puddle. And finally, my bicycle

(*steal*) _____ .

B: You should have stayed in bed.

4-5   USING *USED TO* (HABITUAL PAST) AND *BE USED TO/BE ACCUSTOMED TO*

(a) Jack **used to live** in Chicago.	In (a): At a time in the past, Jack lived in Chicago, but he does not live in Chicago now. *Used to* expresses a habit, activity, or situation that existed in the past but which no longer exists.
(b) Mary **is used to living** in a cold climate. (c) Mary **is accustomed to living** in a cold climate. (d) Mary **is used to (accustomed to) cold weather.**	(b) and (c) have the same meaning: Living in a cold climate is usual and normal to Mary. Cold weather, snow, and ice do not seem strange to her. *Be used to* and *be accustomed to* are followed by an *-ing* verb form (a gerund),* as in (b) and (c), or by a noun object, as in (d).
(e) When Bob moved to Italy, he **got used to (got accustomed to)** Italian food very quickly.	In the expressions *get used to* and *get accustomed to, get* means *become.*

*See 7–2 Using Gerunds as the Objects of Prepositions. Note: In British English, sometimes the simple form may be used following *be accustomed to* rather than the gerund form.

EXERCISE 14—ORAL (BOOKS CLOSED): Answer the questions in complete sentences.

I.   *used to* (*habitual past*)

1. What did you use to do on summer days when you were a child?
2. . . . in class when you were in elementary school?
3. . . . for fun when you were younger?
4. . . . for exercise on weekends?
5. . . . after school was out when you were a teenager?
6. . . . with your family when you were growing up?
7. What was your daily routine when you were living (in Bangkok)?
8. How has your way of life changed in the last few years? What did you use to do that you don't do now?

II. *be used to/be accustomed to*

> *Example:* You have to take a bus to school. Are you accustomed to that?
>
> *Response:* No, I'm not accustomed to taking a bus to school. I'm accustomed to walking to school.

9. You have to get up at 6:30 every morning. Are you used to that? (*No . . .*)
10. You have to eat your big meal at six o'clock. Are you accustomed to that?
11. Last night you went to bed at one A.M. Are you accustomed to that?
12. You are living (in a dormitory). Are you accustomed to that?
13. You have to speak English all the time. Are you used to that?
14. The weather is very cold. You have to wear heavy clothes. Are you used to that?
15. You borrowed your friend's car, so you have to drive a stick shift car. Are you accustomed to that?
16. You have a roommate. You have to share your room with another person. Are you used to that?
17. Many people in the United States drink coffee with their meals. Are you accustomed to doing that?
18. You live in your own apartment now. You have to make your own breakfast. Are you used to that?

III. *get used to/get accustomed to*

19. What adjustments does a person have to make, what does he have to get used to or accustomed to when he moves from his parents' house into his own apartment?
20. A person who moves from a warm to a cold climate?
21. A student who moves into a dormitory?
22. A woman when she gets married or a man when he gets married?
23. You are living in a new environment. You have had to make adjustments. What have you gotten used to? What haven't you gotten used to or can't you get used to?

4-6 USING *-ING* AND *-ED* FORMS AS ADJECTIVES (PARTICIPIAL ADJECTIVES)

-ING (ACTIVE MEANING)	-ED (PASSIVE MEANING)
(a) **The problem confuses** the students. (b) It is **a confusing problem**.	(c) **The students are confused** by the problem. (d) They are **confused students**.

-ING (ACTIVE MEANING)	-ED (PASSIVE MEANING)
(e) **The class bores** the students. (f) It is **a boring class.**	(g) **The students are bored** by the class. (h) They are **bored students.**
(i) **The story amused** the children. (j) It was **an amusing story.**	(k) **The children were amused** by the story. (l) They were **amused children.**

EXERCISE 15: Give the correct form, *-ing* or *-ed*, of the verbs in parentheses.

1. The news surprised me. It was (*surprise*) _____ news.

2. The man was surprised by the sudden noise. The (*surprise*) _____ man sat up quickly.

3. The work exhausted the men. It was (*exhaust*) _____ work.

4. The men were exhausted. The (*exhaust*) _____ men sat down to rest under the shade of a tree.

5. A (*damage*) _____ earthquake occurred recently.

6. The (*damage*) _____ automobile was sold for junk.

7. The dragon was a (*terrify*) _____ sight for the villagers.

8. The (*terrify*) _____ villagers ran for their lives.

9. The sound frightened the child. It was a (*frighten*) _____ sound.

10. The child was frightened by the sound. The (*frighten*) _____ child sought comfort from her father.

11. The window is broken. I have to repair the (*break*) _____ window.

12. I found myself in an (*embarrass*) _____ situation last night.

EXERCISE 16: Same as the preceding exercise.

1. Success in one's work is a (*satisfy*) _____ experience.

2. The (*steal*) _____ jewelry was recovered.

3. I elbowed my way through the (*crowd*) _____ room.

4. The value endures. A gift given in love has (*endure*) _____ value.

5. No one lives in that (*desert*) _____ house except a few ghosts.

6. The thief tried to pry open the (*lock*) _____ cabinet.

7. Parents have a (*last*) _____ effect on their children.

8. The (*injure*) _____ woman was put into an ambulance.

9. I bought some (*freeze*) _____ vegetables at the supermarket.

10. That (*annoy*) _____ buzz is coming from the fluorescent light.

11. I like to talk with her. I think she is an (*interest*) _____ person.

12. Use the (*give*) _____ words in the (*follow*) _____ sentences.

13. The teacher gave us a (*challenge*) _____ assignment, but we all enjoyed doing it.

14. The (*expect*) _____ event did not occur.

15. A (*grow*) _____ child needs a (*balance*) _____ diet.

16. There is an old saying: Let (*sleep*) _____ dogs lie.

17. No one appreciates a (*spoil*) _____ child.

18. At present, the (*lead*) _____ candidate in the senatorial race is Henry Moore.

19. It is sad. She led a (*waste*) _____ life.

20. We had a (*thrill*) _____ but hair-raising experience on our backpacking trip into the wilderness.

21. Last night while we were walking home, we saw an unidentified (*fly*) _____ object.

22. The (*abandon*) _____ car was towed away by the police.

23. Any (*think*) _____ person knows that smoking is a destructive habit.

24. I still have five more (*require*) _____ courses to take.

25. The streets bustled with activity. We made our way through the (*bustle*) _____ streets.

EXERCISE 17—WRITTEN: Write a brief biography of someone you know well and admire—perhaps a parent, spouse, brother or sister, friend, colleague, or neighbor.

EXERCISE 18—ERROR ANALYSIS: Find and correct the errors in the following.

> *Example:* I dressed my clothes.
> *Correction:* I got dressed.

1. I am interesting in his ideas.
2. How many peoples have you been invited to the party?
3. When I returned home, everything is quite. I walk to my room, get undress, and going to bed.
4. I didn't go to dinner with them because I had already been eaten.
5. In class yesterday, I was confusing. I didn't understand the lesson.
6. I couldn't move. I was very frighten.
7. When we were children, we are very afraid of caterpillars. Whenever we saw one of these monsters, we run to our house before the caterpillars could attack us. I am still scare when I saw a caterpillar close to me.
8. One day, while the old man was cutting down a big tree near the stream, his axe was fallen into the water. He sat down and begin to cry because he does not have enough money to buy another axe.

EXERCISE 19—PREPOSITIONS: Supply an appropriate preposition. All of the sentences contain two-word verbs.

1. A: I think we should increase the membership dues from one dollar to two.

   B: That might solve some of our financial problems. Why don't you bring that

   _____ at the next meeting?

2. A: Did you hand _____ your composition?

   B: No. I didn't like it, so I decided to do it _____ .

3. A: What time did you get _____ this morning?

   B: I slept late. I didn't drag myself out of bed until after nine.

4. A: What's the baby's name?

   B: Helen. She was named _____ her paternal grandmother.

5. A: I need to get more exercise.

   B: Why don't you take _____ tennis?

6. A: You can't go in there.

   B: Why not?

A: Look at that sign. It says, "Keep _____ . No trespassing."

7. A: I can't reach Fred. There's a busy signal.

   B: Then hang _____ and try again later.

8. A: The radio is too loud. Would you mind if I turned it _____ a little?

   B: No.

9. A: I can't hear the radio. Could you turn it _____ a little?

   B: Sure.

10. A: What are you doing Saturday night, Bob?

   B: I'm taking Virginia _____ for dinner and a show.

Modal Auxiliaries-I

EXERCISE 1—PRETEST: Add the word *to* where appropriate.

1. I have ___to___ talk to him.

2. They may ___X___ come.

3. You must _____ be quiet.

4. She can _____ come.

5. Mary should _____ finish her work.

6. She could _____ visit them.

7. I ought _____ call her.

8. You had better _____ write them.

9. I have got _____ go home.

10. He has _____ go to the dentist.

5-1 VERB FORMS FOLLOWING MODAL AUXILIARIES

(1) MODALS FOLLOWED BY THE SIMPLE FORM OF A VERB:	
can	(a) I **can do** it.
could	(b) I **could do** it.
had better	(c) You **had better do** it.
may	(d) They **may do** it.
might	(e) She **might do** it.
must	(f) He **must do** it.
shall	(g) I **shall do** it.
should	(h) Mark **should do** it.
will	(i) Barb **will do** it.
would	(j) I **would do** it.

<table>
<tr><td colspan="2">(2) MODALS FOLLOWED BY AN INFINITIVE (TO + SIMPLE FORM)</td></tr>
<tr><td>have to</td><td>(k) I have to do it.</td></tr>
<tr><td>have got to</td><td>(l) We have got to do it.</td></tr>
<tr><td>ought to</td><td>(m) She ought to do it.</td></tr>
</table>

5-2 EXPRESSING ABILITY: *CAN, COULD*

(a) She **can speak** English. (b) Fish **cannot survive** out of water.*	In (a): *can = is able to* (*present*)
(c) He **can come** tomorrow. (d) We **can't go** on vacation until next month.	In (c): *can = will be able to* (*future*)
(e) I **could speak** German when I was a child. (f) I **couldn't open** the window. It was stuck.	In (e): *could = was able to* (*past*)

*The negative of *can* may be written as *cannot*, *can not*, or *can't*.

5-3 GIVING PERMISSION: *CAN, MAY*

FORMAL	INFORMAL	
(g) When you finish the test, you **may leave**.	(h) I'm not quite ready to go, but you **can leave** if you're in a hurry. I'll meet you later.	In giving permission, *may* is usually used in formal situations; *can* is usually used in informal situations.
(i) You **may pay** the bill either in person or by mail.	(j) Sure! You **can borrow** five bucks from me. You **can pay** me back later.	

EXERCISE 2: *Can* is usually pronounced /kən/. *Can't* is usually pronounced /kænt/. Try to determine whether the teacher is saying *can* or *can't* in the following sentences.*

1. The secretary *can/can't* help you.
2. My mother *can/can't* speak English.
3. My friend *can/can't* meet you at the airport.
4. Mr. Smith *can/can't* answer your question.
5. We *can/can't* come to the meeting.
6. *Can/can't* you come?
7. You *can/can't* take that course.
8. I *can/can't* cook.
9. Our son *can/can't* count to ten.
10. I *can/can't* drive a stick-shift car.

---

*Sometimes even native speakers have a little difficulty distinguishing between *can* and *can't*.

5-4 ASKING POLITE QUESTIONS

(1) QUESTIONS WITH "I" AS THE SUBJECT		
MAY I COULD I	(a) **May I (please) borrow** your pen? (b) **Could I borrow** your pen **(please)**?	*May I* and *could I* are used to request permission. They are equally polite. (*May I* is somewhat more appropriate in formal usage than *could I.*) *Please* is often included in the question.
CAN I	(c) **Can I borrow** your pen?	*Can I* is sometimes used informally to request permission, especially if the speaker is talking to someone he/she knows fairly well.
MIGHT I	(d) **Might I borrow** your pen?	*Might I* is less frequently used, but it has the same meaning and usage as *may I* and *could I.*
		Note: In polite questions, all four words—*may, could, can, might*—have a present or future meaning, not a past meaning.

		Typical responses:*
		    Certainly. Yes, certainly.
		    Of course. Yes, of course.
		    Sure. (*informal*)

(2) QUESTIONS WITH "YOU" AS THE SUBJECT		
WOULD YOU WILL YOU	(e) **Would you pass** the salt **(please)**? (f) **Will you (please) pass** the salt?	The meaning of *would you* and *will you* in a polite question is the same. *Would you* is more common and is at times a little more polite than *will you.* The degree of politeness, however, is often determined by the speaker's tone of voice.

COULD YOU	(g) **Could you pass** the salt?	Basically, *could you* and *would you* have the same meaning. The difference is slight:
		    would you = Do you want to do this please?
		    could you = Do you want to do this please, and is it possible for you to do this?

CAN YOU	(h) **Can you pass** the salt?	*Can you* is sometimes used informally.

	Typical responses:*
	Yes, I'd (I would) be happy to.
	Yes, I'd be glad to.
	Certainly.
	Sure. (*informal*)

*Often the response to a polite question consists of an action, a nod or shake of the head, or a simple "uh-huh."

EXERCISE 3–ORAL (BOOKS CLOSED):

STUDENT A: Ask a polite question for the given situation.

STUDENT B: Give a typical response.

1. You are sitting at the dinner table. You want the butter.
2. You want to ask your teacher a question.
3. You are at your friend's apartment. You want to use the phone.
4. You are speaking on the phone to your brother. You want him to pick you up at the airport when you arrive home.
5. You want your friend to meet you in front of the library at three this afternoon.
6. You want to leave class early. You are speaking to your instructor.
7. You knock on your professor's half-open door. He is sitting at his desk. You want to come in.
8. You want to make an appointment to see Dr. North. You are speaking to her secretary.

9. You are at a gas station. You want the attendant to check the oil.
10. You are in your chemistry class. You are looking at your textbook. On page 100 there is a formula which you do not understand. You want your professor to explain this formula to you.
11. You call your friend. Her name is Mary. Someone else answers the phone.
12. You want to see your classmate's dictionary for a minute.

5-5 USING *WOULD YOU MIND*

(1) ASKING PERMISSION	
(a) **Would you mind if I closed** the window?	Notice in (a): ***would you mind if I*** is followed by the simple past.* The meaning in (a): *May I close the window? Is it all right if I close the window? Will it cause you any trouble or discomfort if I close the window?*
	Typical responses: **No.** **Not at all.** **"unh-unh"** (meaning *no*)
(2) ASKING SOMEONE ELSE TO DO SOMETHING	
(b) **Would you mind closing** the window?	Notice in (b): ***would you mind*** is followed by *-ing* (a gerund). The meaning in (b): *I don't want to cause you any trouble, but would you please close the window? Would that cause you any inconvenience?*
	Typical responses: **No. I'd be happy to.** **Not at all. I'd be glad to.** **"unh-unh"** (meaning *no*)

*Sometimes in informal spoken English, the simple present is used.

EXERCISE 4: Using the verb in parentheses, fill in the blank either with *if I + the past tense* or with *the -ing form of the verb*. In some of the sentences, either response is possible but the meaning is different.

1. I'm getting tired. I'd like to go home and go to bed. Would you mind (*leave*)
   _____if I left_____ early?

2. I'm sorry. I didn't understand what you said. Would you mind (*repeat*) _____
   _____repeating_____ that?

3. A: Are you going to the post office?
   B: Yes.

   A: Would you mind (*mail*) _____ this letter for me?
   B: Not at all.

4. A: Are you coming with us?
   B: I know I promised to go with you, but I'm not feeling very good. Would

   you mind (*stay*) _____ home?

148

A: Of course not.

5. A: I still don't understand how to work this algebra problem. Would you mind
    (*explain*) _____ it again?
    B: Not at all. I'd be happy to.

6. A: It's getting hot in here. Would you mind (*open*) _____ the
    window?
    B: No.

7. A: This is probably none of my business, but would you mind (*ask*) _____
    _____ you a personal question?
    B: It depends.

8. A: Would you mind (*smoke*) _____?
    B: I'd really rather you didn't.

9. A: Excuse me. Would you mind (*speak*) _____ a little more
    slowly? I didn't catch what you said.
    B: I'd be happy to.

10. A: I don't like this TV program. Would you mind (*change*) _____
    the channel?
    B: Unh-unh.

EXERCISE 5—ORAL (BOOKS CLOSED): Ask polite questions in the following
situations. Use any appropriate modal: *may, could, would,* etc.

1. Your plane leaves at six P.M. tomorrow. You want your friend to take you to
   the airport.
2. You are sitting at a friend's house. A bowl of fruit is sitting on the table. You
   want an apple.
3. Your friend is driving the car. You want her to stop at the next mailbox so you
   can mail a letter.
4. You are hot. The window is closed.
5. You are trying to study. Your roommate is playing his record player very
   loudly and this is bothering you.
6. You call your friend. Someone else answers and tells you that your friend is
   out. You want to leave a message.
7. You want your pen. You can't reach it, but your friend can. You want your
   friend to hand you the pen.
8. You are at a restaurant. You want some more coffee.
9. You are at your friend's house. You want to help her set the dinner table.
10. You are at the breakfast table. You want the salt and pepper.

11. You want to make a telephone call. You are in a store and have to use a pay phone, but you don't have any change. All you have is a one-dollar bill. You ask a clerk for change.

12. You are at a restaurant. You have finished your meal and are ready to leave. You ask the waiter for the check.

13. You call your boss's house. His name is Mr. Smith. You want to talk to him. His wife answers the phone.

14. You are giving a party. Your guests have just arrived. You want to get them something to drink.

15. You are the teacher. You want a student to shut the door.

16. You are walking down the hall of the classroom building. You need to know what time it is. You ask a student whom you have never met.*

17. You are in the middle of the city. You are lost. You are trying to find the bus station. You stop someone on the street to ask for directions.

18. You call the airport. You want to know what time Flight 62 arrives.

19. You are in a department store. You find a sweater that you like, but you can't find the price tag. You ask the clerk to tell you how much it costs.

20. It is your first day on campus. You are supposed to be at the library for a meeting, but you can't find the library. You ask for information from another student you meet on the sidewalk.

5-6 EXPRESSING ADVISABILITY: *SHOULD, OUGHT TO, HAD BETTER*

(a) I **should lose** some weight. (b) I **ought to lose** some weight.	*Should* and *ought to* have the same meaning: advisability. Basically, they both mean: "This is a good idea. This is good advice."
(c) You **should study** harder. (d) You **ought to study** harder.	In (a) and (b): It is a good idea for me to lose some weight. I've been eating too much and my clothes are getting tight. (Maybe I will lose some weight, and maybe I won't. I am only saying that losing weight is a good idea.)
	Ought to is usually pronounced "otta."
(e) You **shouldn't leave** your keys in the car.	Negative contraction: *shouldn't*. (*Ought to* is not commonly used in the negative.)

---

*The responses to 16 through 20 include noun clauses. For word order in noun clauses see Chapter 9.

(f) The gas tank is almost empty. We **had better stop** at the next service station. (g) You **had better take** care of that cut on your hand, or it will get infected.	In meaning, *had better* is close to *should* and *ought to,* but *had better* is usually stronger. Basically, *had better* means: "This is a *very* good idea." Often *had better* implies a warning or a threat of possible bad consequences.
	In (f): If we don't stop at a service station, there will be a bad result. We will run out of gas.
	Spoken and written contraction: *You'd better take care of it.* Sometimes in speaking, *had* is dropped: *You better take care of it.*

EXERCISE 6: Complete the following.

1. I should study tonight because _____.

2. I ought to study tonight because _____.

3. I had better study tonight. If I don't, _____.

4. I should wash my clothes today, but _____.

5. I'd better wash my clothes today, or _____.

6. It's a beautiful day. We ought to _____.

7. It looks like rain. If you are going out, you _____.

EXERCISE 7—ORAL (BOOKS CLOSED): Give advice in the following situations by using *should, ought to,* or *had better.*

Example: I have a test tomorrow.

Response: You should (ought to, had better) study tonight.

1. I'm writing a composition, and there is a word I don't know how to spell.

2. I don't feel good. I think I'm catching a cold.

3. I can't see the blackboard when I sit in the back row.

4. I'm cold.

5. My foot is asleep.

6. I'm homesick.

7. I have a problem with my student visa.

8. My roommate snores and I can't get to sleep.

9. I need to improve my English.

10. I can't stop yawning.

11. My library book is due today.

12. There's no food in my house, and some guests are coming to dinner tonight.

13. I have only twenty-five cents in my pocket, but I need some money to go out tonight.

14. My apartment is a mess, and my mother is coming to visit me tomorrow.

15. I'm about to leave on a trip, but the gas gauge in my car is on empty.

16. I have a toothache.

17. I have the flu.

18. My friend is arriving at the airport this evening. I'm supposed to pick him up, but I've forgotten what time his plane gets in.

19. I have the hiccups.

5-7   THE PAST FORM OF *SHOULD**

(a) I had a test this morning. I did not do well on the test because I did not study for it last night. **I should have studied** last night.	Past form: ***should have + -ed*** (*past participle*) Usual pronunciation of ***should have:*** "should've" or "shoulda."
(b) You were supposed to be here at 10 P.M. but you did not come until midnight. We were worried about you. You **should have called** us. (You did not call.)	
(c) I hurt my back. **I should not have carried** that heavy box up two flights of stairs. (I carried the box and now I am sorry.)	Usual pronunciation of ***should not have:*** "shouldn't've" or "shouldn't'a."
(d) We went to the movie, but it was a bad movie. We wasted our time and our money. We **should not have gone** to the movie.	

*The past form of ***ought to*** is ***ought to have + -ed.*** (*I ought to have studied.*) It has the same meaning as the past form of *should.* In the past, ***should*** is used more commonly than ***ought to. Had better*** has no past form.

EXERCISE 8–ORAL (BOOKS CLOSED):

Example: You failed the test because you didn't study.

Response: I should have studied.

Example: You didn't study because you went to a movie.
Response: I shouldn't have gone to a movie.

1. You are cold because you didn't wear a coat.
2. You misspelled a word because you didn't look it up in the dictionary.
3. Your friend is upset because you didn't write him a letter.
4. You are broke now because you spent all your money foolishly.
5. The room is full of flies because you opened the window.
6. You don't have any food for dinner because you didn't go to the grocery store.
7. You overslept this morning because you didn't set your alarm clock.
8. Your friends went to (New Orleans) over vacation. They had a good time. You didn't go with them, and now you are sorry.
9. John loved Mary, but he didn't marry her. Now he is unhappy.
10. John loved Mary, and he married her. But now he is unhappy.
11. You didn't have a cup of coffee. Now you are sleepy.
12. You didn't stop for gas, and then you ran out of gas on the highway.
13. You were sick yesterday, but you went to class anyway. Today you feel worse.
14. The weather was beautiful yesterday, but you stayed inside all day.
15. You bought your girlfriend a box of candy for her birthday, but she doesn't like candy.
16. The little girl told a lie. She got into a lot of trouble.
17. You have a stomachache because you ate (five hamburgers).

18. You had to pay a fine because your library book was overdue.

5-8 EXPRESSING NECESSITY: *MUST, HAVE TO, HAVE GOT TO*

(a) Every driver **must have** a valid license. (b) Every driver **has to have** a valid license. (c) All applicants **must take** an entrance exam. (d) All applicants **have to take** an entrance exam.	*Must* and *have to* both express necessity. In (a) and (b): It is necessary for every driver to have a license. There is no other choice. A license is required.

(e) **I must be** home by eight. I'm expecting an extremely important telephone call at eight. (f) **I have to be** home by eight. I have a lot of studying to do tonight.	Sometimes (not always), *must* is a little stronger than *have to.* In (e): By using *must*, the speaker is emphasizing the idea that he has no choice. In (f): The speaker is making a simple statement that it is necessary for him to be home by eight. Note: *Have to* is usually pronounced "hafta"; *has to* is usually pronounced "hasta."
(g) **I have got to go** now. I have a class in ten minutes. (h) No, I can't go downtown with you. I **have got to study.**	*Have got to* has the same meaning as *must* and *have to:* necessity. However, usually *have got to* is used only in spoken English. Generally, *have got to* is not as strong as either *must* or *have to.* Usual pronunciation: "I've gotta go now" or "I gotta go now."

EXERCISE 9: Use either *should* or *must/have to* in the following. In some sentences either is possible, but the meaning is different.

1. A person _____ eat in order to live.

2. A person _____ eat a balanced diet.

3. If you want to become a doctor, you _____ go to medical school for many years.

4. We _____ go to Colorado for our vacation.

5. According to my academic advisor, I _____ take another English course.

6. I _____ write to my folks tonight, but I think I'll wait and do it tomorrow.

7. You _____ have a passport if you want to travel abroad.

8. Everyone _____ have certain goals in life.

9. Rice _____ have water in order to grow.

10. I _____ go to class, but I don't feel good. I think I'd better stay home.

11. If a door is locked, you _____ use a key to open it.

12. I don't have enough money to take the bus, so I _____ walk home.

13. If you don't know how to spell a word, you _____ look it up in the dictionary.

14. This pie is very good. You _____ try a piece.

15. This pie is excellent! You _____ try a piece.*

5-9   EXPRESSING NECESSITY: THE PAST FORM OF
MUST AND *HAVE TO*

(a) **I have to study** tonight. ⟶ **I had to study** last night. (b) **I must study** tonight. ⟶ **I had to study** last night.	In sentences that express necessity, the *past form* of both *must* and *have to* is *had to*.

EXERCISE 10–ORAL (BOOKS CLOSED):   Change the sentences to the past.

Example: I must take a test tomorrow.

Response: I had to take a test yesterday.

1. I don't have any money. I must cash a check.
2. He is sick. He must see a doctor.
3. I have to go to class, so I can't meet you for a cup of coffee.
4. I have to stop at the drugstore because I need some toothpaste.
5. (. . .) has to study, so he/she can't come to my party.
6. I don't have any stamps. I must go to the post office.
7. I can't see the board. I must sit in the front row.
8. I can't go to class because I must pick up my brother at the airport.

5-10   EXPRESSING NECESSITY: USING *MUST* AND
HAVE TO IN THE NEGATIVE

PROHIBITION	(a) You **must not look** in the closet. Your birthday present is hidden there. (b) **I must not forget** to take my key with me. (c) You **must not tell** anyone my secret. Do you promise?	When used in the negative, *must* and *have to* have different meanings.
		must not = *prohibition* (DO NOT DO THIS!) In (a): Do not look in the closet. I forbid it. Looking in the closet is prohibited.
		Negative contraction: *mustn't* (*The first t is not pronounced.*)

*Sometimes in speaking, *must* has the meaning of a very enthusiastic *should*.

(d) I **don't have to study** tonight. I think I'll watch television for a while.	**do not have to** = *lack of necessity*
(e) Tomorrow is a holiday. We **don't have to go** to class.	In (d): It is not necessary for me to study tonight. I have already finished my home-work.
(f) I can hear you. You **don't have to shout**.	

EXERCISE 11: Use *must not* or *do not have to* in the following.

1. A person _____ become rich and famous in order to live a successful life.

2. In order to be a good salesclerk, you _____ be rude to a customer.

3. I _____ go to the doctor. I'm feeling much better.

4. An entering freshman _____ declare a major immediately. The student may wait a few semesters before deciding upon a major.

5. This is an opportunity that comes once in a lifetime. We _____ let it pass. We must act.

6. We have plenty of time. We _____ to hurry.

7. Johnny! You _____ play with sharp knives!

8. Bats _____ see in order to avoid obstacles. They can navigate in complete darkness.

9. A person _____ get married in order to lead a happy and fulfilling life.

10. We _____ forget that the children of today are the world leaders of tomorrow.

11. We _____ go to the concert if you don't want to, but it might be good.

12. If you encounter a growling dog, you _____ show any signs of fear.

13. Tigers are magnificent animals. We _____ allow them to become extinct.

EXERCISE 12: Use a modal auxiliary with each verb in parentheses. More than one auxiliary may be possible. Use the one that seems most appropriate to you.

1. It looks like rain. We (*shut*) _____ the windows.

2. Ann, (*hand, you*) _____ me that dish? Thanks.

3. I returned a book to the library yesterday. It was two weeks overdue, so I (*pay*) _____ a fine of $1.40. I (*return*) _____ the book when it was due.

4. Spring break starts on the thirteenth. We (*go, not*) _____ to classes again until the twenty-second.

5. (*Make, I*) _____ an appointment to see Dean Witherspoon?

6. Neither of us knows the way to their house. We (*take*) _____ a map with us or we'll probably get lost.

7. The baby is only a year old, but she (*say, already*) _____ a few words.

8. You (*tell, not*) _____ Jack about the party. It's a surprise birthday party for him.

9. Excuse me. I didn't understand. (*Repeat, you*) _____ what you said?

10. In the United States, elementary education is compulsory. All children (*attend*) _____ six years of elementary school.

11. When I was younger, I (*run*) _____ ten miles without stopping. But now I (*run, not*) _____ more than a mile or two.

12. There was a long line in front of the theater. We (*wait*) _____ almost an hour before we (*get*) _____ in.

EXERCISE 13: Same as the preceding exercise.

1. Don is putting on a little weight around his middle. He (*get*) _____ more exercise.

2. I'm sleepy. I (*keep, not*) _____ my eyes open. I (*go*) _____ to bed before I fall asleep right here.

3. In my country, a girl and boy (*go, not*) _____ out on a date unless they are accompanied by a chaperone.

4. Jimmy was serious when he said he wanted to be a cowboy when he grew up. We (*laugh, not*) _____ at him. We hurt his feelings.

5. (*Cash, you*) _____ this check for me?

6. This is none of his business. He (*stick, not*) _____ his nose into other people's business.

7. My wife and ten children are coming to join me here. They (*live, not*) _____

   _____ in my dormitory room. I (*find*) _____ an apartment.

8. A: (*Speak, I*) _____ to Peggy?

   B: She (*come, not*) _____ to the phone right now.

   (*Take, I*) _____ message?

9. A: Where are you going?

   B: I (*go*) _____ to the library. I have to do some research for my term paper.

10. A: How are you planning to get to the airport?

    B: By taxi.

    A: You (*take*) _____ a limousine instead. It's cheaper than a taxi. You (*get*) _____ a limo in front of the dormitory. It picks up passengers there on a regular schedule.

11. A: Why didn't you come to the party last night?

    B: I (*study*) _____ .

    A: You (*come*) _____ . We had a good time.

12. A: Should I go to the University of Iowa or Iowa State University?

    B: Think it over for a few days. You (*make, not*) _____ up your mind right now. There's no hurry.

EXERCISE 14—WRITTEN: Choose one of the following.

1. Jim Hansen, a twenty-one-year-old student from the United States, is going to your country to study at a university next year. Write him a letter in which you give him advice and information. You are his new pen pal.

2. Your fifteen-year-old cousin is planning to get married soon, within the coming year. Write him/her a letter in which you give sincere and frank advice.

3. A friend of yours is planning to immigrate to the United States. Write a letter in which you give him/her advice and information.

5-11   IMPERATIVE SENTENCES

(a) **Shut** the door. **Shut** the door, **please**. **Please shut** the door.	Imperative sentences are used to tell someone else to do something; they are used to give orders or make requests.

(b) Don't shut the door. **Don't shut** the door, **please.** **Please don't shut** the door. **(c) Be** careful! You'll hurt yourself! **(d) Please be** here on time. **(e) Don't be** late.	The simple form of the verb is used. The understood subject of the sentence is *you:* (*You*) *shut the door.*
	Negative form: ***Don't*** *+ the simple form of a verb.*
	Please is often added to make a polite request instead of giving an order.
	Sometimes ***won't you*** is added as a tag question to make a polite request: *Have a seat, won't you?*

EXERCISE 15: Supply an appropriate verb (affirmative or negative) in the following. Use *please* if appropriate. All of the sentences are imperative.

1. ____Look____ out! A car is coming.

2. __Please wait__ for me. I'll be ready in just a few minutes.

3. __Don't tell__ anyone my secret. Do you promise?

4. _____ me the salt and pepper.

5. _____ up! It's time to get up.

6. _____ that pot! It's hot. You'll burn yourself.

7. _____ busy! We don't have all day.

8. _____ carefully to my directions. I'll say them only once.

9. _____ pages 35 through 70 for tomorrow's class.

10. _____ it easy. There's no need to get angry.

11. _____ the window.

12. _____! I can hear you. You don't have to yell.

13. _____ this soup. It's delicious.

14. _____ me in front of the Chemistry Building at three o'clock.

15. _____! I'm drowning!

16. _____ the light on. It's getting dark in here.

17. _____ a newspaper on your way home.

18. _____ it over for a few days. You don't have to make a decision now.

19. _____ to bring a No. 2 pencil to the test. You will need one.

20. _____ here tomorrow at nine o'clock.

5-12 MAKING SUGGESTIONS: *LET'S, WHY DON'T, SHALL I/WE*

(a) **Let's go** to a movie. (b) **Let's not go** to a movie. **Let's stay** home instead.	***Let's = let us.*** ***Let's*** is followed by the simple form of a verb. Negative form: ***Let's not*** + *the simple form of a verb.* The meaning of ***let's***: I have a suggestion for us.
(c) **Why don't we go** to a movie? (d) **Why don't you come** around seven? (e) **Why don't I give** Mary a call?	In (c): *Let's go to a movie* has the same meaning. In (d): I suggest that you come around seven. In (e): Should I give Mary a call? Do you agree with my suggestion? ***Why don't*** is used primarily in spoken English. It is often used to make a friendly suggestion.
(f) **Shall I open** the window? (g) **Shall we leave** at five? (h) **Let's go, shall we?** (i) **Let's leave now, okay?**	When ***shall*** is used with ***I*** or ***we*** in a question, the speaker is basically making a suggestion and asking another person if he/she agrees with this suggestion. Sometimes ***shall we?*** is used as a tag question after ***let's***. More informally, ***okay*** is used as a tag question, as in (i).

EXERCISE 16: Use *why don't* in the following dialogues to make an appropriate suggestion. Also use *let's* if possible.

1. A: I'm hungry.

   B: Why don't you have an apple? (OR: Let's order some pizza.)

2. A: I'm sleepy.

   B: _____

3. A: What a beautiful day it is!

   B: I agree. _____

4. A: Where should we go over vacation?

   B: _____

5. A: I don't feel good.

   B: _____

6. A: What time should we leave?

   B: _____

7. A: Have you finished your homework?

   B: Yes.

   A: Then _____

   B: Okay.

8. A: I don't like living in the dorm.

   B: Well, if you don't like living there, _____

EXERCISE 17—ORAL (BOOKS CLOSED): Make suggestions by using *why don't you.*

    Example: I'm tired.

    Response: Why don't you take a nap? Why don't you stop working? (etc.)

1. I'm hungry.
2. I don't know what this word means.
3. It's hot in here.
4. It's cold in here.
5. I don't like my job.
6. I'm tired.
7. I don't want to go to the meeting tonight.
8. I don't feel good.
9. I'm broke.
10. I can't read the board if I sit in the back row.

5-13 USING *DO* FOR EMPHASIS

(a) A: Do you speak another language? Do you speak Spanish? B: No, I don't speak Spanish, but **I do speak** French. (b) The teacher thinks I didn't study for the test, but that's not true. **I did study**!	Using *do* as an auxiliary in an affirmative sentence makes the verb stronger. The speaker uses *do* to emphasize what he/she is saying.
(c) You **did tell** me to be here at ten, **didn't you?** (d) Class **does begin** at nine, **doesn't it?**	*Do* for emphasis is also used in a sentence with a tag question when the speaker wants to make sure that he/she has the right information.
(e) We waited for two hours, but he **never did come.** (f) I **never did understand** trigonometry very well, and I still don't.	Emphatic *do* frequently occurs with *never.*

EXERCISE 18:   Complete the following. Use *do* for emphasis. Say *do* loudly and strongly.

1. I don't have a car, but I _____ a motorcycle.

2. A: Do you know Beth Adams?

   B: No, I don't. But I _____ her brother.

3. I don't like biographies, but I _____ novels.

4. No one expects you to be perfect, but we _____ you to do your best always.

5. I don't like coffee, but I _____ .

6. A: Does he have any vices?

   B: Not really. He doesn't smoke. He doesn't drink. He doesn't lie, steal, or

   cheat, but he (*gamble*) _____ once in a while.

7. A: Do you speak Arabic?

   B: No, but I _____ .

8. The teacher thinks I didn't study, but she is wrong. I _____ .

EXERCISE 19—ORAL: Make sentences with tag questions. Use *do* for emphasis.

   Example: You are speaking to your roommate. You want to make sure that he/she locked the door.

   Response: You did lock the door, didn't you?

1. You are speaking to your teacher. You want to make sure that spring vacation starts next Friday.

2. You are speaking to a classmate. You want to make sure that the teacher assigned Chapter Four.

3. You are speaking to your friend. You want to make sure that the movie begins at 7:30.

4. You are speaking to your husband/wife. You want to make sure that he/she turned off the stove.

5. You are speaking to your daughter. You want to make sure that she apologized for hitting her little brother over the head with a toy airplane.

EXERCISE 20—PREPOSITIONS: Supply an appropriate preposition. All of the sentences contain two-word verbs.

1. A: Omar, would you please pass these papers _____ to the rest of the class?

   B: I'd be happy to.

2. A: When are we expected to be at the hotel?

   B: According to our reservation, we are supposed to check _____

     the hotel before 6 P.M. Monday and check _____ before noon Tuesday.

3. A: How do you get _____ with your roommate?

   B: Fine. He's a nice guy.

4. A: Thanks for the ride. I appreciate it.

   B: Where should I drop you _____?

   A: The next corner would be fine.

5. A: I'm going to be out of town for a couple of days. Would you mind looking

     _____ my cat?

   B: Not at all. I'd be happy to. Just tell me what I'm supposed to do.

6. A: I think I'm going to turn _____ now. Good night.

   B: 'Night. See you in the morning. Sleep well.

7. A: Don't you think it's hot in here?

   B: Not especially. If you're hot, why don't you take your sweater _____

     _____?

8. A: How do you spell "occasionally"?

   B: I'm not sure. You'd better look it _____ in your dictionary.

9. A: How much lettuce should we get?

   B: I think we could use two heads. Pick _____ two that feel fresh and firm.

10. A: Why are you sniffling?

   B: I had a cold last week and I can't seem to get _____ it.

6

Modal Auxiliaries - II

6-1 EXPRESSING POSSIBILITY: MAY, MIGHT

(a) A: Why isn't John in class? B: I don't know. **He may be sick.** (b) A: Why isn't John in class? B: I don't know. **He might be sick.**	*May* and *might* express *possibility*. Their meaning is basically the same, though sometimes *might* indicates a little more uncertainty than *may*. (Note: When used to express possibility, *might* is not the past form of *may*.)
(c) A: What are you going to do tonight? B: I haven't made up my mind yet. **I may (might) go** to the library, **I may (might) visit** some friends, or **I may (might)** just **stay** home.	In (a) and (b): The second speaker is saying: "Perhaps, maybe,* possibly John is sick. I am only making a guess. Maybe John is sick, and maybe John is not sick."
	Notice: In (a) and (b), the meaning of *may* and *might* is present. In (c), the meaning is future.†

Maybe (spelled as one word) is an adverb: *Maybe he is sick*. *May be* (spelled as two words) is a verb form: *He may be sick*.

†Sometimes *could* is also used to express possibility in affirmative sentences. Uses of *could* are discussed further in Chapter 14 (Conditional Sentences).

6-2 EXPRESSING PROBABILITY: MUST

(d) A: Why isn't John in class? B: **He must be sick.** Usually he is in class every day, but when I saw him last night, he wasn't feeling good. So my best guess is that he is sick.	*Must* is used to express *probability*.
	In (d): The speaker is basically saying: "Probably John is sick. I have evidence to make me believe that John is sick. That is my logical conclusion, but I do not know for certain."

(e) I see a man with a white cane walking down the street. **He must be blind.**	In (e): The speaker is making a logical inference. He/she does not know for certain that the man is blind.

EXERCISE 1—ORAL (BOOKS CLOSED): Respond by using "I don't know" + *may* or *might*.

> *Example:* What are you going to do tonight?
> *Response:* I don't know. I may (might) watch TV for a while.

1. What are you going to do tonight? (*I don't know. I . . .*)
2. What are you going to do this weekend?
3. You are going out for dinner tonight. Where are you going to go?
4. You are going shopping later today. What are you going to buy?
5. You don't like your job. Are you going to quit?
6. You have decided that you would like to have a pet. What kind of pet are you going to get?
7. Where are you going to go to school next year?
8. (. . .) isn't in class today. Where is he/she?
9. Your English teacher has assigned a research paper. What subject are you going to write on?
10. You and your fiancé/fiancée haven't told me when you are going to get married. What is the date for your wedding?

EXERCISE 2—ORAL (BOOKS CLOSED): From the given information, make your "best guess" by using *must*.

> *Example:* Alice always gets the best grades in the class. Why?
> *Response:* She must study hard./She must be intelligent.

1. (. . .) is yawning. Why?
2. (. . .) is sneezing and coughing. Why?
3. (. . .) is wearing a wedding ring. Why?
4. (. . .) is shivering and has goose bumps. Why?
5. (. . .)'s stomach is growling. Why?
6. (. . .) is scratching his arm. Why?
7. (. . .) is going to get married in five minutes. His/her hands are shaking. Why?
8. (. . .) has already had one glass of water, but now he/she wants another. Why?
9. (. . .) is smiling. Why?
10. (. . .) is crying. Why?
11. You just picked up a telephone receiver, but there is no dial tone. Why?

165

12. There is a restaurant in town which is always packed (full). Why?

13. I am in my car. I am trying to start it, but the engine won't turn over. I left my lights on all day. What's wrong?

14. Every night there is a long line of people waiting to get into (a particular movie). I wonder why.

15. Don't look at your watch. What time is it?

16. One of your teachers wears an orange shirt every day. Do you think he likes the color orange?

All of the following sentences are about my friend John. Use **must not** in your response.

17. John has flunked every test so far this semester. (Do you think he studies?) (*No, he must not . . .*)

18. I am calling John. The phone is ringing, but there is no answer. (Do you think he is at home?)

19. We are at the dinner table. John isn't eating his food. (Do you think he is hungry?)

20. John usually goes to bed at eleven, but right now it's past midnight and he is still up. (Do you think he is sleepy?)

21. The teacher is asking John a question, but he isn't responding. (Do you think he knows the answer?)

22. John is very lonely. Why is he lonely? (Does he have any friends?)

EXERCISE 3:   Use *may/might* or *must* in the following.

1. A: You're coughing, sneezing, blowing your nose, and running a fever. You

   (*feel*) _____ terrible.

   B: I do.

2. A: Are you going to the party?

    B: I don't know. I (*go*) _____ . How about you?

    A: Definitely. I'm looking forward to it.

3. A: Do you want to come to the cafeteria with us?

    B: I don't know. I'm not especially hungry. Why don't you go ahead? I (*join*)

    _____ you later, but don't expect me.

4. A: Hello. May I speak to Ron?

    B: I'm sorry. You (*have*) _____ the wrong number.* There's no one here by that name.

    A: Is this 555-8922?

    B: No, it's not. This is 555-9822.

5. A: How long has it been since you last saw your family?

    B: Over a year.

    A: You (*miss*) _____ them very much.

    B: I do.

6. A: Ed just bought his wife a diamond necklace.

    B: He (*be*) _____ rich.

7. A: What are you going to major in when you go to the university?

    B: I haven't decided yet. I (*major*) _____ in business administration, but economics is another possibility.

8. A: Are you sure you're going to drop out of school and get a job?

    B: Pretty sure. Something (*happen*) _____ to make me change my mind, but I doubt it.

9. A: Look at the man standing outside the window on the fifteenth floor of the building. He (*be*) _____ crazy.

    B: You're right. He (*be*) _____ nuts.

10. A: How old is their daughter now?

    B: Hmmm. She (*be*) _____ about ten or eleven.

11. A: I've heard that your daughter recently graduated from law school and that your son has gotten a scholarship to the state university. You (*be*)

    _____ very proud.

    B: We are.

---

*Another common response in this situation is: *I'm sorry. I'm afraid you have the wrong number.*

EXERCISE 5: Use *will*, *should*, or *must* in the following.

*Reminder: **Will** indicates there is no doubt in the speaker's mind about a future event.*

> ***Should** is used to mean that something "will probably be true" in the future.*

> ***Must** is used to mean that something "is probably true" at present.*

1. Look. Jack's car is in front of his house. He (*be*) _____ at home. Let's stop and visit him.

2. A: Hello. May I speak to Jack?

   B: He isn't here right now.

   A: What time do you expect him?

   B: He (*be*) _____ home around nine or so.

3. Here are your tickets, Mr. Anton. Your flight (*depart*) _____ from Gate 15 on the Blue Concourse at 6:27.

4. A: Where can I find the address for the University of Chicago?

   B: I'm not sure, but you (*be*) _____ able to find that information at the library. The library carries catalogues of most of the universities in the United States.

5. A: When's dinner?

   B: We're almost ready to eat. The rice (*be*) _____ done in five minutes.

6. A: Who do you think is going to win the game tomorrow?

   B: Well, our team has better players, so we (*win*) _____ , but you never know. Anything can happen in sports.

7. A: What time are you going to arrive?

   B: I (*be*) _____ there at seven o'clock. I promise!

8. A: What time are you going to arrive?

   B: Well, the trip takes about four hours. I think I'll leave sometime around noon, so I (*get*) _____ there around four.

9. Ed has been acting strangely lately. He (*be*) _____ in love.

10. Hmmm. I wonder what is causing the delay. Ellen's plane (*be*) _____

_____ here an hour ago.

11. I thought I had a dollar in my billfold, but I don't. I (*spend*) _____

_____ it.

12. A: Where's your dictionary?

B: Isn't it on my desk?

A: No.

B: Then it must be in the bookcase. You (*find*) _____
it on the second shelf.

6-5 THE PASSIVE FORM OF MODAL AUXILIARIES*

(1) *The passive form: modal + **be** + **-ed** (past participle)*

(a) The window **can't be opened.**

(b) The window **couldn't be opened.**

(c) **May I be excused** from class?

(d) You **might be interested** in this.

(e) Children **should be taught** to respect their elders.

(f) This book **had better be returned** to the library before Friday.

(g) Meat **must be kept** in a refrigerator or it will spoil.

(h) Your application **ought to be sent** before June 1st.

(i) Mary **has to be told** about our change in plans.

(2) *The past-passive form: modal + **have been** + **-ed** (past participle)*

(j) The application **should have been sent** last week.

(k) This house **must have been built** over 200 years ago.

(l) I don't know why the child started to cry, but she **might have been frightened** by the
dog's barking.

(m) Mary **ought to have been** invited to the party.

*See Chapter 4 for a discussion of the passive form and meaning.

EXERCISE 6: Use the verb in parentheses with an appropriate modal auxiliary.
All of the sentences are passive. In many sentences, more than one modal is possible. Use the modal that sounds best to you.

1. The entire valley (*see*) _____ can be seen _____ from their mountain
home.

2. He is wearing a gold band on his fourth finger. He (*marry*) _____

_____ .

3. According to our teacher, all of our compositions (*write*) _____

_____ in ink.

4. I found this book on my desk when I came to class. It (*leave*) _____

_____ by one of the students in the earlier class.

5. Five of the committee members will be unable to attend the next meeting. In

my opinion, the meeting (*postpone*) _____ .

6. A child (*give, not*) _____ everything he or she wants.

7. Your daughter has a good voice. Her interest in singing (*encourage*) _____

_____ .

8. Try to speak slowly when you give your speech. If you don't, some of your

words (*misunderstand*) _____ .

9. What? You tripped over a chair at the party and dropped your plate of food

into a woman's lap? You (*embarrass*) _____ !

10. She is very lazy. If you want her to do anything, she (*push*) _____

_____ .

11. The hospital in that small town is very old and can no longer serve the needs of

the community. A new hospital (*built*) _____ years ago.

12. Some UFO sightings (*explain, not*) _____
easily. No one is able to explain them easily.

13. Whales (*save*) _____ from extinction.

14. We can't wait any longer! Something (*do*) _____
immediately!

15. In my opinion, she (*elect*) _____
because she is honest, knowledgeable, and competent.

6-6   USING *WOULD**

(1) EXPRESSING PREFERENCE: *WOULD RATHER*	
(a) **I would rather go** to a movie tonight **than study** grammar.	*Would rather* means *prefer*. In (a): Notice that the simple form of a verb follows both *would rather* and *than*.
(b) **I'd rather study** history **than** (*study*) biology.	In (b): If the verb is the same, it does not have to be repeated after *than*. Also notice the contracted form: *I would = I'd*.

(c) A: How much do you weigh? B: **I'd rather not tell** you.	Negative form: *would rather + not*

(d) A: Did you enjoy the movie?
    B: It was okay, but I **would rather have**
        gone to the concert.
	The past form (*would rather have + -ed*)
	is usually pronounced "I'd rather've."

(e) I **would rather be lying** on a beach in
    Florida **than (be) sitting** in class right
    now.
	Progressive form: *would rather be + -ing*

(2) USING *WOULD* TO EXPRESS A REPEATED ACTION IN THE PAST	

(f) When I was a child, my father **would read**
      me a story every night before bed.
  (g) When I was a child, my father **used to**
      read me a story every night before bed.
	Would is also used to express an *action*
	that was repeated regularly in the past.
	When *would* is used to express this
	idea, it has the same meaning as *used to*
	(habitual past).

	(f) and (g) have the same meaning.

(h) I used to live in California.
      I used to be a Boy Scout.
      I used to have a Volkswagen.
	When *used to* expresses a *situation* that
	existed in the past, *would* may not be
	used as an alternative. *Would* is used
	only for regularly repeated *actions* in
	the past.

(3) USING *WOULD* IN A "SOFT" STATEMENT	
(i) I **would like** a cup of coffee. **I'd like** a cup of coffee.	*I want* is strong. *I would like* is "soft" and polite.†
(j) I **would prefer** a cup of tea.	*I prefer* is strong and definite. *I would prefer* is "soft."
(k) I **would suggest** you see a doctor.	*I suggest* is strong. *I would suggest* is "soft."
(l) I **would appreciate** hearing from you soon.	In (1): This sentence occurs frequently in formal letters. It is a polite way of say- ing: "Please write to me soon."
(m) I **would be happy (glad, pleased)** to help you.	In (m): *Would* is frequently used in a response to a polite question.

*See Chapter 14 for the use of *would* in conditional sentences.

†Compare: *I like ice cream.* (*Ice cream is one of my favorite kinds of food.*)
           I'd like some ice cream. (*I want some ice cream.*)

EXERCISE 7—ORAL (BOOKS CLOSED): Answer the questions in complete
sentences.

1. Where are you right now? Where would you rather be?

2. What would you rather do than go to class?

3. (*To the teacher: Ask another question based on the previous student's response: e.g., "I'd rather read a book than go to class." Next question: "What would you rather do than read a book?" etc.*)

4. What did you do last night? What would you rather have done?

5. What are you doing right now? What would you rather be doing?

Begin your answer with: "No, I'd rather . . . ."

6. Do you want to go to the movie tonight? (to a concert?) (to the zoo tomorrow?)

7. Do you want to play tennis this afternoon? (go bowling?) (shoot pool?)

8. Do you want to eat at the cafeteria? (at a Chinese restaurant?)

9. Do you want to study tonight? (watch TV?) (stay home?)

10. Would you like to live in New York City? (Alaska?) (Florida?)

EXERCISE 8:   In order to practice using *would* to express a repeated action in the past, use *would* whenever possible in the following sentences. Otherwise, use *used to.*

1. I (*be*) _____ used to be _____ very shy. Whenever a stranger came to our house, I (*hide*) _____ would hide _____ in a closet.

2. I remember my Aunt Susan very well. Every time she came to our house, she (*give*) _____ me a big kiss and pinch my cheek.

3. Illiteracy is still a problem, but it (*be*) _____ much worse.

4. I (*be*) _____ afraid of flying. My heart (*start*) _____ _____ pounding every time I stepped on a plane.

5. When I was a child, I (*take*) _____ a flashlight to bed with me so that I could read comic books without my parents' knowing about it.

6. Last summer, my sister and I took a camping trip in the Rocky Mountains. It was a wonderful experience. Every morning, we (*wake*) _____ _____ up to the sound of singing birds. During the day, we (*hike*) _____ through woods and along moun-

tain streams. Often we (*see*) _____ a deer. On one occasion we saw a bear and quickly ran in the opposite direction.

7. I can remember Mrs. Sawyer's fifth grade class well. When we arrived each morning, she (*sit*) _____ at her desk. She (*smile, always*) _____ and (*say*) _____ hello to each student as he or she entered. When the bell rang, she (*stand*) _____ up and (*clear*) _____ her throat. That was our signal to be quiet. Class was about to begin.

8. I (*be*) _____ an anthropology major. Once I was a member of an archaeological expedition. Every morning, we (*get*) _____ up before dawn. After breakfast, our entire day (*spend*) _____ in the field. Sometimes one of us (*find*) _____ a particularly interesting item, perhaps an arrowhead or a piece of pottery. When that happened, other members of the group (*gather*) _____ around to see what had been unearthed.

6-7 SUMMARY CHART OF MODAL AUXILIARIES

AUXILIARY	USES	PRESENT/FUTURE	PAST
can	(1) ability	I **can speak** French.	I **could speak** French when I was a child.
	(2) permission	**Can I borrow** your pen? You **can use** my car tomorrow.	
could	(1) past ability	(I can speak French.)	I **could speak** French when I was a child.
	(2) polite question	**Could I borrow** your pen? **Could** you please **take** a message?	
may	(1) permission	**May I borrow** your pen? You **may leave** when you are finished.	
	(2) possibility	A: Where's John? B: He **may be** at the library.	A: Where was John? B: He **may have been** at the library.

AUXILIARY	USES	PRESENT/FUTURE	PAST
might	(1) possibility	A: Where's John? B: He **might be** at the library.	A: Where was John? B: He **might have been** at the library.
	(2) polite question of permission (**rare**)	**Might I borrow** your pen?	
should	(1) advisability	I **should study** tonight	I **should have studied** last night.
	(2) expectation	The bus **should be** here soon.	The bus **should have been** here ten minutes ago.
ought to	(1) advisability	I **ought to study** tonight.	I **ought to have studied** last night.
	(2) expectation	The bus **ought to be** here soon.	The bus **ought to have been** here ten minutes ago.
had better	(1) strong advisability	You **had better be** on time, or we will leave without you.	
must	(1) necessity	I **must go** to class today.	I **had to** go to class yesterday.
	(2) probability	Mary isn't in class today. She **must be** sick.	Mary wasn't in class yesterday. She **must have been** sick.
have to	(1) necessity	I **have to go** to class today.	I **had to** go to class yesterday.
have got to	(1) necessity	I've **got to go** to class today.	
will	(1) simple future tense	I **will be** there tomorrow.	
	(2) polite question	**Will** you please **pass** the butter?	
would	(1) polite question	**Would** you please **pass** the butter? **Would you mind** if I left early? **Would you mind** closing the door?	
	(2) preference	I **would rather go** to the park than stay home.	I **would rather have gone** to the park.
	(3) repeated action in the past		When I was a child, **I would visit** my grandparents every weekend.
	(4) "soft" statement	I **would like** a cup of coffee.	I **would have liked** a cup of coffee.
shall	(1) simple future tense with "I" or "we"	I **shall arrive** at nine.	
	(2) polite question to make a suggestion	**Shall I open** the window?	

Note: Use of modal auxiliaries in conditional sentences is discussed in Chapter 14. Use of modal auxiliaries in reported speech is discussed in Chapter 9.

EXERCISE 9: Discuss the differences in meaning, if any, in the following groups of sentences.

1. (a) May I use your phone?
   (b) Could I use your phone?
   (c) Can I use your phone?
2. (a) You should take an English course.
   (b) You ought to take an English course.
   (c) You must take an English course.
   (d) You have to take an English course.
3. (a) You should see a doctor about that cut on your arm.
   (b) You had better see a doctor about that cut on your arm.
4. (a) You must not use that door.
   (b) You don't have to use that door.
5. (a) I will be at your house by six o'clock.
   (b) I should be at your house by six o'clock.
6. *There is a knock at the door. Who do you suppose it is?*
   (a) It might be Sally.
   (b) It may be Sally.
   (c) It must be Sally.
7. (a) Jack might have gone home.
   (b) Jack must have gone home.
   (c) Jack had to go home.
   (d) Jack should have gone home.
8. (a) When I was living at home, I would go to the beach every weekend with my friends.
   (b) When I was living at home, I used to go to the beach every weekend with my friends.

EXERCISE 10: Complete the following dialogues.

1. A: _____
   B: No, he had to go home.
   A: Why?

   B: _____

2. A: Did you hear the news? We don't have to _____
   B: Why not?

   A: _____

3. A: _____

   B: You shouldn't have done that!

   A: I know, but _____

4. A: Whose _____

   B: I don't know. It _____, or it _____

      _____

5. A: _____

   B: Not at all. I'd be happy to.

6. A: _____

   B: That must have been fun!

   A: It was. You should have _____

   B: I would have liked to, but I _____

7. A: You must not _____

   B: Why not?

   A: _____

8. A: _____

   _____

   B: Really? _____ must have ESP! (*ESP* = *extrasensory
      perception*)

9. A: _____

   B: Well, you'd better _____, or_____

      _____

   A: I know, but _____

10. A: _____

    B: _____, but I'd rather not have gone. I'd rather

       _____

EXERCISE 11—ORAL: Work in pairs. Using the given situations, create dialogues
of 10 to 20 sentences or more. Then present your dialogues to the rest of the class.
For each situation, the beginning of the dialogue is given. Try to include appropriate modals in your conversation.

1. **Situation:**   *The two of you are roommates or a married couple. It is late at
   night. All of the lights are turned off. You hear a strange noise.*

You try to figure out what it might or must be, what you should or should not do, etc.

Dialogue: A: Psst. Are you awake?

B: Yes. What's the matter?

A: Do you hear that noise?

B: Yes. What do you suppose it is?

A: I don't know. It . . . .

B: . . .

2. *Situation:* *Your teacher is always on time, but today it is fifteen minutes past the time class begins and he/she still isn't here. You try to figure out why he/she isn't here yet and what you should do.*

Dialogue: A: Mr./Ms./Miss/Mrs./Dr./Professor _____ should have been here fifteen minutes ago. I wonder where he/she is. Why do you suppose he/she hasn't arrived yet?

B: Well, ...

3. *Situation:* *The two of you are planning to go on a picnic. You are almost ready to leave when you hear a loud noise. It sounds like thunder. You are supposed to meet John and Mary at the park for your picnic.*

Dialogue: A: Is the picnic basket all packed?

B: Yes. Everything is ready to go.

A: Good. Let's get going.

B: Wait. Did you hear that?

A: . . . .

4. *Situation:* *It is late at night. The weather is very bad. Your eighteen-year-old son, who had gone to a party with some of his friends, was supposed to be home an hour ago. (The two of you are either a married couple or a parent and his/her friend.) You are getting worried. You are trying to figure out where he might be, what might or must have happened, and what you should do, if anything.*

Dialogue: A: It's already _____ o'clock and _____ isn't home yet. I'm getting worried.

B: So am I. Where do you suppose he is?

A: . . . . .

EXERCISE 12–ORAL: In small discussion groups, debate the following statements. At the end of the discussion time, choose one member of your group to summarize for the rest of the class the principal ideas expressed during the discussion.

Do you agree with the following statements? Why or why not?

1. People of different religions should not marry.
2. No family should have more than two children.
3. Books, films, and news should be censored by government agencies.

EXERCISE 13–WRITTEN: Go to a public place, a place where there are people whom you do not know (a cafeteria, store, street corner, park, zoo, lobby, etc.). Choose three of these people to write a composition about. Using a paragraph for each person, describe his/her appearance briefly and then make "guesses" about this person: age, occupation, personality, activities, etc.

Begin your composition: *I am in/on/at . . . , looking at a man/woman/child.*

EXERCISE 14–WRITTEN: Write a short paragraph on each of the following.

1. Write about when, where, and why you should (or should not) have done something in your life.
2. Write about a time in your life when you did something you did not want to do. Why did you do it? What should you have done? What would you rather have done?
3. Look at tomorrow. Write about what you should, must, might, had better, may, ought to, have to do.
4. Look at your future. What will, might, should it be like? Write about what you should, must, can do now in order to make your life what you want it to be.

EXERCISE 15–PREPOSITIONS: Supply an appropriate preposition. All of the sentences contain two-word verbs.

1. A: Are you ready to leave?

   B: Almost. I'll be ready to go just as soon as I get _____ putting the clean dishes away.

2. A: I'm going crazy! I've been trying to solve this math problem for the last hour and I still can't get it.

   B: Why don't you give _____ for a while? Take a break and then go back to it.

3. A: I hear you had a frightening experience yesterday. What happened?

   B: My roommate suddenly got dizzy and then passed _____.
   I tried to revive him, but he was out cold. Luckily there was a doctor in the building.

4. A: What happened when the pilot of the plane passed out during the flight?

   B: The co-pilot took _____.

5. A: Cindy is only three. She likes to play with the older kids, but when they're

      running and playing, she can't keep _____ with them.

   B: Does she mind?

   A: She doesn't seem to.

6. A: I made a mistake in my composition. What should I do?

   B: Since it's an in-class composition, just cross it _____.

7. A: I need my dictionary, but I lent it to Jose.

   B: Why don't you get it _____ from him?

8. A: I wish the teacher wouldn't call _____ me in class.

   B: Why not?

   A: I get nervous.

   B: Why?

   A: I don't know.

9. I took a plane from Atlanta to Miami. I got _____ the plane in

   Atlanta. I got _____ the plane in Miami.

10. It was a snowy winter day, but I still had to drive to work. First I got _____

    _____ the car to start the engine. Then I got _____

    of the car to scrape the snow and ice from the windows.

11. Last year I took a train trip. I got _____ the train in Chicago. I

    got _____ the train in Des Moines.

12. Phyllis takes the bus to work. She gets _____ the bus at Lind-

    bergh Boulevard and gets _____ the bus about two blocks from

    her office on Tower Street.

7

Gerunds
and Infinitives-I

PART I Using Gerunds and Infinitives

7-1   INTRODUCTION

> **A gerund** is the *-ing* form of a verb used as a noun. Examples: *talking, playing, swimming.* A gerund is used in the same ways as a noun, i.e., as a subject or an object.*
>
> **An infinitive** consists of *to + the simple form of a verb.* Examples: *to talk, to play, to swim.*

*The *-ing* form of a verb is also used as a present participle. Compare the following:

(1) *Playing tennis is fun.* (*playing* = a gerund, used as the subject of the sentence)

(2) *Bob and Ann are playing tennis.* (*playing* = a present participle, used in the present progressive tense)

7-2   USING GERUNDS AS THE OBJECTS OF PREPOSITIONS

(a) We talked **about going** to Canada for our vacation. (b) Sue is in charge **of organizing** the meeting. (c) I am interested **in learning** more about your work.	A gerund is frequently used as the object of a preposition.

(d) I am accustomed **to sleeping** with the window open.	In (d) through (g): *to* is a preposition,
(e) I am used **to sleeping** with the window open.	not part of an infinitive form, so a
(f) I look forward **to going** home next month.	gerund follows.
(g) They object **to changing** their plans at this late date.	

EXERCISE 1: Supply an appropriate preposition and verb form.

1. Allison is not interested _____ in _____ (*look*) _____ looking _____ for a new job.

2. Henry is excited _____ (*leave*) _____ for India.

3. You are capable _____ (*do*) _____ better work.

4. I have no excuse _____ (*be*) _____ late.

5. I am accustomed _____ (*have*) _____ a big breakfast every morning.

6. The rain prevented us _____ (*complete*) _____ the work.

7. Fred is always complaining _____ (*have*) _____ a headache.

8. Instead _____ (*study*) _____, Margaret went to a ball game with some friends.

9. Thank you _____ (*help*) _____ me carry the packages to the post office.

10. I'm looking forward _____ (*see*) _____ my family again.

11. He showed us how to get to his house _____ (*draw*) _____ _____ a map.

12. You should take advantage _____ (*live*) _____ here.

13. Everyone in the neighborhood participated _____ (*search*) _____ for the lost child.

14. I apologized to Diane _____ (*make*) _____ her wait for me.

15. The weather is terrible tonight. I don't blame you _____ (*prefer*) _____ to stay home.

16. The weather is terrible tonight. I don't blame you _____ (*want,*
    not) _____ to go to the meeting.

17. She insisted _____ (*know*) _____ the whole
    truth.

18. Who is responsible _____ (*wash*) _____ the dishes
    after dinner?

19. In addition _____ (*go*) _____ to school full time,
    he has a part-time job.

20. The angry look on his face stopped me _____ (*speak*) _____
    _____ my mind.

21. Where should we go for dinner tonight? Would you object _____
    (*go*) _____ to an Italian restaurant?

22. The mayor made another public statement for the purpose _____
    (*clarify*) _____ the new tax proposal.

23. The thief was accused _____ (*steal*) _____ a
    woman's purse.

24. The jury found her guilty _____ (*murder*) _____
    her rich husband.

EXERCISE 2—ORAL (BOOKS CLOSED): Answer the questions in complete
sentences.

> *Example:* Your friend was late. Did she apologize?
> *Response:* Yes, she apologized (OR: No, she didn't apologize) *for being* late.

1. You were late for class yesterday. Did you have a good excuse?
2. You are going to (Baltimore) to visit your friends this weekend. Are you looking forward to that?
3. (. . .) picked up your pen when you dropped it. Did you thank him/her?
4. You are living in a cold/warm climate. Are you accustomed to that?
5. You are going to Hawaii on vacation. Are you excited?
6. You interrupted (. . .) while he/she was speaking. Did you apologize?
7. The students in the class did pantomimes. Did all of them participate?
8. Someone broke the window. Do you know who is responsible?

9. Americans usually have their biggest meal in the evening. Are you used to doing that?

10. The weather is hot/cold. What does that prevent you from doing?

11. (. . .) doesn't like to do homework. Does he/she complain?

12. (. . .) was sick last week, so he/she stayed home in bed. Do you blame him/her?

EXERCISE 3: Using the verb or expression in parentheses, complete the sentence.

1. (*finish*) Ken went to bed instead _of finishing his work._____

2. (*lend*) I thanked her _____

3. (*go*) I'm excited _____

4. (*live*) I'm not accustomed _____

5. (*have*) He didn't feel good. He complained _____

_____

6. (*want, not*) I don't blame you _____

7. (*be*) I have a good reason _____

8. (*miss*) It's getting late. I'm worried _____

9. (*find out about*) I'm interested _____

10. (*go*) I'm thinking _____

11. (*be*) I apologized _____

12. (*drive*) I am/am not used _____

13. (*take care of*) In that office, who is responsible _____

_____

14. (*go*) Nothing can stop me _____

7-3 USING *BY* AND *WITH* TO EXPRESS HOW SOMETHING IS DONE

(a) Pat turned off the tape recorder **by pushing** the stop button.	*By* + *a gerund* is used to express how something is done.
(b) Mary goes to work **by bus.** (c) Andrea stirred her coffee **with a spoon.**	*By* or *with* followed by a noun is also used to express how something is done.

BY IS USED FOR MEANS OF TRANSPORTATION AND COMMUNICATION:

by (air)plane   *by mail*   *by air*

by boat   *by (tele)phone*   *by land*

by bus   *by special delivery* *by sea*

by car

by subway

by taxi

by train

by foot (or *on foot*)

OTHERS:

by chance

by choice

by mistake

by check (but *in cash*)

*by hand**

WITH IS USED FOR INSTRUMENTS OR PARTS OF THE BODY:

I cut down the tree *with an axe* (by using an axe).

I swept the floor *with a broom*.

She pointed to a spot on the map *with her finger*.

*The expression **by hand** is usually used to mean that something was made by a person, not by a machine: *This rug was made by hand*. (A person, not a machine, made this rug.)

EXERCISE 4: Complete the following by using **by** + *a gerund or gerund phrase.*

1. We show other people that we are happy   by smiling.

2. Both of us wanted the last piece of candy. We decided who would get it _____   by flipping a coin.

3. We satisfy our hunger _____

4. We quench our thirst _____

5. I found out what *quench* means _____

6. Tony improved his listening comprehension _____

7. Alex caught my attention _____

8. Grandma amused the children _____

9. They got rid of the rats in the building _____

10. Sometimes teenagers get into trouble with their parents _____

11. My dog shows me she is happy _____

12. He accidentally electrocuted himself _____

EXERCISE 5: In the following, complete the sentences by using *by* or *with* and an appropriate noun from the given list. Also supply *a/an* or a possessive pronoun where needed. (Note: Possessive pronouns, not articles, are usually used with parts of the body.)

calculator	fist	mistake
car	hand	phone
check	√ heels	screwdriver
choice	hoe	subway
fingers	√ knife	√ train
fire extinguisher		

1. I cut the meat _____ with a/my knife. _____

2. He went to California _____ by train. _____

3. She kicked the horse _____ with her heels. _____

4. I solved the math problem _____

5. At the beach I wrote some words in the sand _____

6. I got in touch with Bill _____

7. He pried open the lid of the paint can _____

8. She weeded the garden _____

9. We traveled to Boston _____

10. Janice put out the fire in the wastebasket _____

11. Jim was extremely angry. He hit the wall _____

12. The package wasn't addressed to me. I opened it _____

13. Mrs. Williams goes to work every day _____

14. He protected his eyes from the sun _____

15. I prefer to pay my bills _____

16. I wasn't forced to attend the meeting. I went there _____

EXERCISE 6–ORAL: Answer the questions.

1. How do you open a locked door? (*with a key*)

    . . . dry dishes?

    . . . stir your coffee?

    . . . open a letter (neatly)?

    . . . dig a hole in the ground?

. . . sew?

. . . sharpen a pencil?

. . . hold a pot if it is hot?

. . . cut a piece of wood?

. . . nail two pieces of wood together?

. . . clean a floor?

. . . take your temperature?

2. How many different ways can you get from London to Paris?

. . . from the suburbs to downtown?

. . . from where you live to school?

7-4 COMMON VERBS FOLLOWED BY GERUNDS

(a) *finish*	We **finished eating** at 6:30.	Gerunds are used as the objects of certain verbs.
(b) *stop**	The baby **stopped crying.**	
(c) *quit (give up)*	Joe **quit (gave up) smoking.**	In (c): *give up* has the same meaning as *quit. Give up* is also followed by a gerund. Other two-word verbs followed by gerunds are given in parentheses.
(d) *avoid*	He **avoided answering** my question.	
(e) *postpone (put off)*	I **postponed (put off) doing** my work.	
(f) *delay*	She **delayed leaving** on vacation.	
(g) *keep (keep on)*	We'd better **keep (keep on) working.**	
(h) *enjoy*	I **enjoy listening** to music.	
(i) *appreciate*	I would **appreciate hearing** from you.	
(j) *mind*	Would you **mind opening** the window?	
(k) *consider (think about)*	She is **considering (thinking about) changing** her major.	
(l) *discuss (talk about)*	We **discussed (talked about) building** a new house.	
(m) *go*	Did you **go shopping?** Did you **go swimming?** Did you **go fishing?** Did you **go hunting?** Did you **go bowling?** Did you **go skiing?** Did you **go hiking?** Did you **go dancing?** Did you **go jogging?** Did you **go mountain climbing?**	*Go* is followed by a gerund in certain idiomatic expressions. Some of the most common expressions are given in the examples. Others are: *boating, camping, canoeing, running, sailing, skating, sledding, skinny dipping, tobogganing, water skiing, window shopping.*

*Compare: (1) *When the professor entered the room, the students **stopped talking.** The room became quiet.*

(2) *While I was walking down the street. I ran into an old friend. I **stopped to talk** to him.* (I stopped walking in order to talk to him.)

EXERCISE 7—ORAL (BOOKS CLOSED):

1. What do you enjoy doing in your free time in the evening?

2. Who has gone shopping lately? When did you go? (Do you enjoy going shopping or avoid going shopping?)

3. Who studied last night? What time did you finish?

4. What do you put off doing? (Do you always answer a letter immediately after you have received one? Do you always wash the dishes immediately after dinner?)

5. What are you thinking about doing this weekend?

6. Who is thinking about going somewhere over the next vacation? Where are you considering going?

7. Who smokes? Would you like to quit?

8. Who likes to bowl? When was the last time you went?

9. If someone wants to lose weight, what should he or she give up eating and drinking?

10. Who likes to fish? Swim? Ski? When was the last time you went?

11. What was (. . .) just talking about?

12. When you are tired, do you keep working or stop?

13. Does anyone like to go window shopping?

14. Is/was it raining/snowing? Has it stopped?/When did it stop?

15. When I enter the room at the beginning of class, do you and your classmates keep talking or stop talking?

16. What do you enjoy doing on weekends?

17. Where are you considering going to school next term?

18. Do you appreciate getting letters from home?

19. Who doesn't like cold weather? Do you avoid going outside when it's cold?

20. Who takes the bus to school? You don't mind taking the bus, do you?

EXERCISE 8: By using a gerund, supply any appropriate completion for each of the following.

1. When Beth got tired, she stopped _____ working/studying. _____

2. When we were at the beach, we went _____

3. We can leave just as soon as it quits _____

4. The policeman told him to stop, but the thief kept _____

5. I enjoy _____ a long walk every morning.

6. Would you mind _____ the door?

7. I would like to have some friends over. I'm thinking about _____ a party.

8. I appreciate _____ able to study in peace and quiet.

9. Jack almost had an automobile accident. He barely avoided _____ another car at the intersection of Fourth and Elm.

10. Where are you considering _____ for vacation?

11. You have to decide where you want to go to school next year. You can't post-pone _____ that decision much longer.

12. Sometimes I put off _____ my homework.

7-5   COMMON VERBS FOLLOWED BY INFINITIVES

(a) I **hope to see** you again soon.
(b) He **promised to be** here by ten.
	VERBS WHICH ARE FOLLOWED IMMEDI-ATELY BY AN INFINITIVE:
	
	hope agree remember ask
	promise offer forget expect
	decide refuse
	
	  seem want
	  appear need

(c) He **promised not to be** late.	Negative form: *not* precedes the infinitive.
(d) Mr. Lee **told us to wait** for him. (e) Mrs. Jackson **warned her son not to touch** the electric wire. (f) The policeman **ordered me to stop.**	VERBS WHICH ARE FOLLOWED BY A (PRO)NOUN AND THEN AN INFINITIVE: *tell permit ask* *remind allow expect* *advise require* *encourage force want* *warn order need*
(g) I **was told to be** here at ten o'clock. (h) We **are not allowed to have** pets in the dormitory.	The verbs above are followed immediately by an infinitive when they are used in the passive, as in (g) and (h).
(i) I **expect to pass** the test. (j) I **expect Mary to pass** the test.	*Ask, expect, want,* and *need* may or may not be followed by a (pro)noun object. Compare: In (i): I think I will pass the test. In (j): I think Mary will pass the test.

EXERCISE 9–ORAL (BOOKS CLOSED): Answer in complete sentences.

Imagine that yesterday you had a long talk with your friend John. Tell us about some of the things he said.

1. What did he want to do?
2. What did he promise to do?
3. What did he decide to do?
4. What did he refuse to do?
5. What did he agree to do?
6. What did he offer to do?
7. What did he forget to do?
8. What did he tell you to do?   (What were you told to do?)
9. What did he remind you to do?   (What were you reminded to do?)
10. What did he advise you to do?   (What were you advised to do?)
11. What did he encourage you to do?   (What were you encouraged to do?)
12. What did he warn you not to do?   (What were you warned not to do?)
13. What did he ask you to do?   (What were you asked to do?)
14. What did he ask you not to do?   (What were you asked not to do?)

EXERCISE 10: Supply any appropriate completion for each sentence. Use *either a gerund or an infinitive,* as appropriate. You may use the verbs suggested in the following list or supply your own.

be	*lend*	*snow*
buy ·	*look for*	*take*
cash	*pick up*	*talk*
drive	*play*	*use*
find	*quit*	*wait*
get	*rain*	*watch*
give	*refer to*	

1. Did you remember _____to cash_____ a check before the bank closed?

2. We can't leave until it stops __raining/snowing.__

3. Jack offered _____ his friend (to, at) the airport.

4. Do you enjoy _____ baseball?

5. Fred didn't have any money, so he decided _____ a job.

6. Joan and David were considering _____ married in June, but they finally decided _____ until August.

7. The teacher seems _____ in a good mood today.

8. I was broke, so Jenny offered _____ me five dollars.

9. Mrs. Allen promised _____ the children (to, at) the zoo.

10. Jane had to go out again because she had forgotten _____ some milk at the grocery store.

11. Even though I asked the people in front of me at the movie _____ quiet, they kept _____ .

12. The teacher encourages us _____ a dictionary whenever we are uncertain of the spelling of a word.

13. The doctor advised me _____ smoking.

14. Jim is a very forgetful person. His wife always has to remind him _____ _____ his briefcase with him to the office.

EXERCISE 11: Using the given ideas and the verb in parentheses, make sentences, both active and passive, by using an infinitive phrase. (Omit the "*by* phrase" in the passive sentences.)

1. The teacher said to me, "You may leave early."

   (*permit*)   ___The teacher permitted me to leave early.___   (active)

   ___I was permitted to leave early.___   (passive)

2. The secretary said to me, "Please give this note to Sue."

   (*ask*)   _____   (active)

   _____   (passive)

3. My advisor said to me, "You should take Biology 109."

   (*advise*)   _____

   _____

4. When I went to traffic court, the judge said to me, "You must pay a thirty-dollar fine."

   (*order*)   _____

   _____

5. During the test, the teacher said to Greg, "Keep your eyes on your own paper."

   (*warn*)   _____

   _____

6. During the test, the teacher said to Greg, "Don't look at your neighbor's paper."

   (*warn*) _____

   _____

7. At the meeting, the head of the department said to the faculty, "Don't forget to turn in your grade reports by the 15th."

   (*remind*) _____

   _____

8. Mr. Lee said to the children, "Be quiet."

   (*tell*) _____

   _____

9. Abe said to me, "You must tell me the truth."

   (*force*) _____

   _____

10. When I was growing up, my parents said to me, "You may stay up late on Saturday night."

    (*allow*) _____

    _____

11. The teacher said to the students, "Speak slowly and clearly."

    (*encourage*) _____

    _____

12. The teacher always says to the students, "You should come to class on time."

    (*expect*) _____

    _____

EXERCISE 12—ORAL: In each of the following, report what someone said by using one of the verbs in the given list to introduce an infinitive phrase.

advise	*expect*	*remind*
allow	*force*	*require*
ask	*order*	*tell*
encourage	*permit*	*warn*

1. The professor said to Alan, "You may leave early."

   Possible response: The professor allowed Alan to leave early.

2. The general said to the soldiers, "Surround the enemy!"

3. Nancy said to me, "Would you please open the window?"

4. Bob said to me, "Don't forget to take your book back to the library."

5. Paul thinks I have a good voice, so he said to me, "You should take singing lessons."

6. Mrs. Anderson was very stern and a little angry. She shook her finger at the children and said to them, "Don't play with matches!"

7. I am very relieved because the Dean of Admissions said to me, "You may register for school late."

8. The law says, "Every driver must have a valid driver's license."

9. My friend said to me, "You should get some automobile insurance."

10. The robber had a gun. He said to me, "Give me all of your money."

11. Before the examination began, the teacher said to the students, "Work quickly."

12. The department chairman said to me, "Come to the meeting ten minutes early."

7-6 COMMON VERBS FOLLOWED BY EITHER GERUNDS OR INFINITIVES

(a) It **began to rain.** (b) It **began raining.**	Certain verbs may be followed by either a gerund or an infinitive, as in (a) and (b). These verbs are: *begin* *like* *intend* *start* *prefer** *try* *continue* *hate* *can't stand*

*Notice the patterns with ***prefer:***

(1) *I would **prefer staying** home **to going** to the concert.*

(2) *I would **prefer to stay** home rather **than to go** to the concert.*

EXERCISE 13—ORAL (BOOKS CLOSED): Make sentences from the following verb combinations. Use "I" or the name of another person in the room. Use any appropriate tense.

Examples: like and *go*   *Response:* I like to go (OR: like going) to the park.

         ask and *open*   *Response:* (. . .) asked me to open the window.

1. *enjoy* and *listen*

2. *offer* and *lend*

3. *start* and *laugh*

4. *remind* and *take*

5. *postpone* and *go*

6. *look forward to* and *see*

7. *forget* and *bring*

8. *seem* and *be*

9. *prefer* and *live*

10. *finish* and *do*

11. *hate* and *wait*

12. *can't stand* and *have to wait*

13. *encourage* and *go*

14. *promise* and *come*

15. *be interested in* and *learn*

16. *be used to* and *speak*

17. *consider* and *go*

18. *like* and *go*

19. *like* and *go* and *swim*

20. *continue* and *walk*

21. *be accustomed to* and *eat*

22. *order* and *stay*

23. *want* and *go*

24. *want* and *go* and *shop*

25. *keep* and *put off* and *do*

EXERCISE 14: Supply an appropriate form, gerund or infinitive, of the verb in parentheses.

1. I decided (*stay*) ＿＿＿＿＿＿＿＿ here over vacation.

2. We went for a walk after we finished (*clean*) ＿＿＿＿＿＿＿＿ up the kitchen.

3. The baby started (*talk*) ＿＿＿＿＿＿＿＿ when she was about a year and a half old.

4. I forgot (*take*) ＿＿＿＿＿＿＿＿ a book back to the library, so I had to pay a fine.

5. Sue asked (*use*) ＿＿＿＿＿＿＿＿ my pen.

6. I asked Sue (*give*) ＿＿＿＿＿＿＿＿ my pen back to me.

7. I'm getting tired. I need (*take*) ＿＿＿＿＿＿＿＿ a break.

8. I don't mind (*wait*) ＿＿＿＿＿＿＿＿ for you. Go ahead and finish (*do*) ＿＿＿＿＿＿＿＿ your work.

9. When do you expect (*leave*) ＿＿＿＿＿＿＿＿ on your trip?

10. Students sometimes avoid (*look*) ＿＿＿＿＿＿＿＿ at the teacher if they don't want (*answer*) ＿＿＿＿＿＿＿＿ a question.

11. The club members discussed (*postpone*) ＿＿＿＿＿＿＿＿ the next meeting until March.

12. He prefers (*watch*) ＿＿＿＿＿＿＿＿ television to (*listen*) ＿＿＿＿＿＿＿＿ to the radio.

13. He prefers (*watch*) ＿＿＿＿＿＿＿＿ television rather than (*listen*) ＿＿＿＿＿ ＿＿＿＿＿＿＿＿ to the radio.

14. I would appreciate (*hear*) _____ from you soon.

15. Did Carol agree (*go*) _____ (*shop*) _____ with you?

16. As the storm approached, the birds quit (*sing*) _____ .

17. The taxi driver refused (*take*) _____ a check. He wanted the rider (*pay*) _____ in cash.

18. The soldiers were ordered (*stand*) _____ at attention.

EXERCISE 15: Same as the preceding exercise.

1. Keep (*talk*) _____ . I'm listening to you.

2. The children promised (*play*) _____ more quietly.

3. Linda offered (*look after*) _____ my cat while I was out of town.

4. You shouldn't put off (*pay*) _____ your bills.

5. Alex promised (*be, not*) _____ late.

6. I appreciated (*have*) _____ the opportunity to meet the president of the university.

7. I'm considering (*go, not*) _____ to class tomorrow.

8. The doctor ordered him (*smoke, not*) _____ .

9. Don't tell me his secret. I prefer (*know, not*) _____ .

10. Could you please stop (*whistle*) _____ ? I'm trying to concentrate.

11. She finally decided (*quit*) _____ her present job and (*look for*) _____ another one.

12. Did you remember (*turn off*) _____ the stove?

13. Jack was allowed (*renew*) _____ his student visa.

14. Pat told us (*wait, not*) _____ for her.

15. Mr. Buck warned his daughter (*touch, not*) _____ the hot stove.

16. Would you please remind me (*call*) _____ Alice tomorrow?

17. Liz encouraged me (*throw away*) _____ my old tennis shoes and (*buy*) _____ a new pair without holes in the toes.

18. I'm considering (*drop out of*) _____ school, (*hitchhike*) _____

_____ to New York, and (*try*) _____ to find a

job.

7-7 USING *ADVISE* AND *REMEMBER/FORGET*

(a) He **advised me to buy** a Fiat. (b) He **advised buying** a Fiat.	If there is no (pro)noun object after *advise*, a gerund is used, as in (b).
(c) Judy always **remembers to feed** the cat. (d) I **remember seeing** the Alps for the first time. The sight was impressive. (e) Judy never **forgets to feed** the cat. (f) I'll never **forget seeing** the Alps for the first time. The sight was impressive.	In (d): A gerund is used after *remember* when the speaker recalls something that happened in the past. In (f): A gerund is used after *forget* when the speaker is referring to a past action.

EXERCISE 16: Use a gerund or infinitive for the words in parentheses.

1. Jack advised me (*find*) _____ a new apartment.

2. Jack advised (*find*) _____ a new apartment.

3. Ann advised her sister (*take*) _____ the plane instead of driving to Oregon.

4. Ann advised (*take*) _____ the plane instead of driving to Oregon.

5. She advised us (*wait, not*) _____ until August.

6. She advised (*wait, not*) _____ until August.

7. I can remember (*be*) _____ very proud and happy when I graduated.

8. A: Did you remember (*give*) _____ Jake my message?
 B: Yes. I gave him your message when I saw him yesterday.

9. I remember (*play*) _____ with dolls when I was a child.

10. What do you remember (*do*) _____ when you were a child?

11. What do you remember (*do*) _____ before you leave for class every day?

12. What did you forget (*do*) _____ before you left for class this morning?

13. I'll never forget (*carry*) _____ my wife over the threshold when we moved into our first home.

14. I can't ever forget (*watch*) _____ our team score the winning goal in the last seconds of the game to capture the national championship.

7-8 USING GERUNDS AND INFINITIVES AS SUBJECTS

(a) **Riding** with a drunk driver **is** dangerous.	A gerund is frequently used as the subject of a sentence, as in (a).
(b) **To ride** with a drunk driver **is** dangerous. (c) **It is** dangerous **to ride** with a drunk driver.	Sometimes an infinitive is used as the subject of a sentence, as in (b). However, an infinitive is more commonly used with *it*, as in (c). The word *it* refers to and has the same meaning as the infinitive phrase at the end of the sentence.*

*Sometimes (primarily in informal usage) a gerund is used with *it*:

   It is dangerous riding with a drunk driver. It is nice to meet you. It is nice meeting you.

EXERCISE 17—ORAL: Give equivalent sentences by changing a sentence with a gerund as the subject to a sentence with *it + an infinitive phrase*, and vice-versa.

> *Examples:* **Teasing** animals is cruel. ⟶ **It is** cruel **to tease** animals.
>
> **It** wasn't difficult **to** ⟶ **Finding** their house wasn't difficult.
> **find** their house.

1. Diving into the sea from a high cliff takes courage.
2. Voting in every election is important.
3. It takes too much time to look up each word in the dictionary.
4. Mastering a second language takes time and patience.
5. If you know how, it is easy to float in water for a long time.
6. Driving to Atlanta will take us ten hours.

7. It is unusual to see you awake early in the morning.
8. Hearing the other side of the story would be interesting.

EXERCISE 18: Complete the following, then give a sentence with the same meaning by using a gerund as the subject.

1. It is fun _____ to ride a horse. _____
   (Riding a horse is fun.)

2. It takes a lot of time _____

3. It is easy _____

4. It is dangerous _____

5. It is important _____

6. It is wrong _____

7. It is a good idea _____

8. It is a bad idea _____

7-9 USING INFINITIVES WITH *TOO* AND *ENOUGH*

(a) That box is **too heavy** for Bob **to lift.** Bob can't lift that box. Compare: (b) That box is very heavy, but Bob can lift it.	In the speaker's mind, the use of *too* implies a negative result. In (a): *too heavy* = It is *impossible* for Bob to lift that box. In (b): *very heavy* = It is *possible but difficult* for Bob to lift that box.
(c) I am **strong enough to lift** that box. I can lift it. (d) I have **enough strength** to lift that box. (e) I have **strength enough** to lift that box.	*Enough* follows an adjective, as in (c). *Enough* may precede a noun, as in (d), or follow a noun, as in (e).

EXERCISE 19: Follow the pattern.

1. That ring is too expensive. *Negative result:* _____ I can't buy it. _____

   That ring is too expensive _____ for me to buy. _____

2. I am too tired. *Negative result:* _____ I can't/don't want to go to the party. _____

   I am too tired _____ to go to the party. _____

3. It is too late. *Negative result:* _____

   It is too late _____

4. The restaurant is too crowded. *Negative result:* _____

   The restaurant is too crowded _____

5. It is too cold. *Negative result:* _____

   It is too cold _____

6. Nuclear physics is too difficult. *Negative result:* _____

   Nuclear physics is too difficult _____

7. I am too busy. *Negative result:* _____

   I am too busy _____

8. My son is too young. *Negative result:* _____

   My son is too young _____

9. That ring is very expensive, but it isn't too expensive. *Positive result:* _____
   _____ I can buy it. It isn't too expensive for me to buy.

10. I am very tired, but I'm not too tired. *Positive result:* _____

11. My suitcase is very heavy, but it's not too heavy. *Positive result:* _____

    _____

12. I am very busy, but I'm not too busy. *Positive result:* _____

EXERCISE 20—ORAL (BOOKS CLOSED):

1. What is a child too young to do, but an adult old enough to do?
2. What did you have enough time to do before class today?
3. Who had a good dinner last night? Was it very good or too good?
4. Is it very difficult or too difficult to learn English?
5. After you wash your clothes, are they very clean or too clean?
6. What is my pocket big enough to hold? What is it too small to hold?
7. Who stayed up late last night? Did you stay up too late or very late?
8. Is the weather today too hot/cold or very hot/cold?
9. Compare a mouse with an elephant. Is a mouse too small or very small?
10. What is the highest mountain in the world? Is it too high or very high?

PART II Special Uses of the Simple Form and the -ing Form of a Verb

7-10 USING VERBS OF PERCEPTION

(a) I could **hear** the rain **fall** on the roof. (b) I could **hear** the rain **falling** on the roof. (c) I **saw** my friend **get/getting** into his car. (d) I **felt** her **touch/touching** my shoulder.	Certain verbs of perception are followed by either the simple form or the *-ing* form* of a verb.
	Common verbs used in this pattern: *see, notice, watch, look at, observe, hear, listen to, feel.*†

*The *-ing* form refers to the present participle (not a gerund) and usually gives the idea of "while": *I could hear the rain* (*while it was*) *falling on the roof.*
†Note the differences in meaning among the following verbs of perception.

(a) I **saw** a book on the desk.	In (a): I saw a book on the desk simply because my eyes were open. Seeing the book was an unconscious and unplanned act.
(b) I **noticed** a mistake in his composition.	The meaning of *notice* is often the same as that of *see,* but *notice* emphasizes the idea of seeing something quickly and completely by chance.
(c) I **watched** television last night.	*Watching* is a conscious, planned act that continues over a period of time. *Watching* does not occur by chance.
(d) I **looked** at the clock.	*Looking at* something is also a conscious, planned act, but it may not last as long as *watching* something.
(e) The psychologist **observed** the children's behavior.	The meaning of *observe* combines the ideas of watching and analyzing (thinking about something without emotion).
(f) I **heard** a noise in the middle of the night. (g) I **listened** to some music after dinner.	*Hearing* is an unconscious, unplanned act. It happens by chance. *Listening* is a conscious, planned act. It does not happen by chance.

EXERCISE 21: Complete the sentences. You may use the verbs suggested in the following list or supply your own.

argue	bark	cheat	knock	laugh	play	sing	talk
arrest	chase	come	land	move	ring	take off	tremble
							walk

1. I watched the students ____play/playing____ soccer.

2. Polly didn't hear the telephone _____.

3. I felt the ground _____ during the earthquake.

4. I like to listen to the birds _____ when I get up early in the morning.

5. When did Max get here? I didn't notice him _____ into the room.

6. I saw a policeman _____ a thief.

7. Did you hear a dog _____?

8. The guard observed a suspicious-looking person _____ into the bank.

9. Last night while I was trying to get to sleep, I could hear the people in the next apartment _____.

10. Mary is honest and never cheats, but during the last exam she saw another student _____.

11. I was almost asleep last night when I suddenly heard someone _____ _____ on the door.

12. While I was waiting for my plane, I watched other planes _____ and _____.

7-11 USING CAUSATIVE VERBS: *LET, MAKE,* AND *HAVE;* USING *HELP*

	(a) I **let** my brother **carry** my suitcase. (b) I **made** my brother **carry** my suitcase. (c) I **had** my brother **carry** my suitcase.	Notice in the examples: *let, make,* and *have* are followed by the simple form of a verb, not an infinitive. The meanings of (a), (b), and (c) are not the same.
LET	(d) Please **let** me **help** you.	In (d): *let = permit.* (*Please permit me to help you.*) INCORRECT: *Please let me to help you.* Do not use an infinitive after *let*.

MAKE	(e) The doctor **made** the patient **stay** in bed. (f) Mrs. Lee **made** her son **clean up** his room.	*Make someone do something* gives the idea that there are no choices, no alternatives. In (e): The patient had no choice. The doctor insisted that the patient stay in bed. In (f): Mrs. Lee's son had no choice.
	(g) The traffic **made** me **late**. (h) The salty food **made** me **thirsty**. (i) The good news **made** us **happy**.	*Make someone + an adjective* gives the same idea. In (g): I was late because of the traffic. I couldn't avoid being late. I had no choice.
HAVE	(j) **I had the jeweler repair my watch.** (k) **I had my watch repaired.** (*by the jeweler*) (l) Mrs. Crane **had someone paint her house.** (m) Mrs. Crane **had her house painted.**	In (j): The jeweler repaired my watch because I asked him to repair it. In (k): The *-ed* form (past participle) is used after *have* to give a passive meaning. Active: *have someone do something* Passive: *have something done by someone*
HELP	(n) My brother **helped** me **carry** my bags. (o) My brother **helped** me **to carry** my bags.	In addition to *let, make,* and *have,* sometimes *help* is followed by the simple form, as in (n). An infinitive is also possible as in (o).

EXERCISE 22: Supply any appropriate completion.

1. The good news made me _____ happy/smile/beam with happiness. _____

2. The bad news made me _____.

3. On our way home, Sue had me _____ the car at the corner so she could buy a newspaper.

4. The teacher had the class _____ a 2000-word research paper.

5. I spilled some tomato sauce on my suit coat. I need to have my suit _____

    _____ .

6. I decided to leave Sunday instead of Saturday, so I had the ticket agent _____

_____ my reservation.

7. I went to the bank to have a check _____ .

8. Ron's father wouldn't let him _____ a motorcycle.

9. The professor let the students _____ their calculators during the examination in Accounting 233.

10. I know we should have left twenty minutes ago. I'm sorry that I made you

_____ for me.

11. Keep working. Don't let me _____ you.

12. Could you help me _____ this window? It seems to be stuck.

13. She stopped at the service station to have the tank _____ with gas.

14. The good smells from the kitchen are making me _____ .

15. I had my friend _____ a letter for me.

EXERCISE 23—ORAL:

1. If a policeman sees a driver who is speeding, what does he make the driver do?
2. What do parents sometimes make their children do?
3. When you were a child and were sick, what did you mother or father make you do?
4. What do teachers sometimes have students do?
5. What do you sometimes have a friend of yours do?
6. What do grandmothers or grandfathers sometimes let children do?

7-12   USING CAUSATIVE *GET*

(a) **I got my friend to drive** me to the airport. (b) **I had my friend drive** me to the airport.	*Get someone to do something* has basically the same meaning as *have someone do something. Get someone to do something* is used informally in speech. (a) and (b) have basically the same meaning.

EXERCISE 24—ORAL: Use *get* and *have* in the following to show the cause of the action.

1. Last week you had to go to the post office to pick up a package. You asked Bob (who is a friend of yours) to take you there. He agreed to do so.

   Response: I got Bob to take me to the post office.

   I had Bob take me to the post office.

2. Yesterday you were carrying some packages. Your arms were full. So you asked Ann to open the door for you. She was happy to do so.

3. Jim invited you to his house. You had never been there before, so you asked him to draw a map for you. He drew a very good map.

4. You wanted to go to a show last night, but you didn't have any money. You asked Mary to lend you some, and she did.

5. You were having some trouble with your homework last night, so you asked your roommate to help you. He/she agreed to do so.

7-13 SPECIAL EXPRESSIONS FOLLOWED BY THE *-ING* FORM OF A VERB

(a) We **had fun** **playing** volleyball. We **had a good time playing** volleyball.	*have fun* *+ -ing* *have a good time + -ing*	
(b) I **had trouble** **finding** his house. I **had difficulty** **finding** his house. I **had a hard time** **finding** his house. I **had a difficult time finding** his house.	*have trouble* *+ -ing* *have difficulty* *+ -ing* *have a hard time* *+ -ing* *have a difficult time + -ing*	
(c) Sam **spends most of his time studying.** (d) Ann **spent all day getting** ready to leave on vacation.	*spend + expression of time + -ing*	
(e) She **sat at her desk writing** a letter. (f) I **stood there wondering** what to do next. (g) He **is lying in bed reading** a novel.	*sit* *+ expression of place + -ing* *stand + expression of place + -ing* *lie* *+ expression of place + -ing*	

EXERCISE 25: Supply an appropriate completion for each of the following.

1. I have trouble _____ him when he speaks.

2. We had a lot of fun _____ games at the picnic.

3. I spent five hours _____ my homework last night.

4. She is standing at the corner _____ for the bus.

5. He is sitting in class _____ notes.

6. Ms. Anderson is a commuter. Every work day, she spends almost two hours

   _____ to and from work.

7. Sometimes Ted has a hard time _____ up his mind.

8. It was a beautiful spring day. Dorothy was lying on the grass _____

   the sunshine and _____ the birds.

9. We had to spend almost an hour _____ in line to buy tickets to
   the game.

10. A: My friend is going to Germany next month, but he doesn't speak German.

    What do you suppose he will have difficulty _____ ?

    B: Well, he might have trouble _____ .

11. A: Did you enjoy your vacation in New York City?

    B: Very much. We had a good time _____ .

12. A: This is your first semester at this school. Have you had any problems?

    B: Not really, but sometimes I have a hard time _____ .

EXERCISE 26:   Supply an appropriate form for each verb in parentheses.

1. She stood on the beach (*look*) _____ out over the ocean.

2. Why don't you let him (*make*) _____ up his own mind?

3. She sat on a park bench (*watch*) _____ the ducks (*swim*)

   _____ in the pond.

4. They refused (*pay*) _____ their taxes, so they were sent to jail.

5. It is foolish (*ignore*) _____ physical ailments.

6. She is going to spend next year (*study*) _____ at a university in
   Japan.

7. The sad expression on his face made me (*feel*) _____ sorry for
   him.

8. I didn't know how to get to his house, so I had him (*draw*) _____
   a map for me.

9. The teacher had the class (*open*) _____ their books to page 185.

10. She lit a cigarette without (*think*) _____ about it.

11. (*Learn*) _____ a second language takes time.

12. It is impossible for me (*come*) _____ with you.

13. I went to the pharmacy to have my prescription (*fill*) _____ .

14. I always enjoy (*go*) _____ to hear the symphony.

15. (*Walk*) _____ alone in that section of the city at night is dangerous.

16. My cousins helped me (*move*) _____ into my new apartment.

17. I was tired, so I just watched them (*play*) _____ volleyball instead of (*join*) _____ them.

18. You can lead a horse to water, but you can't make him (*drink*) _____

    _____ .

19. You shouldn't let children (*play*) _____ with matches.

20. I finally told him (*be*) _____ quiet for a minute and (*listen*) _____ to what I had to say.

21. She was lying in bed (*think*) _____ about what a wonderful time she'd had.

22. Barbara has a wonderful sense of humor. She can always make me (*laugh*)

    _____ .

23. Let's (*have*) _____ Maureen (*join*) _____ us for dinner tonight.

24. When she needed a passport photo, she had her picture (*take*) _____

    _____ by a professional photographer.

25. I'm not accustomed to (*eat*) _____ such bland food.

26. There's a great difference between (*be*) _____ a freshman and

    (*be*) _____ a senior.

27. Sometimes I have trouble (*understand*) _____ lectures.

28. The illogic of his statements made me (*tear*) _____ my hair out.

29. Recently she has been spending most of her time (*do*) _____ research for a book.

30. I was getting sleepy, so I had my friend (*drive*) _____ the car.

EXERCISE 27—WRITTEN: Following are composition topics.

1. Write about your first day or week here (in this city/at this school/in this country). Did you have any unusual, funny, or difficult experiences? What were your first impressions and reactions? Whom did you meet?

2. Write about your childhood. What are some of the pleasant memories you have of your childhood? Do you have any unpleasant memories?

3. Whom do you like to spend some of your free time with? What do you enjoy doing together? Include an interesting experience the two of you have had.

EXERCISE 28—ERROR ANALYSIS: Find and correct the errors in the following.

> *Example:*   I am considering to go to a show tonight.
> *Correction:* I am considering **going** to a show tonight.

1. My parents made me to promise to write them once a week.
2. I don't mind to have a roommate.
3. Most students want return home as soon as possible.
4. When I went to shopping last Saturday, I saw a man to drive his car onto the sidewalk.
5. I asked my roommate to let me to use his shoe polish.
6. To learn about another country it is very interesting.
7. I don't enjoy to play card games.
8. I heard a car door to open and closing.
9. I had my friend to lend me his car.
10. After you combine the milk and eggs, mix them by a spoon.

Adjective Clauses

8-1 INTRODUCTION

(a)	**clause:**	*A clause* is a group of words containing a subject and a verb.
(b)	**independent clause:**	*An independent clause* is a complete sentence. It contains the main subject and verb of a sentence.
(c)	**dependent clause:**	*A dependent clause* is not a complete sentence. It must be connected to an independent clause.
(d)	**adjective clause:**	*An adjective clause* is a dependent clause which modifies a noun. It describes, identifies, or gives further information about a noun. (An adjective clause is also called a *relative clause*.)

PART I Adjective Clause Patterns

8-2 USING SUBJECT PRONOUNS: *WHO, WHICH, THAT*

	I thanked the woman. *She* helped me. ↓	In (a): *I thanked the woman* = an independent clause *who helped me* = an adjective clause The adjective clause modifies the noun *woman*.
(a) I thanked the woman	*who* helped me.	
(b) I thanked the woman	*that* helped me.	In (a): *who* is the subject of the adjective clause. In (b): *that* is the subject of the adjective clause. Note: (a) and (b) have the same meaning.

The book is mine.	who = used for people
It is on the table.	which = used for things
↓	that = used for both people and things
(c) The book *which* **is on the table** is mine.	
(d) The book *that* **is on the table** is mine.	

EXERCISE 1—ORAL: Combine the two sentences. Use the second sentence as an adjective clause.

1. I saw the man. He closed the door.
2. The girl is happy. She won the race.
3. The student is from China. He sits next to me.
4. The students are from China. They sit in the front row.
5. We are studying sentences. They contain adjective clauses.
6. I am using a sentence. It contains an adjective clause.

8–3 USING OBJECT PRONOUNS: *WHO*(*M*), *WHICH*, *THAT*

1. PRONOUN USED AS THE OBJECT OF A VERB	Notice in the examples: The adjective clause pronouns are placed at the *beginning* of the clause. (General guideline: Place an adjective clause pronoun as close as possible to the noun it modifies.)
The man was Mr. Jones.	
I saw *him*.	
(e) The man *who*(*m*) **I saw** was Mr. Jones.	
(f) The man *that* **I saw** was Mr. Jones.	In (e): *who* is usually used instead of *whom*, especially in speaking. *Whom* is generally used only in very formal English.
(g) The man **I saw** was Mr. Jones.	
The movie wasn't very good.	In (g) and (j): An object pronoun is often omitted from an adjective clause. (A subject pronoun, however, may not be omitted.)
We saw *it* last night.	
(h) The movie *which* **we saw last night** wasn't very good.	
(i) The movie *that* **we saw last night** wasn't very good.	*who*(*m*) = used for people
(j) The movie **we saw last night** wasn't very good.	*which* = used for things
	that = used for both people and things

EXERCISE 2—ORAL: Combine the sentences, using the second sentence as an adjective clause. Give all the possible patterns.

1. The book was good. I read it.
2. I liked the woman. I met her at the party last night.
3. I liked the composition. You wrote it.
4. The people were very nice. We visited them yesterday.

2. PRONOUN USED AS THE OBJECT OF A PREPOSITION	
She is the woman. **I told you about** *her.*	In very formal English, the preposition comes at the beginning of the adjective clause, as in (k) and (o). Usually, however, in everyday usage, the preposition comes after the subject and verb of the adjective clause, as in the other examples.
(k) She is the woman *about* *whom* **I told you.** (l) She is the woman *who(m)* **I told you** *about.* (m) She is the woman *that* **I told you** *about.* (n) She is the woman **I told you** *about.*	
The music was good. **We listened** *to it* **last night.**	Note: If the preposition comes at the beginning of the adjective clause, only *whom* or *which* may be used. A preposition is never immediately followed by *that* or *who.*
(o) The music *to which* **we listened** **last night** **was good.** (p) The music *which* **we listened** *to* **last night** **was good.** (q) The music *that* **we listened** *to* **last night** **was good.** (r) The music **we listened** *to* **last night** **was good.**	

EXERCISE 3—ORAL: Combine the sentences, using the second sentence as an adjective clause. Give all the possible patterns.

1. The meeting was interesting. I went to it.
2. The man was very kind. I talked to him yesterday.
3. I must thank the people. I got a present from them.
4. The picture was beautiful. She was looking at it.

8-4 USING *WHOSE*

The student is a good writer. **I read** *her composition.* (s) The student *whose composition* **I read** is a good writer.	*Whose* is used to show possession. It carries the same meaning as other possessive pronouns: *his, her, its,* and *their.*
I am from a country. *Its history* **goes back thousands of years.** (t) I am from a country *whose history* **goes back thousands of years.**	*Whose* usually modifies "people", but it may also be used to modify "things".
	Notice in (s): Both *whose* and the noun (*composition*) are placed at the beginning of the adjective clause.

EXERCISE 4—ORAL: Combine the two sentences, using the second sentence as an adjective clause.

1. I apologized to the woman. I spilled her coffee.
2. The man called the police. His wallet was stolen.

3. I met the woman. Her husband is the president of the corporation.
4. The professor is excellent. I am taking her course.
5. He teaches a class for students. Their native language is not English.
6. I live in a dormitory. Its residents come from many countries.

EXERCISE 5: Identify the adjective clause in each, then give the other possible patterns, if any.

1. The dress which she is wearing is new.

   Adjective clause: which she is wearing
   Other possible patterns: The dress that she is wearing is new.
   The dress she is wearing is new.

2. The doctor who examined the sick child was very gentle.
3. The people I was waiting for were late.
4. The term paper David is writing must be finished by Friday.
5. The man whose opinions I respect most is my father.
6. Did I tell you about the woman I met last night?
7. Did you hear about the earthquake that occurred in California?

8. The woman I was dancing with stepped on my toe.

EXERCISE 6: Combine the following sentences. Use sentence (b) as an adjective clause. Give all the possible adjective clause patterns.*

1. (a) The scientist is well-known for her research. (b) We met her yesterday.

   The scientist we met yesterday is well-known for her research.
   The scientist who(m) we met yesterday is well-known for her research.
   The scientist that we met yesterday is well-known for her research.

---

*In everyday usage, often one pattern is used more commonly than another:
   (1) As a subject pronoun, *who* is more common than *that*.
   (2) As a subject pronoun, *that* is more common than *which*.
   (3) Object pronouns are usually omitted.

2. (a) She lectured on a topic. (b) I know very little about it.

3. (a) The students missed the assignment. (b) They were absent from class.

4. (a) Yesterday I ran into an old friend. (b) I hadn't seen him for years.

5. (a) I explained my absence to the teacher. (b) I had missed his class.

6. (a) The young women are all from Japan. (b) We met them at the meeting last night.

7. (a) I am reading a book. (b) It was written by William Faulkner.

8. (a) The man gave me good advice. (b) I spoke to him.

9. (a) The instructor gives difficult tests. (b) I failed her course.

10. (a) The tape recorder was made in England. (b) I bought it.

11. (a) The dogcatcher caught the dog. (b) It bit my neighbor's daughter.

12. (a) The people are very kind. (b) I am staying at their house.

EXERCISE 7: Same as the preceding exercise.

1. (a) The man is standing over there. (b) I was telling you about him.

2. (a) The secretary can give you the information. (b) She sits at the first desk on the right.

3. (a) The students raised their hands. (b) Their names were called.

4. (a) Did you hear about the storm? (b) We are supposed to have it tomorrow.

5. (a) The girl was very helpful. (b) She explained the chemistry formula to me.

6. (a) I returned the money. (b) I had borrowed it from my roommate.

7. (a) The student is in one of my classes. (b) You just met her parents.

8. (a) During the last vacation, I visited many areas of the United States. (b) I had never seen them before.

9. (a) I talked to the child. (b) His father is the mayor of the city.

10. (a) The speech was informative. (b) We listened to it last night.

8-5 USING *WHERE*

The building is very old.		*Where* is used in an adjective clause to modify a place (*city, country, room, house*, etc.)
He lives *there* (*in that building*).		
(a) The building *where* he lives is very old.		If *where* is used, a preposition is not included in the adjective clause. If *where* is not used, the preposition must be included.
(b) The building in which he lives is very old.		
The building which he lives in is very old.		
The building that he lives in is very old.		
The building he lives in is very old.		

EXERCISE 8—ORAL: Combine the sentences, using the second sentence as an adjective clause.

1. The city was beautiful. We spent our vacation there (in that city).
2. That is the restaurant. I will meet you there (at that restaurant).
3. The town is small. I grew up there (in that town).
4. That is the drawer. I keep my jewelry there (in that drawer).

8-6 USING *WHEN*

		I'll never forget the day. I met you *then* (*on that day*).	*When* is used in an adjective clause to modify a noun of time (*year*, *day*, *time*, *century*, etc.)
(c)	I'll never forget the day	*when* I met you.	
(d)	I'll never forget the day	*on which* I met you.	The use of a preposition in an adjective clause which modifies a noun of time is somewhat different from that in other adjective clauses: A preposition is used preceding *which*, as in (d). Otherwise, the preposition is omitted.
(e)	I'll never forget the day	*that* I met you.	
(f)	I'll never forget the day	I met you.	

EXERCISE 9—ORAL: Combine the sentences, using the second sentence as an adjective clause.

1. Monday is the day. We will come then (on that day).
2. 7:05 is the time. My plane arrives then (at that time).
3. 1960 is the year. The revolution took place then (in that year).
4. July is the month. The weather is usually the hottest then (in that month).

EXERCISE 10—ORAL (BOOKS CLOSED): Begin your response with "That is . . . ." Use *where* in an adjective clause.

Example: You were born in **that** city.
Response: That is **the** city where I was born.

1. We have class in that room.
2. We ate dinner at that restaurant.
3. He works in that building.
4. He lives on that street.
5. You eat lunch at that cafeteria.
6. You keep your money at that bank.
7. You do your grocery shopping at that store.
8. You spent your vacation on that island.
9. You went swimming in that lake.
10. You grew up in that town.
11. The examination will be given in that room.
12. The earthquake occurred in that country.

13. Your sister went to graduate
    school at that university.
14. We are going to have a picnic at
    that park.

15. You lived in that city until you
    were ten years old.

EXERCISE 11—ORAL (BOOKS CLOSED): Begin your response with "She told
me about . . . ." All of the sentences are about your friend Mary and some of the
things she told you about during a conversation.

(To the teacher: Write "She told me about . . . ." on the board.)

Example: She wrote a letter.
Response: She told me about **the** letter she wrote.

1. She wrote a report.
2. She got a letter.
3. She went to a party.
4. She met some people.
5. She took a trip.
6. She went to a movie.
7. She saw a program on TV.
8. She took a test.

9. She read a book.
10. She bought some furniture.
11. She saw an accident.
12. She met a man.
13. She talked to a woman.
14. She had a problem.
15. She took a physics course.

EXERCISE 12—ORAL (BOOKS CLOSED): Begin your response with "She told
me about . . . ."

Example: Did she write a letter to her parents yesterday?
Response: Yes. She told me about **the** letter she wrote to her parents
          yesterday.

1. Did she write a letter to the President of the United States?
2. Did she get a letter from her brother yesterday?
3. Did she go to a party yesterday?
4. Did she meet some people at that party?
5. Did she take a trip to Mexico last summer?
6. Did she have some experiences in Mexico?
7. Did she use to live in a small town?
8. Did she get some presents for her birthday?
9. Did she do an experiment in chemistry lab yesterday?
10. Did she have to write a term paper for her English course?
11. Did she take an American history course last semester?
12. Is she reading a science fiction book?

EXERCISE 13–ORAL (BOOKS CLOSED):

Example: You read a book.
    Response: I read a book.
    Was it interesting?
    Response: Yes, **the** book I read was interesting.

Example: You drank **some** tea.
    Response: I drank **some** tea.
    Did it taste good?
    Response: Yes, **the** tea I drank tasted good.

1. You are sitting in a chair. Is it comfortable?
2. You saw a man. Was he wearing a brown suit?
3. You talked to a woman. Did she answer your question?
4. You had some meat for dinner last night. Was it good?
5. You bought a coat. Does it keep you warm?
6. You went to a soccer game. Was it exciting?
7. You watched a TV program last night. Was it good?
8. You are wearing boots/tennis shoes/loafers. Are they comfortable?
9. You stayed at a hotel. Was it in the middle of the city?
10. You eat at a cafeteria. Does it have good food?
11. You got a package in the mail. Was it from your parents?
12. You are doing an exercise. Is it easy?

EXERCISE 14–ORAL (BOOKS CLOSED):

Example: A waiter served you at a restaurant. Was he polite?
Response: Yes, the waiter who served me at the restaurant was polite.

1. A taxi driver took you to the airport. Was he friendly?
2. A barber cut your hair. Did he do a good job?
3. A clerk cashed your check. Did he ask for identification?
4. A man stopped you on the street. Did he ask you for directions?
5. A student stopped you in the hall. Did she ask you for the correct time?
6. A woman stepped on your toe. Did she apologize?

7. A car drove through a red light. Did it hit another car?
8. Some students took a test. Did most of them pass?
9. Some students are sitting in this room. Can all of them speak English?
10. A woman shouted at you. Was she angry?

11. A policeman helped you. Did you thank him? (*Yes, I thanked . . . .*)
12. A person is sitting next to you. Do you know him/her?
13. A professor teaches Chemistry 101. Do you like him?
14. A taxi driver took you to the bus station. Did you have a conversation with her?
15. A woman came into the room. Did you recognize her?
16. A man opened the door for you. Did you thank him?
17. A student is wearing a (blue shirt/blouse). Are you sitting next to him/her?
18. Some students were sitting on the grass outside the classroom building. Did you join them?
19. You were reading a book. Did you finish it?
20. You went to a party last night. Did you enjoy it?
21. You were looking for a book. Did you find it?
22. (. . .) told a story. Did you believe it?
23. (. . .) gave you a present. Did you open it?
24. You borrowed a pen from (. . .). Did you return it?
25. (. . .) told a joke. Did you laugh at it?

EXERCISE 15—ORAL (BOOKS CLOSED): Follow the pattern and supply your own completion.

Example: You spoke to a woman.
Response: The woman I spoke to . . . (was Mrs. Jones/was very kind/etc.).

1. You are looking at a person.
2. You are sitting at a desk.
3. This book belongs to a student.
4. You are interested in a field of study.
5. (. . .) and you listened to some music.
6. (. . .) went to a movie last night.
7. (. . .) was talking about a movie.
8. The police are looking for a man.
9. (. . .) is married to a man/woman.
10. You are living in a city/town.
11. You waited for a person.
12. You are studying at a school.
13. You got a letter from a person.
14. You grew up in a city/town.
15. I am pointing at a person.
16. (. . .) spoke to some people.
17. You are living with some people.
18. You went to a doctor to get some medicine.

EXERCISE 16—ORAL (BOOKS CLOSED):   You are in a room full of people. You are speaking to a friend. You are identifying various people in the room for your friend. Begin your response with "There is . . . ."

>   *Example:*   That man's wife is your teacher.
>   *Response:*   There is the man whose wife is my teacher.

1. That woman's husband is a football player.
2. That boy's father is a doctor.
3. That girl's mother is a dentist.
4. That person's picture was in the newspaper.
5. That man's dog bit you.
6. That man's daughter won a gold medal at the Olympic Games.
7. That woman's car was stolen.
8. You borrowed that student's lecture notes.
9. You found that woman's keys.
10. You are in that teacher's class.
11. You read that author's book.
12. We met that man's wife.

EXERCISE 17—ORAL (BOOKS CLOSED):   Use *whose* in the response.

>   *Example:*   Dr. Jones is a professor. You are taking his course.
>   *Response:*   Dr. Jones is the professor whose course I am taking.

1. (. . .) is a student. You found his/her book.
2. (. . .) is a student. You borrowed his/her dictionary.
3. Mark Twain is an author. You like his books best.
4. You used a woman's phone. You thanked her.
5. You broke a child's toy. He started to cry.
6. You stayed at a family's house. They were very kind.
7. A woman's purse was stolen. She called the police.

8. A man's beard caught on fire when he lit a cigarette. He poured a glass of water on his face.
9. A girl's leg is in a cast. She has trouble climbing stairs.
10. Everyone tried to help a family. Their house had burned down.

EXERCISE 18—ORAL (BOOKS CLOSED): Begin your response with either "I'll never forget . . ." or "I'll always remember . . . ."

> *Example:* trip
> *Response:* I'll never forget the trip . . . (I took to France).

1. trip	9. woman
2. experiences	10. man
3. day	11. house
4. first day	12. story
5. time	13. accident
6. first time	14. wonderful food
7. person	15. room
8. people	16. friends

EXERCISE 19: In addition to modifying nouns, adjective clauses also modify certain pronouns. Study the examples, then complete the sentences.

> *Examples:* (a) There is **someone I want you to meet.**
> (b) **Everything he said** was pure nonsense.
> (c) **Anybody who wants to come** is welcome.
> (d) Paula is **the only one who knows the answer.**
> (e) Scholarships are available for **those who need financial assistance.**
> (f) I have enough. This is **all I want.**

1. I have a question. There is something _____ .

2. He can't trust anyone. There is no one _____ .

3. Don't ask me any more questions about it. I've already told you all _____

    _____ .

4. I'm powerless to help her. There is nothing _____ .

5. All of the students are seated. The teacher is the only one _____ .

6. I can't give you any more money. This is all _____ .

7. She makes a good first impression. She charms everyone _____ .

8. I studied French many years ago, but I don't remember much. I've forgotten

    almost everything _____ .

9. What was she talking about? I didn't understand anything _____ .

10. The concert had already begun. Those _____ had to wait until intermission to be seated.

11. I listen to everything _____.

12. You can believe him. Everything _____.

8-7 PUNCTUATION OF ADJECTIVE CLAUSES

General guideline for the punctuation of adjective clauses:
(1) *Do not use commas if* the adjective clause is necessary to identify the noun it modifies.*
(2) *Do use commas if* the adjective clause simply gives additional information and is not necessary to identify the noun it modifies.†

(a) **The professor who teaches Chemistry 101 is an excellent lecturer.**	In (a): No commas are used. The adjective clause is necessary to identify which professor is meant.
(b) **Professor Wilson, who teaches Chemistry 101, is an excellent lecturer.**	In (b): Commas are used. The adjective clause is not necessary to identify who Professor Wilson is. We already know who Professor Wilson is: he has a name. The adjective clause simply gives additional information. It may be omitted from the sentence with no change in meaning: *Professor Wilson is an excellent lecturer.*
(c) **People who were born on December 25th must celebrate their birthdays on Christmas Day.**	In (c): No commas are used. The adjective clause identifies which people must celebrate their birthdays on Christmas Day. The adjective clause is necessary to the meaning of *people;* it cannot be omitted from the sentence.
(d) **My father, who was born on December 25th, must celebrate his birthday on Christmas Day.**	In (d): Commas are used. The adjective clause is not necessary to identify *my father;* it simply gives additional information. It may be omitted from the sentence with no change in meaning.
(e) **Hawaii, which consists of eight principal islands, is a favorite vacation spot.** (f) **Mrs. Smith, who is a retired teacher, does volunteer work at the hospital.** (g) **I am reading *The Sun Also Rises,* which was written by Ernest Hemingway.**	Notice that commas are used in (e), (f), and (g). General guideline: Use commas if an adjective clause modifies a proper noun. (*A proper noun* = the name of a person, place, or thing. A proper noun begins with a capital letter, not a small letter.) Note: A comma reflects a pause in speech.

*Adjective clauses that do not require commas are called "essential" or "restrictive."

†Adjective clauses that do require commas are called "nonessential" or "nonrestrictive."

(h) I met **a woman who teaches** at the university. I met **a woman that teaches** at the university. (i) I met **Linda Jennings, who teaches** at the university.	If no commas are used, any possible pronoun may be used in the adjective clause. Object pronouns may be omitted, as in (j). If commas are used, only *wh-* pronouns may be used (*who, which, whose, whom, where, when*); *that* may not be used.
(j) **The woman who(m) I met** yesterday is in the Modern Languages Department. **The woman that I met** yesterday is in the Modern Languages Department. **The woman I met** yesterday is in the Modern Languages Department. (k) **Linda Jennings, whom I met** yesterday, is in the Modern Languages Department at the university.	In (i) and (k): *that* may not be used. In (k): *whom* may not be omitted.

EXERCISE 20: Add commas where necessary. Change the adjective clause pronoun to *that* if possible.

1. Only people who speak Russian should apply for the job.
2. Matthew who speaks Russian applied for the job.
3. Allen and Jackie who did not come to class yesterday explained their absence to the instructor.
4. The students who did not come to class yesterday explained their absence to the teacher.
5. The geologist who lectured at Browning Hall last night predicted another earthquake.
6. Dr. Fields who lectured at Browning Hall last night predicted another earthquake.
7. The rice which we had for dinner last night was very good.
8. Rice which is grown in many countries is a staple food throughout much of the world.
9. I have fond memories of my hometown which is situated in a valley.
10. I live in a town which is situated in a valley.
11. The Mississippi River which flows south from Minnesota to the Gulf of Mexico is the major commercial river in the United States.
12. A river which is polluted is not safe for swimming.

EXERCISE 21: Same as the preceding exercise.

1. We enjoyed the city where we spent our vacation.
2. We enjoyed Mexico City where we spent our vacation.

3. An elephant which is the earth's largest land mammal has few natural enemies other than human beings.

4. One of the elephants which we saw at the zoo had only one tusk.

5. A rebel is a person who resists or fights against authority.

6. A cardinal which is a brightly colored red bird usually does not fly south during winter.

7. Child labor was a social problem in late eighteenth-century England where employment in factories became virtual slavery for children.

8. We had to use a telephone, so we went to the nearest house. The woman who answered our knock listened cautiously to our request.

9. According to a newspaper article which I read, the police arrested the man who had robbed the First National Bank. The man who was wearing a plaid shirt and blue jeans was caught shortly after he had left the bank.

10. The woman who is wearing the green suit is Cynthia Anderson. Marge Jackson is the woman who is standing next to Ms. Anderson. Both Ms. Jackson and Ms. Anderson who are the president and vice-president of the organization respectively are successful businesswomen.

8-8   USING EXPRESSIONS OF QUANTITY IN ADJECTIVE CLAUSES

In my class there are 20 students. *Most of them* are from the Far East. (a) In my class there are 20 students, *most of whom* are from the Far East.	This adjective clause pattern occurs with any expression of quantity: *some of, many of, most of, none of, two of, half of, both of, neither of, each of,* etc.
He gave several reasons. *Only a few of them* were valid. (b) He gave several reasons, *only a few of which* were valid.	Only *whom, which,* and *whose* are used in this pattern. This pattern, which is more common in writing than in speaking, requires commas.
The teachers discussed Jim. *One of his problems* was poor study habits. (c) The teachers discussed Jim, *one of whose problems* was poor study habits.	
We bought an antique table. *The top of it* has jade inlay. (d) We bought an antique table, *the top of which* has jade inlay.	An adjective clause that includes *a noun + of + which* is sometimes an alternative to an adjective clause with *whose.* (d) and (e) have the same meaning.

```
We bought an antique table.
Its top has jade inlay.
```

(e) We bought an antique table *whose top* has jade inlay.

EXERCISE 22: Combine the two sentences. Use (b) as an adjective clause.

1. (a) Last night the orchestra played three symphonies. (b) One of them was Beethoven's Seventh.
2. (a) I tried on six pairs of shoes. (b) I liked none of them.
3. (a) After the riot, over one hundred people were taken to the hospital. (b) Many of them had been innocent bystanders.
4. (a) I bought a book. (b) The title of the book is *Contemporary Architectural Styles.*
5. (a) The professor has assigned the students a research paper. (b) The purpose of the research paper is to acquaint them with methods of scholarly research.

EXERCISE 23: Complete the following sentences.

1. He introduced me to his roommates, both of ___whom are from California.___

2. They own four automobiles, one of _____

3. I have three brothers, all of _____

4. I am taking four courses, one of _____

5. In my apartment building, there are twenty apartments, several of _____

_____

6. I have two roommates, neither of _____

7. They own a Picasso original, the value of _____

8. This semester I had to buy fifteen books, most of _____

EXERCISE 24—WRITTEN: Complete the following sentences. Punctuate carefully. Use an adjective clause in each.

1. One of the men I . . . .
2. My father whose name . . . .
3. I visited the Eiffel Tower which . . . .
4. One of the places I . . . .

5. The doctor he . . . .

6. The city where . . . .

7. The/An author whose . . . .

8. I will never forget the time when
   . . . .

9. I took five courses one of . . . .

10. There is something I . . . .

11. The room in . . . .

12. Mr. Johnson who . . . .

EXERCISE 25—WRITTEN: Write a short composition in which you describe the members of your family. Try to use some adjective clauses but don't force them. Generally, one adjective clause in a sentence (or maybe two) is enough. (Do NOT write: *My father, who owns his own business, which is a clothing store, is a kind man whom I love very much and who takes good care of his family, which consists of six people.*) Begin your composition with: "I would like you to meet my family."

EXERCISE 26—ORAL (BOOKS CLOSED):

(*To the teacher: Use the questions to elicit information from someone in the class. Then ask another student to summarize this information in one sentence beginning with* "The . . . .")

> *Example:* Who got a letter yesterday?
>
> > *Response:*   I did.
> >
> > Who was it from?
> >
> > *Response:*   My brother.
>
> To another
> student: Can you summarize this information? Begin with "The . . . ."
>
> > *Response:*   The letter (Ali) got yesterday was from his brother.

1. Who got a letter last week?
   Where was it from?

2. Who is wearing earrings?
   What are they made of?

3. Who lives in an apartment?
   Is it close to school?

4. Pick up something that doesn't
   belong to you.
   Whose is it?

5. Who grew up in a small town?
   In what part of the country is
   it located?

6. Who has bought something recently?
   What did you buy?
   Was it expensive?

7. Hold up a book.
   What is the title?

8. Who went to a bar/restaurant last
   night?
   Was it crowded?

9. What did you have for dinner
   last night?
   Was it good?

10. Who watched a TV program last night?
What was it about?

11. Who has borrowed something recently?
What did you borrow?
Who does it belong to?

12. Who shops for groceries?
What is the name of the store?

13. Who eats lunch away from home?
Where do you usually eat?
Does it have good food?

14. Who took the bus to class today?
Was it late or on time?

15. Who read a newspaper yesterday?
Which newspaper?

16. Point at a person.
Who is he/she pointing at?

EXERCISE 27: The purpose of this exercise is for you to describe various people in the class by using adjective clauses. Fill in the necessary information for all of the solid lines, but leave the broken lines blank. Then show another student what you have written, and he or she will supply the names for the broken lines. Discuss possible completions for the example sentence.

Example: The name of the _____ who _____

is _ _ _ _ _ _ _ _ _ _ _ _ _.

1. I am thinking about a person in this class who _____

_____ . His/her name is _ _ _ _ _ _ _.

2. Let me introduce you to my classmates. The _____ who

_____ is _ _ _ _ _ _ _ _ _ _ _ _ _.

The _____ who _____

is _ _ _ _ _ _ _ _ _ _ _ _ . And the one who _____

_____ is _ _ _ _ _ _ _ _ _ _ _ _ _.

3. _ _ _ _ _ _ _ _ _ _ _ _ is the name of the person whose _____

_____ .

4. There is only one person in this class who _____

_____ . His/her name is _ _ _ _ _ _ _.

5. In the front/middle/back of the room there are two people, both of whom ____

_____

Their names are _ _ _ _ _ _ _ _ _ _ _ and _ _ _ _ _ _ _ _ _ _ _.

PART II Reduction of Adjective Clauses to Adjective Phrases

8-9 INTRODUCTION

(a) **clause:**	A *clause* is a group of related words that contains a subject and a verb.
(b) **phrase:**	A *phrase* is a group of related words that does not contain a subject and a verb.
(c) **adjective phrase:**	An *adjective phrase* is a reduction of an adjective clause. It modifies a noun. It does not contain a subject and a verb.
	Adjective clause: The girl *who is sitting next to me* is Mary.
	Adjective phrase: The girl *sitting next to me* is Mary.

8-10 CHANGING AN ADJECTIVE CLAUSE TO AN ADJECTIVE PHRASE

There are two ways in which an adjective clause is changed to an adjective phrase:	
(1) *The subject pronoun is omitted AND the **be** form of the verb is omitted:* (a) The **boy who is talking** to John is from Korea. (b) The **boy** talking to John is from Korea. (c) The **ideas which are presented** in that book are interesting. (d) The **ideas** presented in that book are interesting. (e) She is the **woman who is responsible** for the improvement. (f) She is the **woman** responsible for the improvement. (g) The **books that are on that shelf** are mine. (h) The **books** on that shelf are mine. (2) *If there is no **be** form of a verb in the adjective clause, it is sometimes possible to omit the subject pronoun and change the verb to its **-ing** form.* (i) English has an **alphabet which consists** of 26 letters. (j) English has an **alphabet** consisting of 26 letters. (k) **Anyone who wants** to come with us is welcome. (l) **Anyone** wanting to come with us is welcome.	Only adjective clauses that have a subject pronoun—*who, which,* or *that*—are reduced to modifying adjective phrases. There is no difference in meaning between the adjective clause and the adjective phrase in each example.
(m) **George Washington**, who was the first president of the United States, was a wealthy colonist. (n) **George Washington**, the first president of the United States, was a wealthy colonist.	If the adjective clause requires commas, the adjective phrase also requires commas.

EXERCISE 28:   Change the adjective clauses to adjective phrases.

1. Do you know the woman who is coming toward us?

   (*Do you know the woman coming toward us?*)

2. The people who are waiting for the bus in the rain are getting wet.
3. I come from a city which is located in the southern part of the country.
4. The children who attend that school receive a good education.
5. The scientists who are researching the causes of cancer are making progress.
6. The fence which surrounds our house is made of wood.
7. They live in a house which was built in 1890.
8. We have an apartment which overlooks the park.

EXERCISE 29:   Same as the preceding exercise.

1. Dr. Stanton, who is the president of the university, will give a speech at the commencement ceremonies.
2. Did you get the message which concerned the special meeting?
3. Be sure to follow the instructions which are given at the top of the page.
4. The conclusion which is presented in that book states that most of the automobiles which are produced by American industry have some defect.
5. The rules which allow public access to wilderness areas need to be reconsidered.
6. The photographs which were published in the newspaper were extraordinary.
7. There is almost no end to the problems which face a head of state.
8. Nero, who was Emperor of Rome from 54 to 68 A.D., is believed to have murdered both his mother and his wife.
9. The psychologists who study the nature of sleep have made important discoveries.
10. The experiment which was conducted at the University of Chicago was successful.
11. Pictures which showed the brutality of war entered the living rooms of millions of Americans on the nightly news.
12. Freud's wife Martha, who was a plain and gracious woman, did not try to understand her husband's psychoanalytic theories.
13. The Indians who lived in Peru before the discovery of the New World by Europeans belonged to the Incan culture.
14. Many of the students who hope to enter the university will be disappointed because only one-tenth of those who apply for admission will be accepted.
15. There must exist in a modern community a sufficient number of persons who possess the technical skill which is required to maintain the numerous devices upon which our physical comforts depend.

EXERCISE 30: Change the adjective phrases to adjective clauses.

1. David Keller, a young poet known for his sensitive interpretations of human relationships, has just published another volume of poems.

   *(David Keller, **who is** a young poet **who is** known for his sensitive interpretations of human relationships, has just published another volume of poems.)*

2. Corn was one of the agricultural products introduced to the European settlers by the Indians. Some of the other products introduced by the Indians were potatoes, peanuts, and tobacco.
3. He read *The Old Man and the Sea,* a novel written by Ernest Hemingway.
4. The sunlight coming through the window wakes me up early every morning.
5. Mercury, the nearest planet to the sun, is also the smallest of the nine planets orbiting the sun.
6. The pyramids, the monumental tombs of ancient Egyptian pharaohs, were constructed from 3000 to 1800 B.C.
7. The sloth, a slow-moving animal found in the tropical forests of Central and South America, feeds entirely on leaves and fruit.
8. Two-thirds of those arrested for car theft are under twenty years of age.
9. St. Louis, Missouri, known as "The Gateway to the West," traces its history to 1793, when Pierre Laclede, a French fur trader, selected this site on the Mississippi River as a fur-trading post.
10. Any student not wanting to go on the trip should inform the office.

EXERCISE 31: Combine the sentences. Use the second sentence as an adjective phrase.

1. Louisville was founded in 1778. It is the largest city in Kentucky.
   _____ Louisville, the largest city in Kentucky, was founded in 1778. _____

2. John Quincy Adams was born on July 11, 1767. He was the sixth president of the United States.

   _____

   _____

3. Two languages, Finnish and Swedish, are used in Helsinki. It is the capital of Finland.

   _____

   _____

4. The Washington National Monument is a famous landmark in the nation's capital. It is a towering obelisk made of white marble.

   _____

   _____

5. Honolulu has consistently pleasant weather. It is best known to the traveler for Waikiki Beach.

   _____

   _____

6. Libya is a leading producer of oil. It is a country in North Africa.

   _____

   _____

EXERCISE 32–WRITTEN: Complete the following.

1. _____, a country in _____, is _____

   _____

2. _____, the capital city of _____, _____

   _____

3. I would like to read the biography of _____, a/the _____

   _____

4. I was born _____, a/the _____

   _____

5. _____, the (leader/Prime Minister/King/Queen/President, etc.)

   of _____, _____

EXERCISE 33–WRITTEN: Write about some trips you have taken. Describe some of the most enjoyable and interesting places you have visited.

EXERCISE 34–ERROR ANALYSIS: All of the following sentences adapted from student compositions contain errors. Test your skill by seeing how many of the errors you can find and correct.

1. It is important to be polite to people who lives in the same building.

2. She lives in a hotel is restricted to senior citizens.

3. My sister has two childrens, who their names are Ali and Talal.

4. He comes from Venezuela that is a Spanish-speaking country.

5. There are ten universities in Thailand, seven of them locate in Bangkok is the capital city.

6. I would like to write about several problems which I have faced them since I come to United State.

7. There is a small wooden screen separates the bed from the rest of the room.

8. At the airport, I was waiting for some relatives which I had never met them before.

9. It is almost impossible to find two person who their opinions are the same.

10. On the wall, there is a colorful poster which it consists of a group of young people who dancing.

EXERCISE 35–PREPOSITIONS: Supply an appropriate preposition for each of the following two-word verbs.

1. A: Why don't we try to call _____ the O'Briens sometime this weekend? We haven't seen them for a long time.

   B: Sounds like a good idea. I'd like to see them again.

2. A: Did you go _____ your paper carefully before you handed it _____ ?

   B: Yes. I looked it _____ carefully.

3. A: Do you believe his story about being late because he had a flat tire?

   B: No. I think he made it _____ .

4. A: Could you pick _____ a newspaper on your way home from work tonight?

   B: Sure.

5. A: Did you hear the bad news?

   B: About what?

   A: Gary's grandmother passed _____ . Gary went home to be with his family and attend the funeral.

6. A: I like your new shoes.

   B: Thanks. I had to try _____ almost a dozen pairs before I decided to get these.

7. A: Have you decided to accept that new job?

   B: Not yet. I'm still thinking it _____ .

8. A: I'm tired. I wish I could get _____ of going to the meeting tonight.

   B: Do you have to go?

9. A: Why hasn't Mary been in class for the last two weeks?

   B: She dropped _____ _____ school.

10. A: What time does your plane take _____?

    B: 10:40.

    A: How long does the flight take?

    B: I think we get _____ around 12:30.

11. A: Do you like living in the dorm?

    B: It's okay. I've learned to put _____ with all the noise.

12. A: What brought _____ your decision to quit your job?

    B: I couldn't get _____ _____ my boss.

Noun Clauses

9-1 INTRODUCTION

A noun is used as a subject or an object.

A noun clause is used as a subject or an object. In other words, a noun clause is used in the same ways as a noun.

(a) **His story** was interesting.	In (a): *story* is a noun. It is used as the subject of the sentence.
(b) **What he said** was interesting.	In (b): *what he said* is a noun clause. It is used as the subject of the sentence. The noun clause has its own subject (*he*) and verb (*said*).
(c) I heard **his story**.	In (c): *story* is a noun. It is used as the object of the verb *heard*.
(d) I heard **what he said**.	In (d): *what he said* is a noun clause. It is used as the object of the verb *heard*.

The following words are used to introduce noun clauses:

(1) question words: *when*   *who*
                 where *whom*
                 why   *what*
                 how   *which*
                         whose

(2) *whether*
   if

(3) *that*

9-2 NOUN CLAUSES WHICH BEGIN WITH A QUESTION WORD

QUESTION	NOUN CLAUSE	
Where does she live? What did he say?	(a) I don't know **where she lives**. (b) I couldn't hear **what he said**.	In (a): *where she lives* is the object of the verb *know*. Note: Do *not* use question word order in a noun clause. In a noun clause, the subject precedes the verb.
S V Who lives there? What happened? Who is at the door?	S V (c) I don't know **who lives there**. (d) Please tell me **what happened**. (e) I wonder **who is at the door**.	In (c): The word order is the same in both the question and the noun clause because *who* is the subject in both.
V S Who is she? Who are those men? Whose house is that?	S V (f) I don't know **who she is**. (g) I don't know **who those men are**. (h) I wonder **whose house that is**.	In (f): *she* is the subject of the question, so it is placed in front of the verb *be* in the noun clause.*
What did she say? What should they do?	(i) **What she said** surprised me. (j) **What they should do** is obvious.	In (i): *what she said* is the subject of the sentence. Notice in (j): A noun clause subject takes a singular verb.

*For a presentation of subject-verb usage in questions with *be* and a question word, see 1-4.

EXERCISE 1: Change the question in parentheses to a noun clause.

1. (*How old is he?*)   I don't know   <u> how old he is </u> .

2. (*What was he talking about?*)   <u> What he was talking about </u> was interesting.

3. (*Where do you live?*)   Please tell me _____.

4. (*What did she say?*)   _____ wasn't true.

5. (*When are they coming?*)   Do you know _____?

6. (*How much does it cost?*)   I can't remember _____.

7. (*Which one does he want?*)   Let's ask him _____.

8. (*Who is coming to the party?*)   I don't know _____.

9. (*Who are those people?*)   I don't know _____.

10. (*Whose pen is this?*)   Do you know _____?

11. (*Why did they leave the country?*)   _____ is a
                                      secret.

12. (*What are we doing in class?*)   _____ is easy.

13. (*Where did she go?*)   _____ is none
                                      of your business!

14. (*How many letters are there in*   I don't remember _____
    the English alphabet?)   _____.

15. (*Who is the mayor of New York*   I don't know _____.
    City?)

16. (*How old does a person have to*   Could you tell me _____
    be to buy beer?)   _____.

EXERCISE 2—ORAL (BOOKS CLOSED): Begin your response with "I don't know . . . ."

> *Example:* What time is it?
> *Response:* I don't know what time it is.

1. Where does (. . .) live?
2. What country is (. . .) from?
3. How long has (. . .) been living here?
4. What is (. . .)'s telephone number?
5. Where is the post office?
6. How far is it to (Kansas City)?
7. Why is (. . .) absent?
8. Where is my book?
9. What kind of watch does (. . .) have?
10. Why was (. . .) absent yesterday?
11. Where did (. . .) go yesterday?
12. What is (. . .)'s favorite color?
13. How long has (. . .) been married?
14. How did (. . .) meet his wife/her husband?
15. What is the capital of (Texas)?
16. What is the population of (Texas)?
17. Why was (. . .) late to class?
18. Why are we doing this exercise?
19. What kind of government does (Italy) have?
20. Where is (. . .) going to eat lunch/dinner?
21. When does (the semester) end?
22. When does (Thanksgiving) vacation start?
23. Where did (. . .) go after class yesterday?
24. Why is (. . .) smiling?
25. How many questions have I asked in this exercise?
26. How often does (. . .) go to the library?
27. Whose book is that?
28. How much did that book cost?

9-3 NOUN CLAUSES WHICH BEGIN WITH *WHETHER* OR *IF*

YES/NO QUESTION	NOUN CLAUSE	
Will she come?	(a) I don't know **whether she will come.** I don't know **if she will come.**	When a yes/no question is changed to a noun clause, *whether* or *if* is used to introduce the clause. (Note: *whether* is more acceptable in formal English, but *if* is quite commonly used, especially in speaking.)
Does he need help?	(b) I wonder **whether he needs help.** I wonder **if he needs help.**	
	(c) I wonder **whether or not** she will come.	In (c), (d), and (e): Notice the patterns when *or not* is used.
	(d) I wonder **whether** she will come **or not.**	
	(e) I wonder **if** she will come **or not.**	
	(f) **Whether she comes or not** is unimportant to me.	In (f): Notice that the noun clause is in the subject position.

EXERCISE 3—ORAL (BOOKS CLOSED): Begin your response with "I wonder ...."

> *Example:* Does (...) need any help?
> *Response:* I wonder whether/if (...) needs any help.
>
> *Example:* Where is (...)?
> *Response:* I wonder where (...) is.

1. Where is your friend?
2. Should you wait for him?
3. Should you call him?
4. Where is your dictionary?
5. Who took your dictionary?
6. Did (...) borrow your dictionary?
7. Did you leave your dictionary at the library?
8. Who is that woman?
9. Does she need any help?
10. Who is that man?
11. What is he doing?
12. Is he having trouble?
13. Should you offer to help him?
14. How far is it to (Florida)?
15. Do we have enough time to go to (Florida) over vacation?

16. Whose book is this?
17. Does it belong to (...)?
18. Why is the sky blue?
19. How long does a butterfly live?
20. What causes earthquakes?
21. When was the first book written?
22. Why did dinosaurs become extinct?
23. Is there life on other planets?
24. How did life begin?
25. Will people live on the moon someday?

(To the teacher: Continue the exercise by having the students supply their own completions for "I wonder ....")

EXERCISE 4–ORAL (BOOKS CLOSED):   Begin your response with "Could you please tell me . . . ."

> *Example:*   What is this?
> *Response:*   Could you please tell me what this is?

1. Where is the library? The nearest phone? The rest room?
2. How much does this book cost?
3. When is Flight 62 expected to arrive?
4. Does this bus go downtown?
5. Is this word spelled correctly?
6. What time is it?
7. Is this information correct?
8. How much does it cost to fly from (Chicago) to (New York)?
9. Where is the bus station?
10. Whose pen is this?

9–4   QUESTION WORDS FOLLOWED BY INFINITIVES

(a) I don't know **what I should do**. (b) I don't know **what to do**. (c) Pam can't decide **whether she should go or stay home**. (d) Pam can't decide **whether to go or (to) stay home**. (e) Please tell me **how I can get to the bus station**. (f) Please tell me **how to get to the bus station**. (g) Jim told us **where we could find it**. (h) Jim told us **where to find it**.	Question words (***when, where, how, who, whom, whose, what, which***) and ***whether*** may be followed by an infinitive. Each pair of sentences in the examples has the same meaning. Notice that the meaning expressed by the infinitive is either ***should*** or ***can/could***.

EXERCISE 5:   Give sentences with the same meaning by using infinitives.

1. He told me when I should come. (*He told me when to come.*)
2. The plumber told me how I could fix the leak in the sink.
3. Please tell me where I should meet you.
4. Don had an elaborate excuse for being late for their date, but Sandy didn't know whether she should believe him or not.
5. Jim found two shirts he liked, but he had trouble deciding which one he should buy.
6. I've done everything I can think of to help Andy get his life straightened out. I don't know what else I can do.

Complete the following; use infinitives in your completions.

7. I was tongue-tied. I didn't know what _____

8. A: I can't decide what _____ to the reception.

   B: How about your green suit?

9. A: Where are you going to live when you go to the university?

   B: I'm not sure. I can't decide whether _____

10. A: Do you know how _____

    B: No, but I'd like to learn.

11. Tom's wife is very bossy. She tells him how _____,

    when _____, where _____;

    what _____, and who _____.

12. Poor Tom is a very indecisive person. He can't ever decide whether _____

    _____ or _____, whether _____

    _____ or _____, where _____

    _____, nor what _____.

9-5 NOUN CLAUSES WHICH BEGIN WITH *THAT*

STATEMENT (*Expression of an idea or fact*)	NOUN CLAUSE	
He is a good actor.	(a) I think **that he is a good actor.** (b) I think **he is a good actor.**	In (a): *that he is a good actor* is a noun clause. It is used as the object of the verb *think*.
The world is round.	(c) We know **(that) the world is round.**	The word *that*, when it introduces a noun clause, has no meaning in itself. It simply marks the beginning of the clause. Frequently it is omitted, as in (b), especially in speaking. (If used in speaking, it is unstressed.)

STATEMENT (*Expression of an idea or fact*)	NOUN CLAUSE	
She doesn't understand spoken English.	(d) **That she doesn't understand spoken English** is obvious. (e) It is obvious **(that) she doesn't understand spoken English.**	In (d): The noun clause (*That she doesn't understand spoken English*) is used as the subject of the sentence. The word *that* is not omitted when it introduces a noun clause used as the subject of a sentence, as in (d) and (f).
The world is round.	(f) **That the world is round** is a fact. (g) It is a fact **that the world is round.**	More commonly, the word *it* functions as the subject, and the noun clause is placed at the end of the sentence, as in (e) and (g).

EXERCISE 6: Complete sentence (a) by using *it* and any appropriate word or expression from the given list. In (b), give the equivalent sentence by using a "*that* clause" as the subject. Notice the example.

a fact	*surprising*	*a shame*
a well-known fact	*unfair*	*a pity*
true	*obvious*	*too bad*
strange	*apparent*	*unfortunate*

Example: (a) _____It is a fact that_____ the world is round.

(b) _____That_____ the world is round

_____is a fact._____

1. (a) _____ drug abuse can ruin one's health.

(b) _____ drug abuse can ruin one's health

_____

2. (a) _____ Tim hasn't been able to make any friends.

(b) _____ Tim hasn't been able to make any friends

_____

3. (a) _____ some women do not earn equal pay for equal work.

(b) _____ some women do not earn equal pay for

equal work _____

4. (a) _____ the earth revolves around the sun.

   (b) _____ the earth revolves around the sun

   _____

5. (a) _____ Irene failed her entrance examination.

   (b) _____ Irene failed her entrance examination

   _____

6. (a) _____ smoking can cause cancer.

   (b) _____ smoking can cause cancer _____

EXERCISE 7—ORAL: *Student A:* Make an original sentence by using *it* and the given word or expression. *Student B:* Give the equivalent sentence by using a "*that* clause" as the subject.

  1. true

     A: It is true that plants need water in order to grow.

     B: That plants need water in order to grow is true.

  2. a fact   7. strange

  3. surprising   8. unfortunate

  4. obvious   9. true

  5. too bad   10. unlikely

  6. a well-known fact

EXERCISE 8:   A "*that* clause" may follow *be* directly; notice the examples. Complete the sentences with your own ideas by using "*that* clauses."

  (a) He says he is twenty-one, but the truth is ___ that he is only eighteen. ___

  (b) There are two reasons why I do not want to go out tonight. The first

     reason is ___ that I have to study. ___ The second reason is

     ___ that I do not have enough money. ___ *

  1. There are several reasons why I am studying English. One reason is _____

                 that I enjoy learning a new language. _____

---

*Notice: ***That*** is used, not ***because***, to introduce the clause. (***Because*** might occur only in very informal spoken English: *The first reason is because I have to study.*)

Another reason is _____

_____

A third reason is _____

_____

2. I have had three problems since I came here. One problem is that _____

_____

Another problem is that _____

_____

The third problem I have had is that _____

_____

3. One advantage of owning your own car is _____

_____

Another advantage is _____

_____

One disadvantage, however, of owning your own car is _____

_____

EXERCISE 9–WRITTEN: Write paragraphs in which you complete the following with your own ideas. Use "*that* clauses."

1. There are three reasons why I prefer to live (in a dormitory, in an apartment, in a house, at home, with my aunt and uncle, etc.). The first reason is . . . . Another reason is . . . . The third reason why I prefer to live . . . . is . . . .

2. Living (in a city, in a small town, in the suburbs, in the country, on a farm, etc.) offers several advantages. One advantage is . . . . Another advantage is . . . . A third advantage is . . . . There are, however, certain disadvantages. One disadvantage of living . . . . is . . . . Another disadvantage is . . . .

3. If you are living in a foreign country and cannot speak the language of that country, you will face several problems. One problem is . . . . Another problem is . . . . A third problem is . . . .

EXERCISE 10: "*That* clauses" may follow *be + certain adjectives or passive verbs* which express feelings or attitudes. Complete the following with "*that* clauses."

1. I'm sorry (that) I was late for class. _____

2. I'm glad (that) _____

3. I'm disappointed (that) _____

4. I'm pleased (that) _____

5. I'm sure (that) _____

6. I'm surprised (that) _____

7. I'm happy (that) _____

8. I'm worried (that) _____

9. Yesterday I was annoyed (that) _____

10. I'm afraid* (that) _____

EXERCISE 11: A "*that* clause" frequently is used with *the fact*. Complete the following by using *the fact that* with one of the given sentences in parentheses.

> *Example:* (*Ann was late.*)   The fact that Ann was late   didn't surprise me.

(*I'm a little tired.*)
(*Mary didn't come.*)
(*I was supposed to bring my passport to the examination for identification.*)
(*Many people in the world live in intolerable poverty.*)
(*The people of the town were given no warning of the approaching tornado.*)
(*She did not pass the entrance examination.*)

1. The fact that _____ made me angry.

2. Alice was not admitted to the university due to _____

   _____

3. I feel fine except for _____

4. _____ must concern
   all of us.

---

*To be afraid has two possible meanings:

   (1) It can express fear: *I'm afraid of dogs. I'm afraid that his dog will bite me.*

   (2) Colloquially (i.e., in spoken English), it often expresses a meaning similar to *to be sorry; I'm afraid that I can't accept your invitation. I'm afraid you have the wrong number.*

5. Due to _____

_____, there were many casualties.

6. I was not aware of _____

_____. As a result, I was not allowed to take the test.

9-6   QUOTED SPEECH*

Quoted speech refers to reproducing words exactly as they were originally spoken. Quotation marks (") are used.†

QUOTING ONE SENTENCE	
(a) She said, "My brother is a student."	In (a): Use a comma after *she said.* Capitalize the first word of the quoted sentence. Put the final quotation marks outside of the period at the end of the sentence.
(b) "My brother is a student," she said.	In (b): Use a comma, not a period, at the end of the quoted sentence when it precedes *she said.*
(c) "My brother," she said, "is a student."	In (c): If the quoted sentence is divided by *she said,* use a comma after the first part of the quote. Do not capitalize the first word of the second half of the quoted sentence.
QUOTING MORE THAN ONE SENTENCE	
(d) "My brother is a student. He is attending a university," she said.	In (d): Quotation marks are placed at the beginning and end of the complete quote. Notice: There are no quotation marks after *student.*
QUOTING A QUESTION OR AN EXCLAMATION	
(e) She asked, "When will you be here?"	In (e): The question mark is inside the quotation marks.
(f) "When will you be here?" she asked.	In (f): If a question mark is used, no comma is used before *she asked.*
(g) She said, "Watch out!"	In (g): The exclamation point is inside the quotation marks.

---

*Quoted speech is also called *direct speech. Reported speech* (discussed in 9-7) is also called *indirect speech.*

† In British English, quotation marks are called *inverted commas.*

EXERCISE 12:   Add the necessary punctuation and capitalization to the following.

1. Henry said   there is a phone call for you
2. There is a phone call for you   he said.
3. There is   said Henry   a phone call for you *
4. There is a phone call for you   it's your sister   said Henry
5. There is a phone call for you   he said   it's your sister
6. I asked him   where is the phone
7. Where is the phone   she asked

8.   When the policeman came over to my car, he said   give me your driver's license, please

   What's wrong, officer   I asked   was I speeding

   No, you weren't speeding   he replied   you went through a red light at the corner of Fifth Avenue and Main Street   you almost caused an accident

   Did I really do that   I said   I didn't see the red light   †

EXERCISE 13:   Choose two of your classmates to have a brief conversation in front of the class and decide upon a topic for them (what they did last night, what they are doing right now, sports, music, books, etc.). Give them a few minutes to practice their conversation. Then, while they are speaking, take notes so that you can write their conversation. Use quoted speech in your written report. Be sure to start a new paragraph each time the speaker changes.

EXERCISE 14—WRITTEN: Think of an important conversation you have had with a parent, a teacher, a good friend, a brother or sister, etc. Describe the circumstances of that conversation (i.e., where and when it took place) and present the

---

*Notice in sentences 3 and 4: the noun subject (Henry) follows *said*. A noun subject often follows the verb when the subject and verb come in the middle or at the end of a sentence. A pronoun subject almost always precedes the verb.

†Notice: A new paragraph begins each time the speaker changes.

conversation in a written report. (If you cannot think of a memorable conversation, invent a probable exchange.) Use quoted speech. Start a new paragraph each time the speaker changes.

9-7 REPORTED SPEECH AND THE FORMAL SEQUENCE OF TENSES IN NOUN CLAUSES

Reported speech refers to using a noun clause to report what someone has said. No quotation marks are used.

QUOTED SPEECH	REPORTED SPEECH
(a) She said, "I **watch** TV every day."	She said (that) she **watched** TV every day.
(b) She said, "I **am watching** TV."	She said she **was watching** TV.
(c) She said, "I **have watched** TV."	She said she **had watched** TV.
(d) She said, "I **watched** TV."	She said she **had watched** TV.
(e) She said, "I **will watch** TV."	She said she **would watch** TV.
(f) She said, "I **am going to watch** TV."	She said she **was going to watch** TV.
(g) She said, "I **can watch** TV."	She said she **could watch** TV.
(h) She said, "I **may watch** TV."	She said she **might watch** TV.
(i) She said, "I **must watch** TV."	She said she **had to watch** TV.
(j) She said, "I **should watch** TV."	She said she **should watch** TV.
(k) She said, "I **ought to watch** TV."	She said she **ought to watch** TV.
(l) She said, "**Watch** TV."	She **told someone to watch** TV.*
(m) She said, "**Do** you **like** to watch TV?"	She **asked me if** I **liked** to watch TV.

*In reported speech, an imperative sentence is changed to an infinitive. *Tell* is usually used instead of *say*. Also note that *tell* is immediately followed by a (pro)noun object, but *say* is not:

> *He told me (that) he would be late.   He said (that) he would be late.*

> Also possible: *He said to me (that) he would be late.*

GENERAL GUIDELINES ON TENSE USAGE IN A NOUN CLAUSE:

(1) If the main verb of the sentence is in the past (e.g., *said*), the verb in the noun clause will usually also be in a past form.

(2) This formal sequence of tenses in noun clauses is used in both speaking and writing. However, sometimes in spoken English, no change is made in the noun clause verb, especially if the speaker is reporting something *immediately or soon after* it was said.

> Immediate reporting: *A: What did the teacher just say? I didn't hear him.*
>
> *B: He said he **wants** us to read Chapter Six.*
>
> Later reporting: *A: I didn't go to class yesterday. Did Mr. Jones make any assignments?*
>
> *B: Yes. He **said** he **wanted** us to read Chapter Six.*

(3) Also, sometimes the present tense is retained even in formal English when the reported sentence deals with a general truth: *She **said** that Alaska **is** the largest state in the nation.*

EXERCISE 15: Complete the sentences by changing the sentence in quotation marks into a noun clause. Use formal sequence of tenses where appropriate.

1. "I will help you." Bob said <u>(that) he would help me.</u>

2. "Do you need a pen?" Annie asked me <u>if I needed a pen.</u>

3. "Are you hungry?" Sid wanted to know <u>if I was hungry.</u>

4. "What do you want?" Jennifer asked me <u>what I wanted.</u>

5. "I will come to the meeting." Juan promised me _____

6. "I am going to move to Ohio." Bruce informed me _____

7. "What are you talking about?" Dick asked me _____

8. "Did you enjoy your trip?" Connie asked me_____

9. "Have you seen my grammar book?" Nancy wanted to know _____

10. "Can you come to my party?" David asked me _____

11. "Where is Mary?" Sam wanted to know _____

12. "I may be late." Mike told me _____

13. "I don't want to go." Susan said _____

14. "You should study harder." Felix told me _____

15. "I have to go downtown." Barbara said _____

EXERCISE 16: Same as the preceding exercise.

1. "Do you know what time it is?" Fred asked me _____
_____

2. "Someday we will be in contact with beings from outer space." The scientist predicted _____
_____

3. "Does Jim know what he is doing?" I wondered _____
_____

4. "I need to go to the drugstore." Janet suddenly remembered _____
_____

5. "Is there anything I can do to help you?" Sally wanted to know _____
_____

6. "I think I will go to the library   Joe said _____
   to study."

   _____

7. "Have you ever met Ms. Powell?"   Mr. Peterson asked me _____

   _____

8. "Is what I heard true?"   I wondered _____

   _____

9. "What can I do to improve my   Maria wanted to know _____
   pronunciation?"

   _____

10. "I am going to postpone the   Professor Williams announced _____
    examination."

    _____

EXERCISE 17: Change the quoted speech into reported speech, using the pattern shown in the example (*said that . . . and that/said that . . . but that*).

> *Example:* "My father is a businessman. My mother is a teacher."
>
> He *said that* his father was a businessman *and that* his mother was a teacher.

1. "I'm excited about my new job. I've found a nice apartment."

   I got a letter from my sister yesterday. She said _____

   _____

2. "Your Uncle Harry is in the hospital. Your Aunt Sally is very worried about him."

   The last time my mother wrote, she said_____

   _____

3. "I expect you to be in class every day. Unexcused absences may affect your grades."

   Our sociology professor said _____

   _____

4. "Highway 60 will be closed for two months. Commuters should seek alternate routes."

   The mayor of the city said _____

   _____

5. "I'm getting good grades, but I still have difficulty understanding lectures."

My brother is a junior at the state university. In his last letter, he wrote _____

_____

_____

6. "I'll come to the meeting, but I can't stay for more than an hour."

Julia told me _____

_____

7. "Every obstacle is a stepping-stone to success. You should view problems in your life as opportunities to prove yourself."

My father often told me _____

_____

EXERCISE 18—WRITTEN: Think of a letter written in English which you have received recently. In a short paragraph, summarize some of the news or information in this letter. (If you have not received a letter written in English recently, invent one.) Include at least one or two sentences that use the pattern you practiced in the preceding exercise: *said that . . . and that/ said that . . . but that.*

EXERCISE 19—ORAL (BOOKS CLOSED): Begin your response with "He (she) asked me . . . ."

(To the teacher: Suggest to the students that they practice using the formal sequence of tenses.)

Example: Where is your friend?
Response: He (she) asked me where my friend was.

1. What time is it?
2. What is your name?
3. Can you speak Arabic?
4. Have you met my brother?
5. Where are you living?
6. Will you be here tomorrow?
7. What kind of camera do you have?
8. How tall are you?
9. What courses are you taking?
10. Do you feel okay?
11. Have you read any good books lately?
12. How do you like living here?
13. Did you finish your assignment?
14. What are you doing?
15. Whose briefcase is that?
16. May I borrow your dictionary?
17. Where will you be tomorrow around three o'clock?

18. Did you go to class yesterday?
19. What are you going to do over vacation?
20. What is the capital city of your country?
21. Did you go to a party last night?
22. How many people have you met in the last couple of months?
23. Can I use your pen?
24. Where should I meet you after class?
25. Do you understand what I am saying?
26. What country are you from?
27. Is what you said really true?
28. How do you know that it is true?
29. Who do you think will win the game?
30. Is what you want to talk to me about important?

EXERCISE 20–WRITTEN: Complete the following. Use formal sequence of tenses if appropriate.

1. I cannot understand why . . . .
2. One of the students remarked that . . . .
3. I was not sure whose . . . .
4. What . . . surprised me.
5. That she . . . surprised me.
6. One of the students stated that . . . .
7. I could not . . . due to the fact that . . . .
8. What he said was that . . . .
9. No one knows who . . . .
10. My friend convinced me that . . . .
11. The instructor announced that . . . .
12. What I want to know is why . . . .
13. What . . . is not important.
14. We discussed the fact that . . . .
15. I wonder whether . . . .

EXERCISE 21–ORAL:

STUDENT A: Ask a question on the given topic—whatever comes into your mind. Use a question word (*when, how, where, what, why*, etc.).

STUDENT B: Answer the question in a complete sentence.

STUDENT C: Report what Student A and Student B said.

Example: tonight Rosa: What are you going to do tonight?

Ali: I'm going to study.

Yung: Rosa asked Ali what he was going to do tonight, and Ali replied that he was going to study.

1. tonight
2. music
3. courses
4. tomorrow
5. book
6. this city

7. population
8. last year
9. television
10. dinner
11. next year
12. vacation

EXERCISE 22: Give a one-minute impromptu speech. Your classmates will take notes, and then in a short paragraph, or orally, they will report what you said. Choose any topic that comes to mind (pollution, insects, soccer, dogs, etc.) or have your classmates help select a topic.

EXERCISE 23: Break up into small groups and discuss one (or two, or all) of the following topics. At the end of your discussion, make a formal written report of the main points made by each speaker in your group. (Do not attempt to report every word that was spoken.)

In your report, use words such as *think, believe, say, remark*, and *state* to introduce noun clauses. When you use *think* or *believe*, you will probably use present tenses (e.g., *John **thinks** that money **is** the most important thing in life*). When you use *say, remark*, or *state*, you will probably use past tenses (e.g., *Ann **said** that many other things **were** more important than money*).

Do you agree with the given statement? Why or why not?

1. Money is the most important thing in life.
2. A woman can do any job a man can do.
3. When a person decides to get married, his or her love for the other person is the only important consideration.
4. A world government is both desirable and necessary. Countries should simply become the states of one nation, the Earth. In this way, war could be eliminated and wealth could be equally distributed.

EXERCISE 24: You are a newspaper reporter at a press conference. You and your fellow reporters (your classmates) will interview your teacher or a person whom your teacher invites to class. Your assignment is to write a story for the school newspaper. The purpose of your article is to give a professional and personal sketch of the person whom you interview.

Take notes during the interview. It is important to report information accurately. Listen to the answers carefully; write down some of the important sentences so that you can use them for quotations in your article; ask for clarification if you do not understand something the interviewee has said.

When you write the article, try to organize your information into related topics. For example, if you interview your teacher:

    I. General introductory information
   II. Professional life
      A. Present teaching duties
      B. Past teaching experience
      C. Academic duties and activities outside of teaching
      D. Educational background
  III. Personal life
      A. Basic biographical information (e.g., place of birth, family background, places he/she has lived)
      B. Spare-time activities and interests
      C. Travel experiences

The above outline only suggests a possible method of organization. You must organize your own article, depending upon the information you have from the interview and whom you interview.

When you write your report, most of your information will be presented in reported speech; use quoted speech only for the most important or memorable sentences. When you use quoted speech, be sure you are presenting the interviewee's *exact words*. If you are simply paraphrasing what the interviewee said, do not use quotation marks.

EXERCISE 25–ERROR ANALYSIS: All of the following sentences contain errors. These sentences are from student compositions. Test your skill by seeing how many of the errors you can find and correct.

1. Tell the taxi driver where do you want to go.
2. My roommate came into the room and asked me why aren't you in class? I said I am waiting for a telephone call from my family.
3. It was my first day at the university, and I am on my way to my first class. I wondered who else will be in the class. What the teacher would be like?
4. He asked me that what did I intend to do after I graduate?
5. Many of the people in the United States doesn't know much about geography. For example, people will ask you where is Japan located.

6. What does a patient tell a doctor it is confidential.

7. The reason I decided to come here, because this university has a good meteorology department.

8. We looked back to see where are we and how far are we from camp. We don't know, so we decided to turn back. We are afraid that we wander too far.

9. After the accident, I opened my eyes slowly and realize that I am still alive.

10. My country is prospering due to it is a fact that it has become a leading producer of oil.

11. Is true that one must to know english in order to study at an american university.

12. My mother told me what it was the purpose of our visit.

9-8 USING THE SIMPLE FORM OF A VERB IN A NOUN CLAUSE TO STRESS IMPORTANCE

INTRODUCTORY VERB OR EXPRESSION +	SIMPLE FORM OF THE VERB IN THE NOUN CLAUSE	
demand	(a) He **demanded** that we **be** on time.	Certain verbs and expressions require the simple form of a verb in the noun clause that follows. The sentences *stress importance*.
insist	(b) I **insisted** that he **pay** me the money.	
request	(c) He **requested** that he **be told** the news as soon as possible.	
ask	(d) She **asked** that we **be** sure to lock the door behind us.	
suggest	(e) I **suggested** that she **see** a doctor.	*Should* is also used after *suggest* and *recommend*: *I suggested that she should see a doctor.*
recommend	(d) I **recommended** that he **not go** to the concert.	
it is important	(g) **It is important** that you **come** soon.	
it is necessary	(h) **It is necessary** that he **see** a dentist.	
it is essential	(i) **It is essential** that no one **be admitted** to the room without proper identification.	

EXERCISE 26: Complete the following. In many of the sentences, there is more than one possible completion.

1. Mr. Adams insists that we _____ be _____ careful in our writing.

2. They requested that we not _____ after midnight.

3. I recommended that the student _____ to the Dean of Liberal Arts.

4. The policeman demanded that the woman _____ him her driver's license.

5. I suggest that everyone _____ a letter to his/her senator.

6. She suggested that I _____ to another doctor.

7. It is essential that I _____ you tomorrow.

8. It is important that he _____ the director.

9. It is necessary that everyone _____ here on time.

10. She demanded that I _____ her the truth.

EXERCISE 27: Give the correct form of the verb in parentheses. Some of the verbs are passive.

1. Her advisor recommended that she (*take*) _____ five courses.

2. He insisted that the new baby (*name*) _____ after his grandfather.

3. The doctor recommended that she (*stay*) _____ in bed for a few days.

4. The students requested that the test (*postpone*) _____, but the instructor decided against a postponement.

5. I requested that I (*permit*) _____ to change my class.

6. It is essential that pollution (*control*) _____ and eventually (*eliminate*) _____ .

7. It was such a beautiful day that one of the students suggested we (*have*) _____ _____ class outside.

8. The director insisted that everything about his productions (*be*) _____ _____ authentic.

9. She specifically asked that I (*tell, not*) _____ anyone else about it.

10. It is important that you (*be, not*) _____ late.

OTHER VERBS AND EXPRESSIONS USED TO STRESS IMPORTANCE

He *advised* that they not **be told** the bad news.

I *move* that the meeting **be adjourned**.

They *proposed* that a new highway **be built**.

It is advisable that you **be** here on time.

It is desirable that no one else **know** about the problem.
It is imperative that he **return** home immediately.

9-9 USING -*EVER* WORDS

whoever	(a)	**Whoever** wants to come is welcome.
		Anyone who wants to come is welcome.
who(m)ever	(b)	He makes friends easily with **who(m)ever** he meets.
		He makes friends easily with **anyone who(m)** he meets.
whatever	(c)	He always says **whatever** comes into his mind.
		He always says **anything that** comes into his mind.
whichever	(d)	There are four good programs on TV at eight o'clock.
		We can watch **whichever program (whichever one)** you prefer.
		We can watch **any of the four programs that** you prefer.
whenever	(e)	You may leave **whenever** you wish.
		You may leave **at any time that** you wish.
wherever	(f)	She can go **wherever** she wants to go.
		She can go **anyplace that** she wants to go.
however	(g)	The students may dress **however** they please.
		The students may dress **in any way that** they please.

Note: -*ever words* give the idea of "any." Each pair of sentences in the examples has the same
meaning.

EXERCISE 28:   Complete the following by using -*ever words*.

1. He is free to go anyplace he wishes. He can go ____wherever____ he wants.

2. He is free to go anytime he wishes. He can go _____ he wants.

3. I don't know what you should do about that problem. Do _____
seems best to you.

4. There are five flights going to Chicago every day. I don't care which one we

   take. We can take _____ one fits in best with your schedule.

5. I want you to be honest. I hope you feel free to say _____ is on
your mind.

6. _____ leads a life full of love and happiness is rich.

7. No one can tell him what to do. He does _____ he wants.

8. If you want to rearrange the furniture, go ahead. You can rearrange it _____

   _____ you want. I don't care one way or the other.

9. Those children are wild. I feel sorry for _____ has to be their baby-sitter.

10. I have a car. I can take you _____ you want to go.

11. He likes to tell people about his problems. He will talk to _____ will listen to him. But he bores _____ he talks to.

12. I know you're failing all of your courses, but there is nothing I can do about it. It is up to you to do _____ is necessary to improve your grades.

13. I have four. Take _____ one pleases you most.

14. She does _____ she wants to do, goes _____ she wants to go, gets up _____ she wants to get up, makes friends with _____ she meets, and dresses _____ she pleases.

EXERCISE 29: Notice the pattern in the examples and then change the italicized words into sentences that use this pattern.

(a) **What** he told me **to do** was **(to) write** a letter to my embassy.

(b) **What** I want **to do** tomorrow is **(to) stay** home and sleep all day.

(c) **What** I would rather **do** is **go** to a movie.

1. (*I would like to go to the zoo.*)   What I would like to do is (to) go to the zoo.

2. (*She needs to study harder.*)   What _____

3. (*I am planning to start my own business.*)   What _____

4. (*You ought to see a doctor.*)   What _____

5. (*I would rather go on a picnic.*)   What _____

6. (*want*)   A: What are you going to do tonight?

                   B: Well, what I want to do is go to a movie , but I think I'd better study.

7. (*would like*) A: What are you going to do over vacation?

                   B: I don't know yet, but _____

8. (*need*)   A: He's flunking all of his courses.

                   B: I know. _____

9. (*would rather*) A: Are you going to the party tonight?

                   B: I guess so, but _____

10. (*should*)   A: I've asked her to marry me a dozen times, and she's always said no. What am I going to do?

             B: _____

11. (*tell*)   A: Did you follow his advice?

             B: No. _____

12. (*plan*)   A: What are you planning to do after you graduate?

             B: Well, right now _____

               _____, but I haven't made up my mind for certain yet.

13. (*should*)   A: Do you want to come with us tonight? We're going down to the riverfront to listen to some jazz. Then we'll probably stop somewhere for a drink.

             B: That sounds like fun. What _____

               _____, but I think I'll go with you anyway.

EXERCISE 30–PREPOSITIONS: Supply an appropriate preposition for each of the following two-word verbs.

1. A: Guess who I ran _____ today as I was walking across campus.

   B: Who?

   A: Ann Keefe.

   B: You're kidding!

2. A: There will be a test on Chapters Eight and Nine next Friday.

   B: (Groan.) Couldn't you put it _____ until Monday?

3. A: I think that if I learn enough vocabulary I won't have any trouble using English.

   B: That's not necessarily so. I'd like to point _____ that language consists of much more than just vocabulary.

4. A: You'd better put _____ your coat before you leave. It's chilly out.

   B: What's the temperature?

5. A: One billion seconds ago, World War II was being fought. One billion minutes ago, Jesus Christ was living. One billion hours ago, the human race had not yet discovered agriculture.

   B: How did you figure that _____?

A: I didn't. I came _____ that information while I was reading the newspaper.

6. A: I smell something burning in the kitchen. Can I call you _____ in a minute?

   B: Sure. I hope your dinner hasn't burned.

   A: So do I! Bye.

   B: Good-bye.

7. A: Your children certainly love the outdoors.

   B: Yes, they do. We brought them _____ to appreciate nature.

8. A: What forms do I have to fill out to change my tourist visa to a student visa?

   B: I don't know, but I'll look _____ it first thing tomorrow

   and try to find _____ . I'll let you know.

9. A: How long were you in the hospital?

   B: About a week. But I've missed almost two weeks of classes.

   A: It's going to be hard for you to make _____ all the work you've missed, isn't it?

   B: Very.

10. A: Would you mind turning _____ the light?

    B: Not at all.

10

Conjunctions

10-1 PARALLEL STRUCTURE

<table>
<tr>
<td colspan="2">One use of a conjunction is to connect words or phrases that have the same grammatical function in a sentence. This use of conjunctions is called parallel structure. The conjunctions used in this pattern are: and, but, or, nor.*</td>
</tr>
<tr>
<td>
(a) Steve and his friend are coming to dinner.
(b) Susan raised her hand and snapped her fingers.
(c) He is waving his arms and (is) shouting at us.

(d) These shoes are old but comfortable.
(e) He wants to watch TV or (to) listen to some music.
</td>
<td>
In (a): noun + and + noun
In (b): verb + and + verb

In (c): verb + and + verb (The second auxiliary may be omitted if it is the same as the first auxiliary.)
In (d): adjective + but + adjective
In (e): infinitive + or + infinitive (The second to may be omitted.)
</td>
</tr>
<tr>
<td>
(f) Steve, Joe, and Alice are coming to dinner.
(g) Susan raised her hand, snapped her fingers, and asked a question.
(h) The colors in that fabric are red, gold, black, and green.
</td>
<td>
A parallel structure may contain more than two parts. In a series, commas are used to separate each unit. The final comma which precedes the conjunction is optional but is customarily used. (No commas are used if there are only two parts to a parallel structure.)
</td>
</tr>
</table>

*More specifically, **and, but, or, nor** are called *coordinating conjunctions.*

EXERCISE 1: Underline the parallel structure in each sentence and give the pattern that is used, as in the examples.

1. The old man is extremely <u>kind</u> and <u>generous.</u>

   <u>   adjective + and + adjective   </u>

2. He received a pocket <u>calculator</u> and a wool <u>sweater</u> for his birthday.

   <u>   noun   + and +   noun   </u>

3. She spoke angrily and bitterly about the war.

   <u>   + and +   </u>

4. I looked for my book but couldn't find it.

   <u>   + but +   </u>

5. I hope to go to that university and study under Dr. Liu.

   <u>   + and +   </u>

6. In my spare time, I enjoy reading novels or watching television.

   <u>   + or +   </u>

7. He will leave at eight and arrive at nine.

   <u>   + and +   </u>

8. He should have broken his engagement to Beth and married Sue instead.

   <u>   + and +   </u>

EXERCISE 2: Parallel structure makes repeating the same words unnecessary.* Combine the given sentences into one concise sentence which contains parallel structure. Punctuate carefully.

1. Mary opened the door. Mary greeted her guests.

   <u>   Mary opened the door and greeted her guests.   </u>

2. Mary is opening the door. Mary is greeting her guests.

   <u>   </u>

3. Mary will open the door. Mary will close the door.

   <u>   </u>

4. While we were in New York, we attended an opera. While we were in New York, we ate at marvelous restaurants. While we were in New York, we visited some old friends.

   <u>   </u>

   <u>   </u>

---

*This form of parallel structure, in which unnecessary words are omitted but are understood, is termed *ellipsis*.

5. Alice is kind. Alice is generous. Alice is trustworthy.

_____

6. Please try to speak more loudly. Please try to speak more clearly.

_____

7. He gave her flowers on Sunday. He gave her candy on Monday. He gave her a ring on Tuesday.

_____

8. He decided to quit school. He decided to go to California. He decided to find a job.

_____

_____

9. I am looking forward to going to the United States. I am looking forward to beginning my graduate work.

_____

_____

10. I like coffee. I do not like tea.

I like coffee but not tea.*
_____

11. I have met his mother. I have not met his father.

_____

12. He would like to live in Florida. He would not like to live in Alaska.

_____

EXERCISE 3—WRITTEN: Combine the given sentences into one concise sentence which contains parallel structure. Punctuate carefully.

1. The country lane was narrow. The country lane was steep. The country lane was muddy.

_____

*Sometimes a comma precedes **but not;** _I like coffee, but not tea._

2. I should have finished my homework. I should have cleaned up the apartment.

3. I like to become acquainted with the people of other countries. I like to become acquainted with the places of other countries. I like to become acquainted with the customs of other countries.

4. He stared at me for a long time. He never said a word. (*use but*)

5. A calculator makes it easy to figure gas mileage. A calculator makes it easy to figure sales taxes. Or a calculator makes it easy to figure your bank balance.

6. The boy was old enough to work. The boy was old enough to earn some money.

7. He preferred to play baseball. Or he preferred to spend his time in the streets with other lazy boys.

8. I dislike living in a city because of the air pollution. I dislike living in a city because of the crime. I dislike living in a city because of the heavy traffic.

9. We discussed some of the social problems of the United States. We discussed some of the political problems of the United States. We discussed some of the economic problems of the United States.

10. A university education will enable you to increase your knowledge. A university education will enable you to prepare for a profession. A university education will enable you to learn more about yourself.

11. I decided to become a math tutor because I wanted to help others. I decided to become a math tutor because I wanted to give myself the opportunity to review the material. I decided to become a math tutor because I wanted to earn some pocket money.

12. Hawaii has beautiful beaches. Hawaii has many interesting tropical trees. Hawaii has many interesting tropical flowers. Hawaii has nice weather.

10-2   USING PAIRED CONJUNCTIONS: *BOTH . . . AND / NOT ONLY . . . BUT ALSO / EITHER . . . OR / NEITHER . . . NOR**

(a) *Both* my mother *and* my sister **are** here.	Two subjects connected by *both . . . and* take a plural verb.
(b) *Not only* my mother *but also* my sister **is** here.	When two subjects are connected by *not only . . . but also, either . . . or,* or *neither . . . nor,* the subject that is closer to the verb determines whether the verb is singular or plural.
(c) *Not only* my sister *but also* my parents **are** here.	
(d) *Neither* my mother *nor* my sister **is** here.	
(e) *Neither* my sister *nor* my parents **are** here.	
(f) The research project will take *both* time *and* money.	Notice the parallel structure in the examples. The *same* grammatical form should follow each word of the pair.
(g) Yesterday it *not only* rained *but (also)* snowed.	In (f): *both + noun + and + noun*

*Paired conjunctions are also called *correlative conjunctions.*

(h) I'll take *either* chemistry *or* physics next quarter.	In (g): *not only + verb + but also + verb*
(i) That book is *neither* interesting *nor* accurate.	In (h): *either + noun + or + noun*
	In (i): *neither + adjective + nor + adjective*

EXERCISE 4: Supply *is* or *are* in the following.

1. Both the teacher and the student _____ here.

2. Neither the teacher nor the student _____ here.

3. Not only the teacher but also the student _____ here.

4. Not only the teacher but also the students _____ here.

5. Either the students or the teacher _____ planning to come.

6. Either the teacher or the students _____ planning to come.

EXERCISE 5: What is wrong with the following sentences?

1. Either John will call Mary or Bob.

2. Not only Sue saw the mouse but also the cat.

3. Both my mother talked to the teacher and my father.

EXERCISE 6: Combine the following into sentences which contain parallel structure. Use appropriate paired conjunctions: *both . . . and / not only . . . but also / either . . . or / neither . . . nor.*

1. He does not have a pen. He does not have paper. (*He has neither a pen nor paper.*)*

2. Ron enjoys horseback riding. Bob enjoys horseback riding.

3. You can have tea, or you can have coffee.

4. The library does not have the book I need. The bookstore does not have the book I need.

5. Arthur is not in class today. Pam is not in class today.

6. Arthur is absent. Pam is absent.

7. We can fix dinner for them here, or we can take them to a restaurant.

8. She wants to buy a Chevrolet, or she wants to buy a Toyota.

9. The leopard faces extinction. The tiger faces extinction.

10. Mike didn't tell his mother about the trouble he had gotten into. Mike didn't tell his father about the trouble he had gotten into.

---

*If you use *neither . . . nor,* omit *not.* See 10-7 for a discussion of "double negatives".

11. We could fly, or we could take the train.

12. Donald can give you the information, or Carol can give you the information.

13. The President's assistant will not confirm the story. The President's assistant will not deny the story.

14. Small pox is a dangerous disease. Malaria is a dangerous disease.

15. Coal is an irreplaceable natural resource. Oil is an irreplaceable natural resource.

EXERCISE 7–ORAL (BOOKS CLOSED):   Use *both . . . and* in the response.

> *Example:*   John is going to the movie. Is Mary going to the movie?
> *Response:*   Yes, both John and Mary are going to the movie.

1. You have met his father. Have you met his mother?

2. Your brother is living in (name of this city). Is your sister living in (. . .)?

3. She can sing. Can she dance?

4. You are going to visit Los Angeles on your trip. Are you going to visit San Francisco on your trip?

5. Wheat is grown in Kansas. Is corn grown in Kansas?

6. He buys used cars. Does he sell used cars?

7. You had lunch with your friends. Did you have dinner with them?

8. The city suffers from air pollution. Does it suffer from water pollution?

9. Your daughter is in elementary school. Is your son in elementary school?

10. The driver was injured in the accident. Was her passenger injured in the accident?

EXERCISE 8–ORAL (BOOKS CLOSED):   Use *not only . . . but also* in the response.

> *Example:*   I know you are studying math. Are you also studying chemistry?
> *Response:*   Yes, I am studying not only math but also chemistry.

1. I know John attended the party. Did Mary also attend the party?

2. I know he speaks Japanese. Does he speak Chinese too?

3. I know she goes to school. Does she also have a full-time job?

4. I know your country has good universities. Does the United States have good universities too?

5. I know you like classical music. Do you also like popular music?

6. I know his cousin is living with him. Is his mother-in-law living with him too?

7. I know you lost your wallet. Did you also lose your keys?

8. I know you washed the dishes after dinner. Did you also clean up the kitchen?
9. I know he bought a coat. Did he also buy a new pair of shoes?
10. I know the book covers the history of France during the Middle Ages. Does it also cover the history of England during the Middle Ages?

EXERCISE 9—ORAL (BOOKS CLOSED): Use *either . . . or* in the response.

Example: You will ask John, or you will ask Mary.
Response: I will ask either John or Mary.

1. John has your book, or Mary has your book.
2. You are going to major in biology, or you are going to major in chemistry.
3. We will go to New Orleans for our vacation, or we will go to Miami.
4. Your sister will meet you at the airport, or your brother will meet you at the airport.
5. You are going to give your friend a book for her birthday, or you are going to give her a pen.
6. We can go swimming, or we can play tennis.
7. A student can enter the university in September, or a student can enter the university in January.
8. According to the news report, it will snow tonight, or it will rain tonight.
9. You are going to vote for Mr. Smith, or you are going to vote for Mr. Jones.
10. You will rent an apartment, or you will live in the dorm.

EXERCISE 10—ORAL (BOOKS CLOSED): Use *neither . . . nor* in the response.

Example: John won't be here. Will Mary be here?
Response: No, neither John nor Mary will be here.

1. She doesn't eat breakfast. Does she eat lunch?
2. He doesn't drink. Does he smoke?
3. He doesn't like coffee. Does he like tea?
4. Chapter One isn't hard. Is Chapter Two hard?
5. They don't have a refrigerator for their new apartment. Do they have a stove?
6. The students aren't wide awake today. Is the teacher wide awake today?
7. Her husband doesn't speak English. Do her children speak English?
8. She doesn't enjoy hunting. Does she enjoy fishing?
9. Her roommates don't know where she is. Does her brother know where she is?
10. The result wasn't good. Was the result bad?

10-3 COMBINING INDEPENDENT CLAUSES WITH CONJUNCTIONS

(a) It was raining hard. There was a strong wind.	Example (a) contains two independent clauses (i.e., two complete sentences). Notice the punctuation. A period,* *not a comma,* is used to separate two independent clauses.
(b) It was raining **hard, and** there was a strong wind. (c) It was raining **hard and** there was a strong wind. (d) It was raining **hard. And** there was a strong wind.	A conjunction may be used to connect two independent clauses. *Punctuation:* In (b): Usually a comma immediately precedes the conjunction. In (c): Sometimes in short sentences the comma is omitted. In (d): Sometimes in informal writing a conjunction may begin a sentence.
(e) He was tired, **so** he went to bed. (f) The child hid behind his mother's skirt, **for** he was afraid of the dog. (g) He did not study, **yet** he passed the exam.	In addition to *and, but, or,* and *nor,* three other conjunctions are used to connect two independent clauses: *so* (meaning *therefore, as a result*) *for* (meaning *because*) *yet* (meaning *but, nevertheless*) A comma almost always precedes *so, for,* and *yet* when they are used as conjunctions.†

*In British English, *a period* is called *a full stop.*

†*So, for,* and *yet* have other meanings in other structures: e.g., *He is not so tall as his brother.* (*so = as*) *We waited for the bus.* (*for* = a preposition) *She hasn't arrived yet.* (*yet* = an adverb meaning *up to this time*)

EXERCISE 11: Punctuate the following sentences by adding commas or periods. Capitalize letters where necessary.

1. The boys walked the girls ran.

   The boys walked. The girls ran.

2. The teacher lectured the students took notes.
3. The teacher lectured and the students took notes.
4. Jessica came to the meeting but Ron stayed home.
5. Jessica came to the meeting her brother stayed home.
6. Her academic record was outstanding yet she was not accepted by the university.
7. I have not finished writing my term paper yet I will not be finished until sometime next week.
8. We had to go to the grocery store for some milk and bread.

9. We had to go to the grocery store for there was nothing in the house to fix for dinner.

10. Frank did not have enough money to buy an airplane ticket so he borrowed fifty dollars from his uncle.

EXERCISE 12:   Same as the preceding exercise.

1. A thermometer is used to measure temperature a barometer measures air pressure.

2. The king made many promises but he had no intention of keeping them.

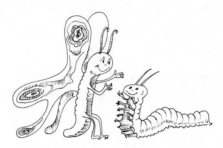

3. The butterfly is a marvel it begins as an ugly caterpillar and turns into a work of art.

4. I always enjoyed studying mathematics in high school so I decided to major in it in college.

5. Both John and I had many errands to do yesterday John had to go to the post office and the bookstore I had to go to the drugstore the travel agency and the bank.

6. Anna is in serious legal trouble for she had no car insurance at the time of the accident.

7. Last night Martha had to study for a test so she went to the library.

8. I did not like the leading actor yet the movie was quite good on the whole.

9. The team of researchers has not finished compiling the statistics yet their work will not be made public until later.

10. The ancient Egyptians had good dentists archaeologists have found mummies that had gold fillings in their teeth.

11. We have nothing to fear for our country is strong and united.

12. He slapped his desk in disgust he had failed another examination and had ruined his chances for a passing grade in the course.

13. I struggled to keep my head above water I tried to yell for help but no sound came from my mouth.

14. The earthquake was devastating tall buildings crumbled and fell to the earth.

15. It was a wonderful picnic the children waded in the stream collected rocks and insects and flew kites the teenagers played an enthusiastic game of baseball the adults busied themselves preparing the food supervising the children and playing a game or two of volleyball.

EXERCISE 13—WRITTEN: Write a paragraph on one of the following topics.

TOPICS: 1. Give a physical description of your place of residence (apartment, dormitory room, etc.).

2. Describe the characteristics and activities of a successful student.

3. Give your reader directions for making a particular dish.

After you have finished the first draft of your paragraph, reread it and look for sentences that can be "tightened up" (made more concise). Do you see any places where two or three sentences could be combined into one by effective use of parallel structure? Also, when you are making your revision, pay special attention to punctuation. Are all of your commas and periods used correctly? After you have finished making your revisions, rewrite the paragraph on another piece of paper.

Example:

First draft: To make spaghetti sauce, you will need several ingredients. First, you will need some ground beef. One pound of ground beef is enough. You should also have an onion. If the onions are small, use two. Also find a green pepper. And of course you need some tomato sauce or tomatoes.

Revision: The ingredients you will need to make spaghetti sauce are one pound of ground beef, one large or two small onions, a green pepper, and some tomato sauce or tomatoes.

(*Note:*   "Tightening up" and "effective use of parallel structure" do *not* mean combining a series of short sentences with *and.* Example of a wordy, stringy sentence: *You will need one pound of ground beef, and you will also need an onion, and of course you need some tomato sauce or tomatoes.*)

EXERCISE 14—PRETEST: Complete the following with an appropriate verb form.

1. Bob studies hard, and so _____ do _____ I.

2. Bob studies hard, and so _____ Sandra.

3. Bob studied hard, and so _____ Tom.

4. Kathy will study, and so _____ Jim.

5. Jack should study, and so _____ you.

6. Pam is studying, and so _____ Mary and Tom.

7. Pam is studying, and so _____ I.

8. Linda has studied, and so _____ Fred.

9. Fred has been studying hard, and so _____ Alex and Alice.

10. Barb and Lynn are at home, and so _____ Bill.

11. The students were pleased, and so _____ the teacher.

12. I had a good time at the party, and so _____ Larry.*

13. Amelia has her book with her, and so _____ Perry.

14. Jason has finished his work, and so _____ Angela.

10-4 REPEATING THE SAME IDEA: USING *AND* + *SO/TOO/NEITHER/EITHER*

(a) John likes milk, *and so does Mary.* (b) John likes milk, *and Mary does too.* (c) John doesn't like milk, *and neither does Mary.* (d) John doesn't like milk, *and Mary doesn't either.*	(a) and (b) have the same meaning: *Both John and Mary like milk.* (c) and (d) have the same meaning: *Neither John nor Mary likes milk.* Notice: After *so* and *neither,* the verb precedes the subject. Notice: An affirmative verb is used with *neither.* A negative verb is used with *either.*

EXERCISE 15: Complete the following by using *so/too* or *neither/either.* Give both possible forms.

1. Barb wants to come, and _____ so does Steve. _____ (*Steve*)

    and _____ Steve does too. _____

2. Barb doesn't want to come, and _____ neither does Steve. _____ (*Steve*)

    and _____ Steve doesn't either. _____

---

*In American English, a form of *do* is usually used as an auxiliary verb when the main verb is *have.*

3. Martha isn't in her room, and _____ (*her roommate*)

      and _____

4. I'd like to go to the art museum, and _____ (*Sid*)

      and _____

5. Henry didn't go to class, and _____ (*I*)

      and _____

6. I won't be there, and _____ (*my brother*)

      and _____

7. Jackie wants to go to Arizona, and _____ (*I*)

      and _____

8. Mark never came, and _____ (*Sally*)

      and _____

9. I have a test today, and _____ (*Marcia*)

      and _____

10. I have seen that movie, and _____ (*Marcia*)

      and _____

11. I had to study last night, and _____ (*she*)

      and _____

12. Ann used to live here, and _____ (*Jack*)

      and _____

13. I couldn't understand the lecture, and _____ (*Sue*)

      and _____

EXERCISE 16: Use *so* or *neither.* Use "I."* (Do not use *and; and* is not used when there are two speakers.)

1. A: I didn't eat breakfast this morning.

    B: _____ Neither did I. _____

---

*Sometimes in informal speaking, "me too" is used instead of *so am I, I did too,* etc.; and "me neither" is used instead of *I don't either, neither will I,* etc. "Me too" and "me neither" are not considered grammatically correct.

2. A: I'm hungry.

    B: _____ So am I. _____

3. A: I couldn't hear her.

    B: _____.

4. A: I'd like some iced tea.

    B: _____.

5. A: I have a lot of homework to do tonight.

    B: _____.

6. A: I've never met him.

    B: _____.

7. A: I can't understand why Bob said that.

    B: _____.

8. A: It's late. I should leave soon.

    B: _____.

EXERCISE 17—ORAL (BOOKS CLOSED): Agree with the statement. Use *so* or *neither.*

Example: I'm hungry.
Response: So am I.

Example: I'm not hungry.
Response: Neither am I.

1. I'm going to study tonight.
2. I missed class last Thursday.
3. I didn't do the homework.
4. I've never been in (Mexico).
5. I'm tired.
6. I don't want to go to class today.
7. I'd rather go to the park.
8. I don't have a car.
9. I walk to school every day.
10. I'd like a cup of coffee.
11. I like fresh fruit.
12. I don't watch TV very much.
13. I couldn't understand what he said.
14. I've never visited (New York).
15. I should go to the library tonight.
16. I always have tea with my meals.
17. I don't have to go to class this afternoon.
18. I went shopping yesterday.
19. I have a test tomorrow.
20. I used to live in a small town.
21. I have to get a driver's license.
22. I've never taken a course in physics.
23. I prefer living in a big city.
24. I'd rather live in the country.
25. I don't know what that word means.
26. I'm taking chemistry this semester.
27. I couldn't help laughing at his joke.
28. I'm staying here over vacation.

29. I need to renew my visa.
30. I've already seen that movie.
31. I don't want to see it again.
32. I'd rather stay home tonight.
33. I can't speak (Chinese).
34. But I can speak English.

35. I won't be here on Saturday.
36. I enjoy studying grammar.
37. I'll be here tomorrow.
38. I had a good time at the party.
39. I've already eaten (lunch).
40. I've never met (. . .)'s husband/wife.

41. (. . .) is sitting in the front row. (*Response:* So is (. . .).)
42. (. . .) is sitting in the back row.
43. (. . .) has a mustache/beard.
44. (. . .) never sits in the front row.
45. (. . .) always seems to be happy and cheerful.
46. (. . .) is from (name of country).
47. (. . .) doesn't speak (Arabic).
48. (. . .) has curly hair.
49. (. . .) is married.
50. (. . .) isn't married.
51. (. . .) has long hair.
52. (. . .) speaks English very well.
53. (. . .) is wearing (blue jeans/a sweater/a blue shirt).
54. (. . .) is sitting near (the windows, the door).
55. (. . .) carries a briefcase to class.

10-5 CONVERSATIONAL RESPONSES USING *SO*

(1) RESPONSE TO A YES/NO QUESTION		
QUESTION	RESPONSE	
Does John live in the dorm?	(a) **I think so.** **I believe so.**	In (a): *I think so* means *I think that John lives in the dorm* (*but I am not 100 percent sure*).
Is he married?	(b) **I don't think so.** **I don't believe so.**	
Did you pass the test?	(c) **I hope so.**	
(2) RESPONSE TO A STATEMENT OF OPINION		
STATEMENT	RESPONSE	
This food is delicious.	(d) **I think so too.**	The meaning in (d) and (e): *I agree with you.*
This food isn't very good.	(e) **I don't think so either.**	

STATEMENT	RESPONSE	
I think this food is delicious.	(f) **So do I.** **I do too.** **I think so too.**	In (f): Notice that if the statement begins with "I think," there are three possible responses of agreement using *so* or *too*.
I think this food is delicious.	(g) **Oh?** **Really?** **You do?**	The responses in (g) may indicate disagreement or surprise.

EXERCISE 18: Complete the dialogues by adding *so* or *so too* or *so either*.

1. A: Ms. Kelly is a good teacher.
   B: I think _____ so too _____.

2. A: Is Frank at the library?
   B: I think _____.

3. A: He can't sing very well.
   B: I don't think _____.

4. A: Is today the twentieth?
   B: I think _____.

5. A: The weather has been terrible lately.
   B: I think _____.

6. A: Is it supposed to rain today?
   B: I don't think _____.

7. A: I think that book is very well written.
   B: I think _____.

8. A: Will you be home in time for dinner?
   B: I think _____, but the meeting might run late.

9. A: I think Tom is wrong.
   B: I think _____.

10. A: Why did she turn on the air-conditioner? I don't think it's hot in here.
    B: I don't think _____.

EXERCISE 19—ORAL (BOOKS CLOSED): Give possible responses to the given statement in which you (1) agree and (2) disagree, as in the example.

Example: I think (a particular TV show) is very good.

Agree: So do I.
I do too.
I think so too.
I agree.

Disagree: Oh? Why?
You do? Hmmm.
Really? I don't think so.
I'm not sure I agree with you.

1. I think teachers should give tests every day.
2. I think baseball requires more skill than soccer.

3. I think it is possible to judge a person by what he or she wears.

4. I think husbands and wives should share housework.

5. I think all health care should be free.

SOME NOTES ON USING NEGATIVES FOLLOW:

10–6 *NOT* VERSUS *NO*

(a) **I don't have any** money.	*Not* is used to make a verb negative, as in (a): *do not have.*
(b) I have **no money.**	*No* is used as an adjective in front of a noun, as in (b): *no money.*

EXERCISE 20: Change the following into the negative in two ways: use *not . . . any* in one sentence and *no* in the other.

1. I have some problems.   I don't have any problems.

                                        I have no problems.

2. There was some food.   _____

      _____

3. The children made some noise.   _____

      _____

4. I need some help.   _____

      _____

5. We have some time to waste.   _____

      _____

6. There is a way to do it.   _____

      _____

7. I received some letters from home.   _____

      _____

8. I will give you some money.   _____

      _____

9. I trust someone.   I don't trust anyone.

                                    I trust no one.

10. I saw someone. _____

_____

11. There was someone in his room. _____

_____

12. She can find somebody who _____
knows about it.

10-7   AVOIDING "DOUBLE NEGATIVES"

> *One clause* should generally contain only *one negative*. A "double negative" means that the speaker or writer has made a confusing and grammatically incorrect sentence by using two negatives in the same clause.*
>
> Example of a "double negative": *I don't have no money.*   (Does that mean the speaker has *some* money???)

*Note: Negatives in two different clauses in the same sentence cause no problems:
   A person who doesn't have love can't be truly happy.   I don't know why he isn't here.

EXERCISE 21: Correct the following sentences, all of which contain double negatives.

1. I don't need no help.
2. I didn't see nobody.
3. I can't never understand him.
4. He doesn't like neither coffee nor tea.
5. I didn't do nothing.
6. I can't hardly hear the radio. Would you please turn it up?

10-8   BEGINNING A SENTENCE WITH A NEGATIVE WORD*

(a) **Never will I do** that again.
(b) **Rarely have I eaten** better food.
(c) **Hardly ever does he come** to class on time.
	When a negative word begins a sentence, the subject and verb are inverted (i.e., question word order is used).
	The negative words used in this pattern are:
	   never *hardly (ever)*†
	   rarely *scarcely (ever)*
	   seldom *barely (ever)*

*Beginning a sentence with a negative word is relatively uncommon in everyday usage, but is used when the speaker/writer wishes to emphasize the negative element of the sentence.
†*Hardly ever, scarcely ever,* and *barely ever* mean *almost never.*

(d) I can't come today, **nor can I come** tomorrow.	Subjects and verbs are inverted after *nor*, and *and neither*.
(e) The governor does not support the legislation, **and neither does the senator** (**support** the legislation).	

EXERCISE 22: Change each sentence so that it begins with a negative word.

1. I have never known Pat to be dishonest.

    Never have I known Pat to be dishonest.

2. I seldom sleep past seven o'clock.

3. I hardly ever agree with her.

4. I will never forget the wonderful people I have met here.

5. He has never turned his assignments in on time.

6. The mail scarcely ever arrives before noon.

7. We rarely go to movies.

EXERCISE 23—ERROR ANALYSIS: Each of the following sentences contains at least one error. Test your skill by finding and correcting as many of these errors as possible.

1. When I refused to help her, she became very angry and shout at me.
2. My home offers me a feeling of security, warm, and love.
3. The whole place was deserted, you couldn't see nothing but sand.
4. I admire him because of his kindness and patience, and he is gentle.
5. He likes to come up behind me and tickles me.
6. Because I had to sit in the back row of the auditorium, I could not hardly hear the speaker.
7. She asked me a question, but I couldn't say nothing, I just stood there with my mouth open.
8. As a child, he labored with his father to clear away the forest and planting crops.
9. By obeying the speed limit, we can save energy, lives, and it costs us less.
10. In my spare time, I enjoy taking care of my aquarium and to work on my stamp collection.

EXERCISE 24—PREPOSITIONS: Supply an appropriate preposition for each of the following.

1. Do you believe _____ ghosts?

2. Anthony is engaged _____ my cousin.

3. Ms. Ballas substituted _____ our regular teacher yesterday.

4. I can't distinguish one twin _____ the other.

5. Did you forgive him _____ lying to you?

6. Children rely _____ their parents for food and shelter.

7. He wore sunglasses to protect his eyes _____ the sun.

8. Chris excels _____ sports.

9. Andrea contributed her ideas _____ the discussion.

10. I hope you succeed _____ your new job.

11. I'm very fond _____ their children.

12. The firemen rescued many people _____ the burning building.

13. I don't care _____ spaghetti. I'd rather eat something else.

14. He doesn't seem to care _____ his bad grades.

15. Sometimes Bobby seems to be jealous _____ his brother.

EXERCISE 25—PREPOSITIONS: Supply an appropriate preposition for each of the following two-word verbs.

1. A: Who do you take _____ the most, your father or your mother?

    B: My mother, I think. I can see many similarities between the two of us.

2. A: Hey, cut it _____ , you guys! I'm trying to sleep.

    B: What's the matter? Are we making too much noise?

3. A: Could I help you clean _____ ?

    B: Sure. Would you mind taking _____ the garbage?

4. A: Miss Ward, what seems to be the problem?

    B: Well, Doctor, for the last two days I haven't been able to keep any food down. Everytime I try to eat something, I throw _____ soon afterwards.

5. A: Where's my jacket?

   B: I hung it _____ in the closet.

6. A: Why are you going to see Professor Kelly?

   B: He called me _____ to talk about my research project.

7. A: Is that man's story true?

   B: Yes. A newspaper reporter checked _____ his story and found that it was true.

8. A: The city government is planning to redevelop a large section of the inner city.

   B: What's going to happen to the buildings that are there now?

   A: They are going to be torn _____ .

9. A: Some people tried to crash our party last night.

   B: What did you do?

   A: We kicked them _____ .

10. A: The test is about to begin. Please put _____ all of your books and notebooks.

Adverb Clauses and Related Structures—1: Time and Cause and Effect

11-1 INTRODUCTION

(a) **When we were in New York,** we saw several plays. (b) We saw several plays **when we were in New York.**	*When we were in New York* is an adverb clause. It is a dependent clause. It cannot stand alone as a sentence. It must be connected to an independent clause. *Punctuation:* When an adverb clause precedes an independent clause, as in (a), a comma is used to separate the clauses. When the adverb clause follows, as in (b), usually no comma is used.
(c) **Because he was sleepy,** he went to bed. (d) He went to bed **because he was sleepy.**	Like *when, because* introduces an adverb clause. *Because he was sleepy* is an adverb clause.

SUMMARY LIST OF WORDS USED TO INTRODUCE ADVERB CLAUSES*

TIME	CAUSE AND EFFECT	OPPOSITION	CONDITION
after	*because*	*even though*	*if*
before	*since*	*although*	*unless*
when	*now that*	*though*	*only if*
while	*as*		*whether or not*
as	*as/so long as*	*whereas*	*even if*
by the time (*that*)	*inasmuch as*	*while*	*providing* (*that*)
whenever			*provided* (*that*)
since			*in case* (*that*)
until	*so* (*that*)		*in the event* (*that*)
as soon as	*in order that*		
once			
as/so long as			

*Words that introduce adverb clauses are called *subordinating conjunctions*.

11-2 USING ADVERB CLAUSES TO SHOW TIME RELATIONSHIPS

after	(a) **After she (had) graduated**, she got a job. (b) **After she graduates**, she will get a job.	A present tense, *not* a future tense, is used in an adverb clause of time. Notice examples (b) and (d). (See 3–19 for tense usage in future time clauses.)
before	(c) I (had) left **before he came**. (d) I will leave **before he comes**.	
when	(e) **When I arrived**, he was talking on the phone. (f) **When I got there**, he had already left. (g) **When it began to rain**, I stood under a tree. (h) **When I was in Chicago**, I visited the museums. (i) **When I see him tomorrow**, I will ask him to come.	*when* = *at that time* (Notice the different time relation-ships expressed by the tenses.)
while *as*	(j) **While I was walking home**, it began to rain. (k) **As I was walking home**, it began to rain.	*while*, *as* = *during that time*
by the time (*that*)	(l) **By the time he arrived**, we had already left. (m) **By the time he arrives**, we will already have left.	*by the time* = *one event is com-pleted before another event*
whenever	(n) I use my umbrella **whenever it rains**.	*whenever* = *every time when*
since	(o) I haven't seen him **since he left this morning**.	*since* = *from that time to the present* (Use the present perfect tense with *since*.)
until *till*	(p) We stayed there **until we finished our work**. (q) We stayed there **till we finished our work**.	*until*, *till* = *to that time and then no longer* (Usually *till* is used in speaking rather than writing.)

as soon as once	(r) **As soon as it stops raining**, we will leave. (s) **Once it stops raining**, we will leave.	*as soon as, once = when one event happens, another event happens soon afterwards*
as long as so long as	(t) I will never speak to him again **as long as I live**. (u) I will never speak to him again **so long as I live**.	*as long as, so long as = during all that time, from beginning to end.*

EXERCISE 1: Complete the following. Pay special attention to verb tenses.

1. Last night I went to bed after I _____ my homework.

2. Tonight I will go to bed after I _____ my homework.

3. Ever since I was a child, I _____ afraid of dogs.

4. Jane's contact lens popped out while she _____ basketball.

5. Be sure to reread your composition for errors before you _____

   _____ it in to the teacher tomorrow.

6. By the time I left my apartment this morning, the mailman _____

   _____ the mail.

7. I have known Jim Bates since he _____ ten years old.

8. A black cat ran across the road as I _____ my car to school this morning.

9. By the time I leave this city, I _____ here for four months.

10. Whenever Mark _____ angry, his nose gets red.

11. I _____ to the beach whenever the weather was nice, but now I don't have time to do that because I have to study.

12. We will have a big party when _____ .

EXERCISE 2:   Make sentences with *until* from the given situations.

1. I can't pay my bills. I haven't gotten my paycheck yet.

   _____ I can't pay my bills _____ until ____ my paycheck comes. ____

2. We can't leave yet. We have to wait for Nancy.

   _____ until _____.

3. Tell me the truth, or I am not going to leave this room.

   _____ until _____.

4. Finally, Donald arrived. Before that, it had been a dull party.

   _____ until _____.

5. Dinner won't be ready for a while. I think we should just sit here by the fire.

   Let's _____ until _____.

6. When I go to bed at night, I like to read. After a while, I get sleepy.

   _____ until _____.

EXERCISE 3:   Combine the ideas by using either *as soon as* or *once*. (*As soon as* and *once* basically have the same meaning, but *as soon as* is more immediate. Often, *just* is used with *as soon as* to emphasize the idea of "immediately": *I'll call him just as soon as I get home.*)

1. The taxi will get here in five minutes or so. Then we can leave for the airport.

   _____ As soon as the taxi gets here, we can leave for the airport. _____

2. The rice will be done in about ten minutes. Immediately after that, we can eat.

   _____

3. First, I have to graduate. Then I can return home.

   _____

4. Spring will come and the weather will be nice again. Then we can start playing tennis every morning before class.

   _____

5. My roommate walked into the room. Immediately, I knew that something was wrong.

   _____

6. Your English will get better. Then you will begin to feel more comfortable living in the United States.

   _____

7. Immediately after the singer finished her song, the audience burst into applause.

_____

8. I'm watching a baseball game on TV, but it will be over in a few minutes. Then I'll take out the garbage.

_____

EXERCISE 4: Using the given information, make a sentence in which you use *just after, just before,* or *just as.* Notice that *just* adds the idea of "immediately."

1. I got to the airport at 8:15. My plane left ten minutes later.

               I got to the airport just before my plane left. _____

2. You shouldn't eat a heavy meal and then go to bed immediately afterwards.

_____

3. I went to bed at 11:00. The phone rang at 11:05.

_____

4. We were sitting down to eat. At that moment, someone knocked on the door.

_____

5. I was getting on the bus. At that moment, I remembered that I had left my briefcase at home.

_____

6. I got up to give my speech. Immediately before that, I got butterflies in my stomach.

_____

7. The guests will come at 7:00. At 6:55, I'll light the candles.

_____

8. I was bending over to pick up my pencil. My pants split.

_____

EXERCISE 5–WRITTEN: Complete the following. Punctuate carefully. Pay special attention to verb tense usage.

1. Since I came to . . . .
2. Just as I was falling asleep last night . . .
3. I'll help you with your homework as soon as . . . .
4. I was late. By the time I got to the airport . . . .
5. After I finish writing this exercise . . . .

6. One of my friends gets nervous whenever . . . .
7. I will be here until I . . . .
8. As long as I live . . . .
9. I heard . . . while I . . . .
10. Once summer/winter comes . . . .
11. Just before I . . . .
12. I have been in . . . for . . . . By the time I leave, I . . . .

11-3 USING ADVERB CLAUSES TO SHOW CAUSE AND EFFECT RELATIONSHIPS

because	(a) **Because he was sleepy,** he went to bed. (b) He went to bed **because he was sleepy.**	An adverb clause may precede or follow the independent clause. Notice the punctuation in (a) and (b).
since	(c) **Since he's not interested in classical music,** he decided not to go to the concert.	In (c): *since* means *because.*
now that	(d) **Now that the semester is finished,** I'm going to rest a few days and then take a trip.	In (d): *now that* means *because now.* *Now that* is used for present and future situations.
as	(e) **As she had nothing in particular to do,** she called up a friend and asked her if she wanted to take in a movie.	In (e): *as* means *because.*
as/so long as	(f) **As long as (So long as) you're not busy,** could you help me with this work?	In (f): *as long as* means *because.*
inasmuch as	(g) **Inasmuch as the two government leaders could not reach an agreement,** the possibilities for peace are still remote.	In (g): *inasmuch as* means *because.* *Inasmuch as* is usually found only in formal writing and speech.

EXERCISE 6:   Using the given information, make sentences using *now that.*

1. Peggy used to take the bus to school, but last week she bought a car. Now she can drive to school.

    _____Now that Peggy has a car, she can drive to school._____

2. You just had your sixteenth birthday. Now you can get a driver's license.

    _____Now that you are_____

3. We have to wear warm clothes. It's winter now.

    _____

4. Bob used to live in the dorm, but a couple of weeks ago he moved into an apartment. Now he can cook his own food.

_____

5. John used to be overweight, but recently he has lost twenty pounds. He looks better and he feels better.

_____

6. I can get a job as a bilingual secretary. I know English now.

_____

7. My brother got married last month. He's a married man now, so he has more responsibilities.

_____

8. Do you want to go for a walk? The rain has stopped.

_____

9. It's been a long, hard week, but final exams are finally over. We can relax.

_____

10. The civil war has ended. A new government is being formed.

_____

EXERCISE 7:   Complete the following.

1. As long as it's such a nice day, why don't _____

2. As long as the movie is free, let's _____

3. As long as it's raining, I think I'll _____

4. As long as the coffee is already made, I guess I'll _____

5. As long as you're here, why don't _____

6. As long as you're up, would you mind _____

EXERCISE 8:   Combine the given ideas by using *since*. Also, decide which sentences might be found in somewhat formal writing and use *inasmuch as*.

1. Monday is Bob's birthday. Let's give him a party.

_____

2. Monday is a national holiday. All government offices will be closed.

_____

3. The guys I live with don't know any Arabic. I have to speak English with them.

_____

4. Oil is an irreplaceable natural resource. We must do whatever we can in order to conserve it.

_____

5. Mary, maybe you could help me with this calculus problem. You're a math major.

_____

6. Many young people move to the cities in search of employment. There are few jobs available in the rural areas.

_____

EXERCISE 9–WRITTEN: Complete the following. Punctuate carefully.

1. Now that I . . . .
2. The teacher didn't . . . because . . . .
3. Since heavy fog is predicted for tonight . . . .
4. He was not admitted to the university inasmuch as . . . .
5. Jack can't stay out all night with his friends now that . . . .
6. Since we don't have class tomorrow . . . .
7. Inasmuch as her application arrived after the deadline . . . .

PART II Other Ways of Showing Cause and Effect Relationships

11-4 USING *SUCH . . . THAT* AND *SO . . . THAT*

(a) **Because the weather was nice,** we went to the zoo. (b) It was **such nice weather that** we went to the zoo. (c) The weather was **so nice that** we went to the zoo.	Examples (a), (b), and (c) have the same meaning.
(d) It was **such good coffee that** I had another cup. (e) It was **such a foggy day that** we couldn't see the road.	*Such . . . that* encloses a modified noun: *such + adjective + noun + that*

(f) The coffee is **so hot that** I can't drink it.
 (g) I'm **so hungry that** I could eat a horse.
	So . . . that encloses an adjective or adverb:
	
	          adjective
	 so + or *+ that*
	          adverb

(h) She speaks **so fast that** I can't understand her. (i) He walked **so quickly that** I couldn't keep up with him.	
(j) She made **so many mistakes that** she failed the exam. (k) He has **so few friends that** he is always lonely. (l) She has **so much money that** she can buy whatever she wants. (m) He had **so little trouble** with the test **that** he left twenty minutes early.	*So . . . that* is used with *many, few, much,* and *little*.
(n) It was **such a good book (that)** I couldn't put it down. (o) I was **so hungry (that)** I didn't wait for dinner to eat something.	Sometimes, primarily in speaking, *that* is omitted.

EXERCISE 10: Combine the following sentences by using *so . . . that* or *such . . . that*.

> *Example:* This is a boring book. I don't think I'll finish it.
>
> This is *such a boring book that* I don't think I'll finish it.

1. This tea is good. I think I'll have another cup.
2. This is good tea. I think I'll have another cup.
3. The weather was hot. You could fry an egg on the sidewalk.
4. I don't feel like going to class. We are having beautiful weather.
5. I couldn't understand him. He talked too fast.
6. She is a kind person. Everyone loves and respects her.

7. I have gained too much weight. I can't wear any of my old clothes.

8. I've met too many people in the last few days. I can't possibly remember all of their names.

9. It took us only ten minutes to get here. There was little traffic.

10. I always eat more than I should. The food my mother cooks is delicious.

EXERCISE 11: Same as the preceding exercise.

1. The classroom has comfortable chairs. The students find it easy to fall asleep.

2. Ted couldn't get to sleep last night. He was worried about the exam.

3. Jerry got angry. He put his fist through the wall.

4. I have many problems. I can use all the help you can give me.

5. The tornado struck with great force. It lifted automobiles off the ground.

6. During the summer, we had hot and humid weather. It was uncomfortable just sitting in a chair doing nothing.

7. I can't figure out what this sentence says. His handwriting is illegible.

8. David has too many girlfriends. He can't remember all of their names.

9. Too many people came to the meeting. There were not enough seats for everyone.

10. In some countries, few students are accepted by the universities. As a result, admission is virtually a guarantee of a good job upon graduation.

EXERCISE 12—ORAL (BOOKS CLOSED): Use *so . . . that* or *such . . . that*.

Example: You are sleepy.
Response: I am so sleepy that . . . (I could fall asleep in five minutes).

Example: "Book" is a common word.
Response: "Book" is such a common word that . . . (everyone knows what it means).

1. The weather is hot/cold/nice today.

2. Mary is a good student.

3. John speaks too softly.

4. You are tired.

5. On your way to class this morning/afternoon/evening, the traffic was heavy.

6. The teacher in one of your classes speaks too fast.

7. Your instructor assigned too much homework.

8. You and your husband/wife have a baby. The baby had a high temperature last night.

9. You took a test last week. It was an easy test.

10. You were home alone last night. You heard a noise. You were frightened.

11. You went to a movie last night. It was a good movie.

12. Your roommate makes too much noise at night.

13. Yesterday, there were too many students absent due to the flu.

14. You waited too long to mail your application to the university.

15. Think of a time you were nervous. How nervous were you?

16. Think of a time you were angry. How angry were you?

17. Think of a time you were happy. How happy were you?

18. Think of a time you were exhausted. How exhausted were you?

19. Think of a time you were surprised. How surprised were you?

20. Think of a time you were unhappy/embarrassed/glad/disappointed/sick.

EXERCISE 13:   Complete the following.

1. This box is so heavy _____ that I can't lift it. _____

2. This box is too heavy _____ (for me) to lift.* _____

3. That car is too expensive _____

4. That car is so expensive _____

5. The coffee was too hot _____

6. The coffee was so hot _____

7. It is so dark in here _____

8. It is too dark in here _____

11-5 USING *IN ORDER TO*

(a) He came here because he wanted to study English. (b) He came here **(in order) to study** English.	(*In order*) *to* is used to express *purpose*. It answers the question "Why?" Sentences (a) and (b) have essentially the same meaning.
(c) *Incorrect:* He came here for studying English. (d) *Incorrect:* He came here for to study English.	To express *purpose*, use (*in order*) *to*, not *for*, with a verb.
(e) I went to the store **for some bread.** (f) I went to the store **to buy some bread.**	*For* is sometimes used to express *purpose*, but it is a preposition and is followed by a noun object, as in (e).

---

*Reminder: *So . . . that* is followed by a clause. (See 11-4.) *Too* is followed by an infinitive. (See 7-9.)

EXERCISE 14—ORAL (BOOKS CLOSED): Answer the question. Use (*in order*) *to.*

To the teacher: Use the students' names and put the sentences into typical contexts. Examples:

(*1*) *Ali is a good student. He studies every night. Last night he went to the library. He wanted to study grammar. Why did Ali go to the library?*

(*2*) *Yesterday Tania was at home. Dinner was all ready, but her husband still wasn't home. He was at his office. She decided to call him. Why did Tania pick up the phone?*

1. (. . .) went to the library. He/she wanted to study.
2. (. . .) picked up the phone. She wanted to call her husband./He wanted to call his wife.
3. Before class, (. . .) walked to the front of the room. He/she wanted to ask me a question.
4. (. . .) took out his/her dictionary. He/she wanted to look up a word.
5. (. . .) wants to improve his/her English. He/she reads a lot a books and magazines.
6. (. . .) wanted to pay his/her bill at the restaurant. He/she took out his/her wallet.
7. (. . .) turned off the lights. He/she wanted to save energy.
8. (. . .) turned on the stove. He/she wanted to heat some water for tea.
9. Why did (. . .) go to the library last night?
10. Why did (. . .) pick up the phone?
11. Why did (. . .) walk to the front of the room before class?
12. Why did (. . .) take out his/her dictionary?
13. Why does (. . .) read a lot of books and magazines?
14. Why did (. . .) take out his/her wallet?
15. Why did (. . .) turn off the lights?
16. Why did (. . .) turn on the stove?

11-6 USING *SO THAT**

so that + *can*	(a) I'm going to cash a check **in order to be able to buy my textbooks.** (b) I'm going to cash a check **so (that) I can buy my textbooks.**	*So that* has the same meaning as *in order to.* However, *so that* is often used, rather than *in order to,* when the idea of "ability" is being expressed. (a) and (b) have the same meaning, but (b) is the more common way of expressing ability.

*Note: **In order that** has the same meaning as **so that** but is less commonly used.
Example: *She turned off the record player (in order) that her roommate could study.*

So that and *in order that* introduce adverb clauses. It is possible, but unusual, to put these adverb clauses at the beginning of a sentence: *So that her roommate could study, she turned off the record player.*

so that + could	(c) She turned off the record player **in order to enable her roommate to study.** (d) She turned off the record player so **(that) her roommate could study.**	*Could* is used after *so that* in past sentences.
		Note: *May* and *might* may also be used after *so that*, but are not as common as *can* and *could*. 　　*I'm going to cash a check so that I may buy my textbooks.* 　　*She turned off the record player so that her roommate might study.*
so that + will	(e) We keep milk in a refrigerator **in order to make sure that it will not spoil.** (f) We keep milk in a refrigerator so **(that) it will not spoil.**	The use of *will* after *so that* gives the idea that someone does something *in order to make sure* that something else is the result.
so that + would	(g) Yesterday he put the meat in the oven at five **in order to make sure that it would be ready by six.** (h) Yesterday he put the meat in the oven at five so **(that) it would be ready by six.**	*Would* is used in past sentences.

EXERCISE 15:　Combine the ideas by using *so (that).*

1. Please turn down the TV. I want to be able to get to sleep.

   Please turn down the TV so (that) I can get to sleep.

2. When it began to rain, Harry opened his umbrella. He wanted to make sure he did not get wet.

   When it began to rain, Harry opened his umbrella so (that) he wouldn't get wet.

3. Ann and Larry have a six-year-old child. Tonight they are going to hire a baby-sitter. They want to be able to go out with some friends.

4. Last week Ann and Larry hired a baby-sitter. They wanted to be able to go to a dinner party at the home of Larry's boss.

5. I am going to cash a check. I want to make sure that I have enough money to go grocery shopping.

6. I cashed a check yesterday. I wanted to make sure that I had enough money to go grocery shopping.

7. Please be quiet. I want to hear what Sharon is saying.

8. Bill is a student at the university. Last summer he learned how to type. He wanted to be able to type his own term papers.

9. A: Millie, are you going to come with us to the fair this afternoon?

   B: No, I can't. I have to stay home. I want to make sure that I am here to answer the phone when my parents call.

10. Ed took some change from his pocket. He wanted to buy a newspaper.

11. A: How long are you going to stay here (at this party)?

    B: Well, I'm pretty tired tonight. I think I'll leave around eleven. I want to be able to get to bed by midnight.

12. Lynn tied a string around her finger. She wanted to make sure that she didn't forget to take her book back to the library.

13. The little boy pretended to be sick. He wanted to stay home from school.

14. Yesterday Linda was driving on the highway when her car started making strange noises. After she pulled over to the side of the road, she raised the hood of her car in order to make sure that other drivers knew that she had car trouble.

EXERCISE 16:   Complete the following.

1. I am going to take my camera to the zoo so (that) . . . .
2. I stayed home last night so (that) . . . .
3. Please be quiet so (that) . . . .
4. You'd better put the food in the refrigerator so (that) . . . .
5. I'm going to go on a diet so (that) . . . .
6. I'll give you my phone number so (that) . . . .
7. She sang a lullaby so (that) the baby . . . .
8. It's winter. Yesterday I put on two pairs of socks under my boots so (that) . . . .

11-7   USING *BECAUSE OF* AND *DUE TO*

(a) **Because** the **weather was** cold, we stayed home.	*Because* introduces an adverb clause; it is followed by a subject and verb.
(b) **Because of** the cold **weather**, we stayed home. (c) **Due to** the cold **weather**, we stayed home.	*Because of* and *due to* are prepositions; they are followed by a noun object.
(d) **Due to the fact that** the **weather was** cold, we stayed home.	Sometimes, usually in more formal writing, *due to* is followed by a noun clause introduced by *the fact that*.

EXERCISE 17:   Using the ideas given in parentheses, complete the sentences.

1. (*My parents are generous.*) Because of _____ my parents' generosity _____ , all of the children in our family have received the best of everything.

2. (*The traffic was heavy.*) We were late to the meeting due to _____

   _____ .

3. (*Bill's wife is ill.*) Bill has to do all of the cooking and cleaning because of _____

_____ .

4. (*Dr. Robinson has done excellent research on wolves.*) Due to _____

_____ , we know much more today about
that endangered species than we did even five years ago.

5. (*It was noisy in the next apartment.*) I couldn't get to sleep last night because of

_____ .

6. (*Circumstances are beyond my control.*) Due to _____

_____ , I regret to say that I cannot be
present at your daughter's wedding.

11-8   USING *THEREFORE*

(a) I failed the test because I did not study.	
(b) I did not study. **Therefore,** I failed the test. (c) I did not study. I, **therefore,** failed the test. (d) I did not study. I failed the test, **therefore.**	In grammar, *therefore* is called a *transition* (or *conjunctive adverb*).
(e) I did not study; **therefore,** I failed the test.	A semicolon (;) may be used instead of a period.
(f) I did not study. **Consequently,** I failed the test.	*Consequently* is also a transition and has the same meaning as *therefore*.

EXERCISE 18:   Give sentences with the same meaning by using *therefore* or *consequently*. Use several alternative patterns, as shown in 11-8. Punctuate carefully.

1. The children had to stay home because a storm was approaching.

2. Because the Fourth of July is a national holiday, the university will be closed.

EXERCISE 19: Punctuate the following sentences. Add capital letters if necessary.

1. Because it was cold she wore a coat.	(*adverb clause*)
2. She wore a coat because it was cold.	(*adverb clause*)
3. Because of the cold weather she wore a coat.	(*prepositional phrase*)
4. She wore a coat because of the cold weather.	(*prepositional phrase*)
5. The weather was cold therefore she wore a coat.	(*transition*)
6. The weather was cold she therefore wore a coat.	(*transition*)
7. The weather was cold she wore a coat therefore.	(*transition*)
8. The weather was cold so she wore a coat.	(*conjunction*)

EXERCISE 20: Punctuate the following sentences. Add capital letters if necessary.

1. Pat always enjoyed studying sciences in high school therefore she decided to major in biology in college.
2. Due to recent improvements in the economy fewer people are unemployed.
3. Last night's storm damaged the power lines consequently the town was without electricity for several hours.
4. Because of the snowstorm only five students came to class the teacher therefore cancelled the class.
5. Anna always makes numerous spelling mistakes in her compositions because she does not use a dictionary when she writes.

11-9 SUMMARY OF PATTERNS AND PUNCTUATION

ADVERB CLAUSE	(a) **Because it was hot,** we went swimming. (b) We went swimming **because it was hot.**	*An adverb clause may precede or follow an independent clause.* *Punctuation: A comma is used if the adverb clause comes first.*
PREPOSITION	(c) **Because of the hot weather,** we went swimming. (d) We went swimming **because of the hot weather.**	*A preposition is followed by a noun object, not by a subject and verb.* *Punctuation: A comma is usually used if the prepositional phrase precedes the subject and verb of the independent clause.*

TRANSITION	(e) It was hot. **Therefore**, we went swimming. (f) It was hot. We, **therefore**, went swimming. (g) It was hot. We went swimming, **therefore**. (h) It was hot; **therefore**, we went swimming. (i) It was hot; we, **therefore**, went swimming. (j) It was hot; we went swimming, **therefore**.	*A transition is used with the second sentence of a pair.* It shows the relationship of the second idea to the first idea. A transition is movable within the second sentence. *Punctuation:* Either a period or a semicolon may be used between the two independent clauses. A comma may *not* be used to separate the clauses. Commas are usually used to set the transition off from the rest of the sentence.
CONJUNCTION	(k) It was hot, **so** we went swimming.	*A conjunction comes between two independent clauses.** *Punctuation:* Usually a comma is used immediately in front of a conjunction.

*See 10–3 for the use and punctuation of conjunctions.

EXERCISE 21: Using the given words, combine these two ideas:

We postponed our trip. The weather was bad.

    Example: because   We postponed our trip because the weather was bad.
                            (Because the weather was bad, we postponed our trip.)

1. therefore
2. since
3. because of
4. so

5. due to
6. consequently
7. so . . . that
8. due to the fact that

EXERCISE 22: Using the given words, combine these two ideas:

She missed class. She was ill.

1. therefore
2. due to the fact that
3. since

4. due to
5. consequently
6. so

EXERCISE 23–WRITTEN: Using the given words, write about yourself, your friends, your family, your classes, today's weather, current events in the world, etc.

1. now that
2. therefore
3. inasmuch as

4. as (meaning *because*)
5. consequently
6. in order to

7. so (that)	11. because
8. since	12. because of
9. so . . . that	13. due to
10. such . . . that	14. due to the fact that

PART III Reduction of Adverb Clauses to Modifying Phrases

11-10 CHANGING TIME CLAUSES TO MODIFYING PHRASES

INTRODUCTION

In Chapter 8, we discussed changing adjective clauses to modifying phrases. (See 8–10.) Some adverb clauses may also be changed to modifying phrases, and the ways in which the changes are made are the same:

    (1) Omit the subject of the dependent clause and the *be* form of the verb.

        ADVERB CLAUSE: *While I was walking to class,* I ran into an old friend.

        MODIFYING PHRASE: *While walking to class,* I ran into an old friend.

    (2) Or, if there is no *be* form of a verb, omit the subject and change the verb to *-ing*.

        ADVERB CLAUSE: *Before I left for work,* I ate breakfast.

        MODIFYING PHRASE: *Before leaving for work,* I ate breakfast.

(a) **While I was sitting** in class, **I** fell asleep. (b) **While sitting** in class, **I** fell asleep. (c) **While Bob was sitting** in class, **he** fell asleep. (d) **While sitting** in class, **Bob** fell asleep.	In (a): an adverb clause. In (b): a modifying phrase. It modifies the subject. (a) and (b) have the same meaning. In (b): The subject of the adverb clause (which is the *same subject* found in the independent clause) and the *be* form of the verb have been omitted.
(e) While **the teacher** was lecturing to the class, **I** fell asleep.	In (e): The adverb clause *cannot be changed* to a modifying phrase because the two clauses have *different subjects.*
(f) **When the child was told** to go to bed, he started to cry. (g) **When told** to go to bed, **the child** started to cry.	Notice in (f) and (g): When the adverb clause is changed to a modifying phrase, the noun in the adverb clause (*the child*) becomes the subject of the independent clause.
(h) **Since Mary came** to this country, **she** has made many friends. (i) **Since coming** to this country, **Mary** has made many friends.	In (h): an adverb clause. In (i): a modifying phrase. It modifies the subject. In (i): The subject of the adverb clause (which is the *same subject* found in the independent clause) has been omitted, and the verb has been changed to its *-ing* form.

(j) **Before he went** to bed, **he** turned off all the lights.	
(k) **Before going** to bed, **he** turned off all the lights.	
(l) **He** turned off all the lights **before going** to bed.	In (l): Notice that the modifying phrase may follow the independent clause.

EXERCISE 24: Change the adverb clauses to modifying phrases. Make no change if the subjects of the two clauses in each sentence are different.

Examples: *While John was driving* to school yesterday, he had an accident.
While driving to school yesterday, *John* had an accident.

Before I came to class, I had a cup of coffee.
Before coming to class, I had a cup of coffee.

After he (had) finished his homework, he went to bed.
After finishing his homework, he went to bed.
After having finished his homework, he went to bed.*

While I was watching television last night, *the telephone* rang. (*no change*)

1. While I was living in Japan last year, I learned many things about Japanese customs.
2. Before I went to Yellowstone Park, I had never seen a black bear in the wild.
3. After she (had) completed her shopping, she went home.
4. Since I came here, I have learned a lot of English.
5. Before the student came to class, the teacher had already given a quiz.
6. Alex hurt his back while he was chopping wood.
7. You should always read a contract before you sign your name.
8. When young children are left alone, they can get themselves into all sorts of trouble very quickly.
9. When an American woman meets someone for the first time, she may or may not offer her hand.
10. Since I arrived here, I have found an apartment, registered for school, explored the city, and made some new friends.
11. After I heard Mary describe how cold it gets in Minnesota in the winter, I decided not to go there over Christmas vacation.
12. While Susan was climbing the mountain, she lost her footing and fell onto a ledge several feet below.

---

*Note: There is no difference in meaning between *After he finished* and *After he had finished*. There is no difference in meaning between *After finishing* and *After having finished*.

13. While I was trying to get to sleep last night, a mosquito kept buzzing in my ear.

14. Before you ask the librarian for help, you should make every effort to find the materials yourself.

15. After she saw a documentary film on the way of life of a primitive tribe in the Philippines, Kristen decided to become an anthropologist.

11-11 EXPRESSING THE IDEA OF "DURING THE SAME TIME" IN MODIFYING PHRASES

(a) **While I was walking** down the street, **I** ran into an old friend.	Sometimes *while* is omitted but the *-ing* phrase at the beginning of the sentence gives the same meaning (i.e., "during the same time"). (a), (b), and (c) have the same meaning.
(b) **While walking** down the street, **I** ran into an old friend.	
(c) **Walking** down the street, **I** ran into an old friend.	
(d) **Hiking** through the woods yesterday, **we** saw a bear.	
(e) **Pointing** to the sentence on the board, **the teacher** explained the meaning of modifying phrases.	

11-12 EXPRESSING CAUSE AND EFFECT RELATIONSHIPS IN MODIFYING PHRASES

(f) **Because she needed** some money to buy a book, **Sue** cashed a check.	Often an *-ing* phrase at the beginning of a sentence gives the meaning of "because." (f) and (g) have the same meaning.
(g) **Needing** some money to buy a book, **Sue** cashed a check.	*Because* is not used in a modifying phrase. It is omitted, but the resulting phrase expresses a cause and effect relationship.
(h) **Because he lacked** the necessary qualifications, **he** was not considered for the job.	
(i) **Lacking** the necessary qualifications, **he** was not considered for the job.	
(j) **Because I have seen** that movie before, **I don't want** to go again.	*Having + past participle* gives the meaning not only of "because" but also of "before."
(k) **Having seen** that movie before, **I don't want** to go again.	

(l) **Because I had seen** that movie before, **I didn't want** to go again.	
(m) **Having seen** that movie before, **I didn't want** to go again.	
(n) **Having worked** hard all day, **I am** tired now.	In (n): *having worked* = *because* and *before now*
(o) **Having worked** hard all day, **I was** tired last night.	In (o): *having worked* = *because* and *before last night*
(p) **Because she was unable** to afford a car, **she** bought a bicycle. (q) **Being unable** to afford a car, **she** bought a bicycle. (r) **Unable** to afford a car, **she** bought a bicycle.	A form of *be* in the adverb clause is often changed to *being*. The use of *being* makes the cause and effect relationship clear.

EXERCISE 25: Discuss the meaning of the following sentences. Which ones give the meaning of *because*? Which ones give the meaning of *while*? Do some of the sentences give the idea of both *because* and *while*?

1. Sitting on the airplane and watching the clouds pass beneath me, I let my thoughts wander to the new experiences that were in store for me during the next two years of living in the United States.

2. Being a self-supporting widow with three children, she has no choice but to work.

3. Lying on her bed in peace and quiet, she soon forgot her troubles.

4. Having already spent all of his last paycheck, he does not have any more money to live on for the rest of the month.

5. Watching the children's energetic play, I felt like an old man even though I am only forty.

6. Having brought up ten children of their own, the Smiths may be considered experts on child behavior.

7. Being totally surprised by his proposal of marriage, Carol could not find the words to reply.

8. Driving to my grandparents' house last night, we saw a young woman who was selling flowers. We stopped so that we could get some flowers for my grandmother.

9. Struggling against fatigue, I forced myself to put one foot in front of the other.

10. Having guessed at the correct answers for a good part of the test, I did not expect to get a high score.

11. Realizing that I had made a dreadful mistake when I introduced him as George Johnson, I went over to him and apologized. I know his name is John George.

12. Tapping his fingers loudly on the desk top, he made his impatience and dissatisfaction known.

EXERCISE 26:   Change the adverb clauses to modifying phrases.

> *Example:*   Because he didn't want to hurt her feelings, he didn't tell her the bad news.
>
> Not wanting to hurt her feelings, he didn't tell her the bad news.

1. Because the little boy believed that no one loved him, he ran away from home.
2. Because she was not paying attention to where she was going, she stepped into a hole and sprained her ankle.
3. Because I had forgotten to bring a pencil to the examination, I had to borrow one.
4. Because she is a vegetarian, she does not eat meat.
5. Because he has already flunked out of school once, he is determined to succeed this time.

EXERCISE 27:   Combine the two sentences, making a modifying phrase out of the first sentence, if possible.

> *Example:*   The children had nothing to do. They were bored.
>
> Having nothing to do, the children were bored.

1. I heard that Judy was in the hospital. I called her family to find out what was wrong.
2. The little boy was trying his best not to cry. He swallowed hard and began to speak.
3. I did not want to inconvenience my friend by asking her to drive me to the airport. I decided to take a taxi.
4. I was sitting on a large rock at the edge of a mountain stream. I felt at peace with the world.
5. John had run a red traffic light. The policeman arrested him.
6. I am a married man. I have many responsibilities.
7. I was reading the paper last night. I saw an article on solar energy.
8. I had not understood what he said. I asked him to repeat the directions.
9. I was watching the children fly their kites in the park. Suddenly the wind blew my hat off my head.
10. Ann was convinced that she could never learn to play the piano. She stopped taking lessons.

EXERCISE 28:   Change the adverb clauses to modifying phrases.

1. Before I talked to you, I had never understood that formula.
2. Because he did not want to spend any more money that month, John decided against going to a restaurant for dinner. He made himself a sandwich instead.
3. After I read the chapter four times, I finally understood the author's theory.

4. Because I remembered that everyone makes mistakes, I softened my view of his seemingly inexcusable error.

5. Since he completed his Bachelor's degree, he has had three jobs, each one better than the last.

6. While I was traveling across the United States, I could not help being impressed by the great differences in terrain.

7. Before he gained national fame, the union leader had been an electrician in a small town.

8. Because we were enjoying the cool evening breeze and listening to the sounds of nature, we lost track of time.

9. Because she had never flown in an airplane before, the little girl was surprised and a little frightened when her ears popped.

10. Before he became vice-president of marketing and sales, Peter McKay worked as a sales representative.

EXERCISE 29:   Complete the following. Add commas where needed.

1. Before going to class _____

2. After coming home from the party _____

3. Having failed the entrance examination _____

4. Since arriving in this city _____

5. Driving home last night _____

6. Being new on the job _____

7. After traveling for four hours _____

8. Receiving no answer when he knocked on the door _____

9. Having been told that there were no more rooms available in the dormitory __

_____

10. Being the largest city in the United States _____

EXERCISE 30—WRITTEN: Complete the following. Punctuate carefully.

1. After having finished my . . . .

2. Before going to . . . .

3. Since coming to : . . .

4. Sitting in the park the other day . . . .

5. Having heard a strange noise in the other room . . . .

6. Being only four years old . . . .

7. Being disturbed by the noise from the neighbor's apartment . . . .

8. Not having read the directions carefully . . . .
9. Exhausted by the long hours of work . . . .
10. Before leaving on vacation . . . .

EXERCISE 31—ERROR ANALYSIS: The errors in the following are adapted from student compositions. Test your skill by finding and correcting as many of the errors as possible.

1. The weather was such cold that I don't like to leave my apartment.
2. I have to study four hour every day because of my courses are difficult.
3. In the evening, I usually go downstairs for watching television.
4. On the third day of our voyage, we sailed across a rough sea before to reach the shore.
5. I can't understand the lectures in my psychology class, therefore my roommate lets me borrow her notes.
6. According to this legend, a man went in search of a hidden village, he finally found it after walk two hundred mile.
7. Because my country is located in a subtropical area, so the weather is hot.
8. I will stay at the united state for two more year. Because I want finish my degree before go home.
9. After graduating from college, my father wants me to join his business firm.
10. We were floating far from the beach, suddenly my mother cried out "shark! a shark is coming," we could see a black fin cutting the water and coming toward us, we are paralyzed with fear.

EXERCISE 32—WRITTEN: Read today's newspaper. Find three articles—one on local news, one on national news, and one on international news—that you think are interesting. Read these articles several times, and then, without looking at the newspaper, summarize them. Use one paragraph for each summary. Be prepared to share your summaries orally with the rest of the class.

EXERCISE 33—WRITTEN: Using one of the following topics, try to communicate in writing an emotion you have felt. Describe the situation that caused this emotion, your actions (and those of other people who were involved), and your feelings.

1. Describe an occasion when you felt nervous.
2. Describe an occasion when you experienced fear.
3. Describe a time when you felt completely at peace.
4. Describe an occasion when you worried needlessly.
5. Describe a time when you felt very surprised.

12

Adverb Clauses and Related Structures - II: Opposition and Condition

12-1 SHOWING OPPOSITION (UNEXPECTED RESULT)*

ADVERB CLAUSES	even though although though	(a) **Even though it was cold**, I went swimming. (b) **Although it was cold**, I went swimming. (c) **Though it was cold**, I went swimming.
CONJUNCTIONS	but . . . anyway but . . . still yet . . . still	(d) It was cold, **but** I went swimming **anyway**. (e) It was cold, **but I still** went swimming. (f) It was cold, **yet I still** went swimming.
TRANSITIONS	nevertheless nonetheless however	(g) It was cold; **nevertheless**, I went swimming. (h) It was cold. **Nonetheless**, I went swimming. (i) It was cold; **however**, I still went swimming.
PREPOSITIONS	despite in spite of	(j) I went swimming **despite the cold weather**. (k) I went swimming **in spite of the cold weather**.
Note: All of the above example sentences have the same meaning.		

*Compare: Expected result: *Because the weather was cold, I did not go swimming.* Unexpected (or opposite) result:
Even though the weather was cold, I went swimming.

EXERCISE 1: Combine the ideas in the two sentences. Use the given words. Discuss correct punctuation.

1. *We went to the zoo. It was raining.*
   even though
   but . . . anyway
   nevertheless
   in spite of
   because

2. *His grades were low. He was admitted to the university.*
   although
   yet . . . still
   nonetheless
   despite
   because of

EXERCISE 2: Complete the following. Add commas where appropriate.

1. I had a cold but I _____ anyway.

2. Even though I had a cold I _____

3. Although I didn't study _____

4. I didn't study but _____ anyway.

5. I got an "A" on the test even though _____

6. Even though Howard is a careful driver _____

7. Even though the food they served for dinner tasted terrible _____

8. My shirt still has coffee stains on it even though _____

9. I still trust him even though _____

10. Even though he was drowning no one _____

11. Although I tried to be very careful _____

12. Even though Ruth is one of my best friends _____

13. It's still hot in here even though _____

14. Even though I had a big breakfast_____ still _____

EXERCISE 3—ORAL (BOOKS CLOSED):   Use *even though*. Be sure to begin your response with either *yes* or *no*.

> *Example:*   It was raining. Did you go to the zoo anyway?
> *Response:*   Yes, even though it was raining, I went to the zoo.

> *Example:*   You studied hard. Did you pass the test?
> *Response:*   No, even though I studied hard, I didn't pass the test.

1. You weren't tired. Did you go to bed anyway?
2. The telephone rang many times, but did John wake up?
3. The food was terrible. Did you eat it anyway?
4. You didn't study. Did you pass the test anyway?
5. The weather is terrible today. Did you stay home?
6. You fell down the stairs. Did you get hurt?
7. You took a nap. Do you still feel tired?
8. You told the truth, but did anyone believe you?
9. You took an aspirin. Do you still have a headache?
10. You turned on the airconditioner. Is it still hot in here?
11. You mailed the letter three days ago. Has it arrived yet?
12. You have a lot of money. Can you afford to buy an airplane?
13. Your grandmother is ninety years old. Is she still young at heart?
14. You lived in (Mexico) for a whole year. Did you learn to speak (Spanish)?
15. Your house burned down. You lost your job. Your wife/husband left you. Are you still cheerful?

EXERCISE 4:   Change the sentences by using *nevertheless.* *

> *Example:*   He wasn't tired, but he went to bed anyway.
> *Response:*   He wasn't tired; nevertheless, he went to bed.

1. It was cold, but we went on a picnic anyway.
2. She wasn't hungry, but she ate two dishes of ice cream anyway.

---

*Nevertheless and *but . . . anyway* have the same meaning; *but . . . anyway* occurs primarily in speaking and *nevertheless* occurs primarily in writing.

3. Even though Jack wasn't feeling good, he went to class.

4. I still trust him even though he lied to me.

5. Sally was very sad, but she smiled and pretended to be having a good time.

6. George did not panic even though he was alone and lost in the woods.

7. Elizabeth is not a citizen of the United States, but she has to pay income taxes anyway.

8. Even though Henry Johnson is an honest politician, I would never vote for him because I do not agree with his positions on foreign policy.

9. The crime rate has continued to rise even though the local police department has implemented several new crime prevention programs.

10. Even though math has always been easy for him, he understands that it is not easy for everyone. As a result, he is a good teacher.

EXERCISE 5: Give sentences with the same meaning by using *in spite of* or *despite.*

> *Example:* Even though her grades were low, she was admitted to the university.
>
> *Response:* In spite of her low grades, } she was admitted to the university.
> Despite her low grades,
>
> In spite of the fact that her grades were low, } she was admitted to the university.
> Despite the fact that her grades were low,

1. He continued to go to class even though he had a broken leg.

2. I like living in the dorm even though it is noisy.

3. Even though the work was hard, they enjoyed themselves.

4. They wanted to climb the mountain even though it was dangerous.

5. Although the weather was extremely hot, they went jogging in the park.

6. He is unhappy even though he has a vast fortune.

EXERCISE 6–WRITTEN: Complete the following. Punctuate carefully. (Correct punctuation is not indicated in the given cues.)

1. I didn't . . . but . . . anyway.

2. He is very old yet he still . . . .

3. . . . nevertheless we arrived on schedule.

4. Even though she wanted . . . .

5. I wanted . . . however I . . . because . . . .

6. The teacher . . . even though . . . .

7. Although . . . only . . . years old . . . .

8. She never went to school however she . . . despite her lack of education.

9. Despite the fact that my . . . .

10. I have decided to . . . even though . . . .

12-2 SHOWING DIRECT OPPOSITION

ADVERB CLAUSES	whereas while	(a) Mary is rich, **whereas John is poor.** (b) Mary is rich, **while John is poor.** (c) John is poor, **while Mary is rich.** (d) **Whereas Mary is rich,** John is poor.	*Whereas* and *while* are used to show direct opposition: "this" is exactly the opposite of "that." *Whereas* and *while* may be used with the idea of either clause with no difference in meaning. Note: A comma is usually used even if the adverb clause comes second.
CONJUNCTION	*but*	(e) Mary is rich, **but** John is poor. (f) John is poor, **but** Mary is rich.	In (e) through (j): As with *whereas* and *while*, it does not make any difference which idea comes first and which idea comes second. The two ideas are directly opposite.
TRANSITIONS	*however* *on the other hand*	(g) Mary is rich; **however,** John is poor. (h) John is poor; **however,** Mary is rich. (i) Mary is rich. John, **on the other hand,** is poor. (j) John is poor. Mary, **on the other hand,** is rich.	

EXERCISE 7: Complete the following. Discuss other ways of expressing the same idea by moving the position of *whereas* or *while.*

> *Example:* Some people are fat, whereas . . . .
>
> Some people are fat, whereas others are thin.
>
> (Whereas some people are fat, others are thin.)
>
> (Some people are thin, whereas others are fat.)

1. While some students think physics is easy, others . . . .

2. Some people are tall, whereas . . . .

3. Some people prefer to live in the country, while . . . .

4. While some people know only their native language, ...

5. A mouse is small, whereas . . . .

6. The planet Mercury always keeps the same side toward the sun. Therefore, one side of Mercury is always extremely hot, whereas the part of the planet that never faces the sun . . . .

EXERCISE 8: Give sentences with the same meaning by using *however* or *on the other hand*. Punctuate carefully.

1. Florida has a warm climate, whereas Alaska has a cold climate.
2. While Fred is a good student, his brother is lazy.
3. Sue and Ron are expecting a child. Sue is hoping for a boy, whereas Ron is hoping for a girl.

4. In the United States, gambling casinos are not legal in most states, while in my country it is possible to gamble in any city or town.
5. Old people in my country usually live with their children, whereas the old in the United States often live by themselves.

EXERCISE 9—ORAL and/or WRITTEN: What aspects of your country and the United States are in contrast? Use *while, whereas, however, on the other hand*.

1. Size?
2. Population?
3. Food?
4. Time of meals?
5. Climate?
6. Political system?
7. Economic system?
8. Educational system?
9. Religion?
10. Student life?
11. Coffee-tea?
12. Role of women?
13. Language?
14. Educational costs?
15. Medical care?
16. Family relationships?
17. Public transportation?
18. Length of history?
19. Dating customs?
20. Predictability of the weather?

12-3 USING *ON THE CONTRARY*

(a) They are not rich. **On the contrary,** they are poor.	*On the contrary* gives the idea that "just the opposite is true." It frequently follows a negative sentence.
(b) He is not a cruel man. **On the contrary,** he is exceedingly kind.	
(c) A: I thought you enjoyed the movie.	*On the contrary* is a transition.
B: Where did you get that idea? **On the contrary,** I thought it was terrible.	

EXERCISE 10: Complete the following.

1. I'm not sleepy. On the contrary, _____

2. She's not selfish. On the contrary, _____

3. A: It's too late to go to the movie now, isn't it?

   B: No. On the contrary, _____

4. A: Do you mean to say that you think money is the most important thing in life?

   B: No. On the contrary, I was trying to say that _____

5. You seem to be under the impression that I disagree with you. On the contrary,

   _____

6. A: I thought everyone in your country was rich.

   B: Where did you get that idea? On the contrary, _____

PART II Condition

12-4 EXPRESSING CONDITIONS IN ADVERB CLAUSES

if	(a) I will come tomorrow **if I have enough time.** (b) **If it doesn't rain**, the party will be held outside.	In (a): Notice that the simple present, not the simple future, is used in the "*if* clause."
unless	(c) **Unless it rains**, the party will be held outside.	*Unless* = *if not* In (c): *unless it rains* = *if it doesn't rain*
only if	(d) The party will be held inside **only if it rains.**	In (d): Rain is the only condition under which the party will be held inside. If it is cold, the party will be outside. If it is windy, the party will be outside. Only rain will cause the party to move inside.
whether or not	(e) The party will be held outside **whether it rains or not.** (f) The party will be held outside **whether or not it rains.**	In (e) and (f): If it rains, the party will be held outside. If it doesn't rain, the party will be held outside. In other words, rain does not matter.

even if	(g) **Even if it rains**, the party will be held outside.	*even if* = *whether or not* In (g): Maybe it will rain, but rain will not make any difference. Under any conditions, even rain, the party will be held outside.
providing/provided *(that)*	(h) **Providing (that) no one has any further questions**, the meeting will adjourn. (i) **Provided (that) no one has any further questions**, the meeting will adjourn.	*Providing that* and *provided that* have the same meaning and usage. *Providing that* and *provided that* mean *if.*
in case (that) *in the event (that)*	(j) I'll be at my uncle's house **in case you need to reach me.** (k) **In the event that you need to reach me**, I'll be at my uncle's house.	*in case* = *if by any chance this should happen* *in the event* = *if, in case*

EXERCISE 11: Complete the following.

1. Joan has no alternative. She has to get a scholarship. If she doesn't, she can't go to school. Joan can go to school only if _____ she gets a scholarship. _____

2. Max would like to get a scholarship, but it doesn't matter. He can go to school whether _____

3. Alice would like to get a scholarship, but it doesn't matter. She can go to school even if _____

4. John will be very pleased if _____ a scholarship to go to school next year.

5. Your approval doesn't matter to me. I am going to marry Harry whether _____

6. When the time is up, you have to hand in your examination paper whether _____

7. It doesn't matter whether or not Ed graduates from school. He can get a good job even if _____

8. Yes, John, I will marry you—but only if _____

9. I stay up and finish my homework even if _____

10. Usually Sam doesn't lift a finger around the house. He'll do housework only if _____

11. You shouldn't scratch a mosquito bite even if _____ _____

12. I'm exhausted. Please don't wake me up even if _____

13. Even if _____

14. _____ only if _____

15. I will _____ whether _____

16. I will take the six-thirty flight to Atlanta providing that _____

    _____

17. Only students can apply for this low-cost health insurance policy. You are eligible for the insurance provided that _____

18. You probably won't need to get in touch with me, but I'll give you my phone number in case _____

19. I think I have given you all of the information you need, but in case you need more information, _____

20. I'll be in my office tomorrow morning around ten in the event that _____

    _____

12–5 EXPRESSING NEGATIVE CONDITIONS

ADVERB CLAUSES	(a) **If you don't hurry,** you will be late. (b) **Unless you hurry,** you will be late.	*unless* = *if not* (a) and (b) have the same meaning.
TRANSITION	(c) You'd better hurry; **otherwise,** you will be late.	In (c): *otherwise* = *if you don't.*
CONJUNCTION	(d) You'd better hurry, **or (else)** you will be late.	Note: (a), (b), (c), and (d) all have the same meaning.

EXERCISE 12: Complete the following.

1. I will go to the zoo if it isn't cold.

   I will go to the zoo unless _____

2. You can't get a driver's license if you are not at least sixteen years old.

   You can't get a driver's license unless _____

3. You can't travel abroad if you do not have a passport.

   You can't travel abroad unless _____

4. Your letter won't be delivered unless _____

5. I can't attend school unless _____

6. Unless I have a flashbulb, _____

7. I'm sorry, but you can't see the doctor unless _____

8. _____ unless I get a raise.

9. Certain species of animals, birds, and fish will soon become extinct unless

_____

10. The political situation in _____ will continue to deteriorate unless _____

11. Tomorrow I'm going to _____ unless _____

_____

12. Unless you _____

EXERCISE 13: Combine the given ideas by using **unless** and **otherwise.** With **otherwise,** use a modal auxiliary (*should, had better, must, have to*) with the first idea.

1. *leave now — be late for class*

    Unless you leave now, you will be late for class.

    You'd better leave now; otherwise, you will be late for class.

2. *call my mother — be worried*

_____

_____

3. *wash my clothes tonight — not have any clean clothes to wear tomorrow*

_____

_____

4. *go to bed – your cold . . . get worse*

_____

_____

5. *leave now – be dark before . . . get home*

_____

_____

6. *speak both Japanese and Chinese fluently – not be considered for the job*

_____

_____

EXERCISE 14–WRITTEN: Complete the following. Punctuate correctly. (Correct punctuation is not indicated in the cues.) Use capital letters where appropriate.

1. I am going to . . . even if . . . .
2. We have no choice we have to . . . whether . . . .
3. I will go to . . . providing that . . . .
4. . . . is very inconsiderate he plays his record player even if . . . .
5. I can't . . . unless . . . .
6. Tomorrow I'd better . . . otherwise . . . .
7. You should . . . in case . . . .
8. I will . . . only if . . . .
9. I will . . . unless . . . .
10. . . . must . . . otherwise . . . .

EXERCISE 15:   Using the two ideas of *to study* and *to pass or fail the exam*, complete the following. Punctuate correctly.

1. Because I did not study _____

2. I failed the exam because _____

3. Although I studied _____

4. I did not study therefore _____

5. I did not study however _____

6. I studied nevertheless _____

7. Even though I did not study _____

8. I did not study so _____

9. Since I did not study _____

10. If I study for the test _____

11. Unless I study for the test _____

12. I will pass the test providing that _____

13. I must study otherwise _____

14. Even if I study _____

15. I did not study consequently _____

16. I did not study nonetheless _____

17. Inasmuch as I did not study for the test _____

18. I will probably fail the test whether _____

19. I failed the exam for _____

20. I have to study so that _____

EXERCISE 16: Using the ideas of *to be hungry* (or *not to be hungry*) and *to eat breakfast* (or *not to eat breakfast*), complete the following. Punctuate correctly.

1. Because I was not hungry this morning _____

2. Because I ate breakfast this morning _____ now.

3. Because I was hungry this morning _____

4. I did not eat breakfast this morning even though _____

5. Although I was hungry this morning _____

6. I was hungry this morning therefore _____

7. I was hungry this morning nevertheless _____

8. I was so hungry this morning _____

9. I was not hungry this morning but _____

10. I ate breakfast this morning even though _____

11. Since I did not eat breakfast this morning _____

12. I ate breakfast this morning nonetheless _____

13. I was not hungry so _____

14. Even though I did not eat breakfast this morning _____

15. I never eat breakfast unless _____

16. I always eat breakfast whether or not _____

17. I eat breakfast even if _____

18. Now that I have eaten breakfast _____

19. I eat breakfast only if _____

20. I ate breakfast this morning yet _____

21. Even if I am hungry _____

22. I was not hungry however _____

EXERCISE 17–ORAL: Using the given words, combine the following two ideas. The time is *now*, so use present and future tenses.

(1) *to go (or not to go) to the beach*
(2) *hot, cold, nice weather*

Example: because *Because the weather is cold, we aren't going to go to the beach.* OR: *We're going to go to the beach because the weather is hot.*

1. so . . . that	12. since
2. so	13. but . . . anyway
3. nevertheless	14. unless
4. despite	15. therefore
5. now that	16. only if*
6. once	17. nonetheless
7. although	18. in spite of
8. because of	19. even if
9. consequently	20. yet . . . still
10. as soon as	21. whether . . . or not
11. such . . . that	22. as long as . . . let's (why don't)

EXERCISE 18: Complete the following. Add necessary punctuation and capitalization.

1. While some people are optimists _____

2. Even though he has lost a lot of weight _____ still _____

3. Even if she invites me to her party _____

———————

*When *only if* begins a sentence, the subject and verb of the main clause are inverted: *Only if it rains will the party be held inside.*

4. I have never been to Hawaii my parents however _____

5. She goes to her room and closes the door whenever _____

6. I need to borrow some money so that _____

7. The airport was closed due to fog therefore _____

8. _____ therefore the airport was closed.

9. As soon as the violinist played the last note at the concert _____

10. Since neither my roommate nor I know how to cook _____

11. I am not a superstitious person nevertheless _____

12. The crops will fail unless _____

13. Just as I was getting ready to eat my dinner last night _____

14. Now that she is married _____

15. We must work quickly otherwise _____

16. Some children are noisy and wild my brother's children on the other hand ____

_____

EXERCISE 19—WRITTEN: Complete the following. Punctuate carefully.

1. According to the newspaper, now that . . . .

2. Ever since I can remember . . . .

3. Although my apartment . . . .

4. The United States . . . whereas . . . .

5. I was tired however I . . . because . . . .

6. I . . . my friend on the other hand . . . .

7. You must . . . whether . . . .

8. Even though I . . . .

9. As soon as I . . . .

10. In spite of the fact that . . . .

11. . . . therefore I have decided to . . . .

12. . . . nevertheless I could not understand what . . . .

EXERCISE 20—ERROR ANALYSIS: Try to find and correct the errors in the following.

1. Although I usually don't like french food, but I liked the food I had at the french restaurant last night.

2. Although my room in the dormitory is very small, but I like it. Because it is a place where I can be by myself and studying in peace and quiet.

3. Despite I prefer to be a history teacher, I am studying in the Business School in order for I can get a job in industry.

4. A little girl approached the cage however when the tiger shows his teeth and growls she run to her mother. Because she was frightened.

5. Many of the people working to save our environment think that they are fighting a losing battle. Because big business and the government have not joined together to eliminate pollution.

EXERCISE 21:   Complete the following.

1. If what he said _____

2. Because the man who _____

3. Even though she didn't understand what _____

4. Now that all of the students who _____

5. Since the restaurant where we _____

PART III   Showing Other Relationships

12-6   GIVING EXAMPLES

(a) There are many interesting places to visit in the city. **For example**, the botanical garden has numerous displays of plants from all over the world.	*For example* and *for instance* have the same meaning. Usually they are used as transitions.
(b) There are many interesting places to visit in the city. The art museum, **for instance**, has an excellent collection of modern paintings.	
(c) There are many interesting places to visit in the city, **e.g.**, the botanical garden and the art museum.	*e.g.* = *for example* (*E.g.* is an abbreviation of the Latin phrase *exempli gratia*.)
(d) There are many interesting places to visit in the city; **e.g.**, you could go to the botanical garden or the art museum.	In (d): A semicolon is used if a complete clause follows *e.g.*
(e) I prefer to wear casual clothes, **such as** jeans and a sweatshirt.	*such as* = *for example*
(f) **Some sports, such as** football and hockey, are often violent.	In (f), (g), and (h): Notice the patterns for using *such as*. All three sentences have the same meaning.
(g) **Sports such as** football and hockey are often violent.	
(h) **Such sports as** football and hockey are often violent.	

EXERCISE 22:   Complete the following. Use *such as.*

1. You need a hobby. There are many hobbies you might enjoy _____ , such as _____ ceramics or stamp collecting. _____

2. There are certain products which almost everyone buys regularly _____ _____

3. You should buy a small, economical car _____

4. Medical science has made many advances, yet there are still serious diseases which have not been conquered _____

5. Some countries _____ and _____ are rich in oil.

6. I enjoy such sports _____

7. Such inventions _____ have contributed greatly to the progress of civilization. However, other inventions _____ _____ have threatened human existence.

8. There are certain times when I wish to be alone _____ when _____ or when _____

9. Some subjects have always been easy and enjoyable for me _____ _____ . However, other subjects _____ _____

10. In certain situations, _____ when _____ _____ or when _____ _____ , my English still gives me a little trouble.

11. Numbers _____ are odd numbers, where-as numbers _____ are even numbers.

12. Some languages _____ and _____ are closely related to English, while others _____ and _____ are not.

EXERCISE 23—ORAL (BOOKS CLOSED):   Use *such as* in the response.

Example: Give me some examples of sports you enjoy. (*I enjoy . . . .*)
Response: I enjoy sports such as (soccer and boxing).

(*To the teacher: Prompt the response with the words in parentheses only if necessary.*)

1. Give me some examples of places you would like to visit. (*I would like* . . . .)
2. Who enjoys watching television? Give me some examples of programs you enjoy. (*I enjoy* . . . .)
3. Do you like bright colors or dark colors? Can you give me some examples? (*I like* . . . .)
4. What are some examples of gifts that a woman likes to receive? (*A woman* . . . .)
5. And examples of gifts that a man likes to receive? (*A man* . . . .)
6. Give me some examples of problems a foreign student can easily overcome. (*A foreign student can easily overcome problems* . . . .)
7. Are there many sources of protein? Can you give me some examples? (*There are many* . . . .)
8. Give me some examples of emotions we all experience. (*We all* . . . .)
9. Should I buy a big car or a small car? For example? (*You should buy* . . . .)
10. What qualities do you appreciate in a friend? (*I appreciate* . . . .)

12-7 CONTINUING THE SAME IDEA

(a) The city provides many cultural opportunities. It has an excellent art museum. **Moreover, Furthermore, In addition, Besides,** it has a fine symphony orchestra.	*Moreover, furthermore, in addition,* and *besides* mean *also.* They are transitions.
(b) The city provides many cultural opportunities. **In addition to (Besides)** an excellent art museum, it has a fine symphony orchestra.	In (b): *In addition to* and *besides* are used as prepositions. They are followed by an object (*museum*), not a clause.*

*__Besides__ means *in addition (to).* __Beside__ means *next to: I sat __beside__ my friend.*

EXERCISE 24: Combine the ideas in the following by using *moreover, furthermore, in addition (to), besides,* or *also* where appropriate.

1. I like to read that newspaper. One reason is that the news is always reported accurately. It has interesting special features.
2. There are many ways you can work on improving your English outside of class. For example, you should speak English as much as possible, even when you are speaking with friends who speak your native language. You should read as many magazines in English as you have time for. Watching television can be helpful.

3. Along with the increase in population in the city, there has been an increase in the rate of crime. A housing shortage has developed. There are so many automobiles in the city that the expressways are almost always jammed with cars, regardless of the time of day.

4. Good health is perhaps one's most valuable asset. To maintain good health, it is important to eat a balanced diet. The body needs a regular supply of vitamins, minerals, protein, carbohydrates, and other nutrients. Physical exercise is essential. Sleep and rest should not be neglected.

EXERCISE 25—WRITTEN: Write a paragraph of approximately 100 to 150 words in which you give specific examples to support one of the following general ideas. Use connecting words such as *for example, for instance, such as, moreover, furthermore, in addition (to)*, and *also*.

1. A newspaper contains a variety of articles to appeal to the different interests of its readers.

2. Some television programs are not suitable for viewing by children.

3. There are several things you should consider before you decide to get married.

4. There are several problems foreign students face when they first arrive in (the United States).

Comparisons

13-1 COMPARATIVE AND SUPERLATIVE FORMS OF ADJECTIVES AND ADVERBS

		COMPARATIVE	SUPERLATIVE	
ONE-SYLLABLE ADJECTIVES	old wise strange	older than wiser than stranger than	the oldest the wisest the strangest	For most one-syllable adjectives: *comparative form:* use *-er* *superlative form:* use *-est*
TWO-SYLLABLE ADJECTIVES	recent famous boring confused	more recent than more famous than more boring than more confused than	the most recent the most famous the most boring the most confused	For most two-syllable adjectives: *comparative form:* use **more** *superlative form:* use **most**
	pretty busy lazy	prettier than busier than lazier than	the prettiest the busiest the laziest	For two-syllable adjectives that end in *-y*, use *-er* and *-est*. (Notice: The *y* is changed to *i*.)
	clever	cleverer than more clever than	the cleverest the most clever	Certain two-syllable adjectives are used with either form: *-er* or **more**/*-est* or **most**.

		COMPARATIVE	SUPERLATIVE	
TWO-SYLLABLE ADJECTIVES	simple	simpler than more simple than	the simplest the most simple	Some common adjectives used with either form: *able, angry, clever, cruel, friendly, gentle, handsome, narrow, obscure, polite, quiet, secure, simple, stupid.*
ADJECTIVES WITH THREE OR MORE SYLLABLES	important responsible fascinating	more important than more responsible than more fascinating than	the most important the most responsible the most fascinating	*More* and *most* are used with adjectives that have three or more syllables.
IRREGULAR FORMS OF ADJECTIVES	good bad little far	better than worse than less than farther than	the best the worst the least the farthest	
-*LY* ADVERBS	slowly commonly carefully	more slowly than more commonly than more carefully than	the most slowly the most commonly the most carefully	*More* and *most* are used with adverbs that end in -*ly*. *
ADVERBS THAT DO NOT END IN -*LY*	fast hard soon close	faster than harder than sooner than closer than	the fastest the hardest the soonest the closest	The -*er* and -*est* forms are used with one-syllable adverbs.
IRREGULAR FORMS OF ADVERBS	well badly far	better than worse than farther than	the best the worst the farthest	

*Exception: *early* is both an adjective and an adverb.
Forms: *earlier, earliest*

EXERCISE 1: Supply the comparative and superlative forms of the following adjectives and adverbs.

1. natural (*more natural, the most natural*)
2. slow
3. slowly
4. active
5. funny
6. courageous
7. good

8. bad
9. wise
10. wisely
11. heavy
12. recent
13. confusing
14. polite
15. gentle

13-2 USING *FARTHER* AND *FURTHER*

(a) I walked six blocks. My friend walked three blocks. I walked *farther* than my friend did.	*Farther* is used to compare physical distances.*
(b) I need *further* information.	*Further* means "additional."*

*Informally, native speakers often use *further* and *farther* interchangeably to compare physical distances.

EXERCISE 2: Use either *farther* or *further* in the following.

1. Ron and his friend went jogging. Ron ran two miles, but his friend got tired after one mile. Ron ran _____ than his friend did.

2. If you have any _____ questions, please do not hesitate to ask.

3. Earth is _____ from the sun than Mercury is.

4. I like my new apartment, but it is _____ away from school than my old apartment was.

5. Thank you for your help, but I don't want to cause you any _____ trouble.

6. New York is _____ from Los Angeles than Chicago is.

7. I have no _____ need of this equipment. I'm going to sell it.

8. I've already told you what I think. If you don't agree with me, that's fine. But I don't want to discuss it any _____ .

13-3 COMPLETING A COMPARISON

(a) I am older **than my brother is.** (b) I am older **than my brother.** (c) I am older **than he is.** (d) I am older **than he.** (e) I am older **than him.** (*very informal*)	A subject and verb may follow *than*, as in (a), but the verb may sometimes be omitted, as in (b). In formal English, a subject pronoun follows *than*, as in (c) and (d).* Sometimes in spoken English, an object pronoun follows *than*, as in (e). This usage, although fairly common, is not considered to be grammatically correct.
(f) My apartment is larger **than Tom's.** My apartment is larger **than his.**	A possessive may follow *than*. In (f), the understood completion is: *than Tom's apartment.*
(g) He works harder than **I do.** He works harder than **I work.** (h) He can type faster than **she can.** He can type faster than **she can type.**	Frequently only an auxiliary verb follows the subject after *than*, but the main verb may be repeated.

*Usually when a pronoun follows *than*, the verb is not omitted, as in example (c).

EXERCISE 3: Use a pronoun in completing the following.

1. He was late. I got there earlier than _____he/he did._____

2. Their house is large. Our house is smaller than _____theirs/their house._____

3. My sister is only ten. She is younger than _____

4. She lives two miles away from school. I live closer to school than _____
   _____

5. You speak English very well, but I don't. Your English is much better than _____
   _____ You speak English better than _____

6. Her hair is short. My hair is longer than _____

7. I don't study very hard. My roommate studies much harder than _____
   _____

8. They aren't very friendly. Anna is much friendlier than _____

9. Your class is large. Our class is much smaller than _____

10. He's out of shape. I can run faster and farther than _____

13-4 RECOGNIZING "UNDERSTOOD" COMPARISONS

(a) A: Do you like coffee?
    B: Yes, but I like tea **better**.
(b) I like my history class, but my physics
    class is **more interesting**.
(c) Chris is a fine person. I have never met
    a **finer** person.
	Often it is not necessary to complete a comparison by using *than* if the meaning is clearly understood, as in the examples.
	In (a): *. . . better than I like coffee* is clearly understood.

13-5 AVOIDING UNCLEAR COMPARISONS

(d) UNCLEAR: Buy Bright-White toothpaste. It is better for your teeth. (e) UNCLEAR: I hope you can visit my country because it is more beautiful.	If it is not clear what two "things" are being compared, the comparison should be completed. In (d): . . . better for your teeth than what? In (e): . . . more beautiful than what?

(f) UNCLEAR:
He likes football better than his wife.
Possible meanings:
  (1) He likes football better than he likes his wife.
  (2) He likes football better than his wife does.
	Sometimes it is necessary to use both a subject and a verb after *than* in order to avoid unclear comparisons.

EXERCISE 4: Which of the following comparisons are unclear?

1. I know John better than Mary.
2. The next time you go to a drugstore to buy aspirin, get *Nopain*. It relieves pain faster.
3. A: How are you feeling today?
   B: A little better.
4. Since I began to exercise regularly, I have felt more energetic.
5. Ann likes her dog better than her husband.
6. Jan is tall, but her sister is even taller.
7. When I saw my friend for the first time in a year, the first thing I noticed was that his hair was longer.
8. I have decided to become a scientist because science is more beneficial to humankind.
9. A: Was your chemistry test difficult?
   B: I'll say it was! I've never taken a more difficult test.
10. Come to our store to do your shopping! Lower prices! Faster service!
11. You need to improve your study habits. You need to learn how to work more efficiently.
12. My parents like to get letters from me, but I usually write them only once a month. I should write home more often.

13-6 USING *MORE* WITH NOUNS

(a) Would you like some **more coffee?** (b) Not everyone is here. I expect **more people** to come later.	When *more* is used with nouns, it often has the meaning of "additional." It is not necessary to use *than.*
(c) There are **more people** in China **than** there are in the United States. (d) We had **more snow** this winter **than** last winter.	*More* is also used with nouns to make complete comparisons by using *than.*
(e) Do you have enough coffee, or would you like some **more?** (f) I'm full. I can't eat any **more.**	When the meaning is clear, the noun may be omitted and *more* used by itself.

13-7 USING *LESS* AND *FEWER*

(g) This book has little information. It has **less information** than that other book.	*Less* is the comparative form of *little.* It is used with noncount nouns.
(h) If you want to lose weight, you should eat **less** (food).	The noun may be omitted if the meaning is clear, as in (h).
(i) My class has **fewer students** than your class.	*Fewer* is the comparative form of *few.* It is used with count nouns. (Note: *less* is sometimes used with count nouns informally: *less students.* This usage is not considered grammatically correct.)
(j) A compact car is **less expensive** than a full-sized sedan. (k) She visits us **less frequently** than she used to.	*Less* is also used with adjectives and adverbs. Note: *Less* is usually not used with one-syllable adjectives. Instead, *not as . . . as* is usually used. (See 13–11.) Unusual: *He is less kind than Jack.* Usual: *He is not as kind as Jack.*

EXERCISE 5:   Use *more, less,* or *fewer* in the following; then complete the comparison if necessary.

1. A city has _____more_____ traffic _____than a small town._____

2. We have only two chairs, a table, and a bed in our new apartment. We need to buy some _____more_____ furniture.

3. A small town has _____ traffic _____

4. A twelve-year-old has _____ responsibilities _____

_____

5. Too much salt is not good for you. You should add _____ salt to your food.

6. I hope the teacher doesn't give any _____ tests this semester.

7. When you drive to Kansas City from here, don't take Highway 92. It's an old, two-lane road. It will take you _____ time to get there if you take Interstate 70.

8. This dictionary contains five thousand _____ words _____

_____

9. A new medical school has recently been established because the country needs

_____ doctors.

10. This winter has been mild. We have had much _____ snow ____

_____

11. I am very pleased. I made _____ mistakes on this composition

_____

12. I know much _____ about the history of _____

_____

13. In the writer's opinion, parents today have _____ control over their teenage children.

14. When I was in high school, I had to study _____

_____

EXERCISE 6: Using the word(s) in parentheses, complete the following. Use *more/-er* or *less,* as appropriate. In some, either *more/-er* or *less* is possible.

1. (*difficult*)   This test wasn't hard. It was much ___less___

    difficult than the last test.

2. (*difficult*)   Dr. Franklin gives hard tests. Her tests are ___

    more difficult than Dr. Barton's.

3. (*dense*)   Salt water is _____

4. (*convincing*)   What Joan said in her speech wasn't, in my

opinion, credible. Her speech was _____

_____

5. (*refreshing*)

When you are hot and tired, nothing is _____

_____

6. (*practice*)

I haven't mastered tennis yet. I need much ____

_____

7. (*a selfish person*)

Lois Rand is an extremely generous woman. I
have never known _____

8. (*an extraordinary
individual*)

Alex Hart is an unusual person. I have never

met _____

9. (*fortunate*)

In my life, I have always tried to help those

who are _____

10. (*a good conversationalist*)

I am a good writer, but Sue is _____

_____

11. (*a dangerous sport*)

Skiing is _____

_____

12. (*nutritious*)

White bread is _____

13. (*fluent*)

Because I have been speaking English every day
outside of the classroom, my spoken English is

becoming _____

_____

14. (*water*)

This house plant seems to be dying. Perhaps

you should give it _____

15. (*interested in*)

I am _____

_____

EXERCISE 7–ORAL (BOOKS CLOSED): Answer the question. Begin your response with "*Not really, but at least . . . .*"

(*To the teacher: Write "Not really, but at least . . ." on the board.*)

 Example: Is the mayor of this city famous?
 Response: Not really, but at least he/she is more famous than I am.

1. Is the weather warm/cold today?

2. Is a mouse big?
3. Is this room large?
4. Is your bed comfortable?
5. Is an elephant intelligent?
6. Was the last exercise easy?
7. Do you know a lot about chemistry?
8. Is a pen expensive?
9. Is this book heavy?
10. Are you relaxed right now?
11. Is riding a bicycle fast (transportation)?
12. Is (name of a city) far from here?

EXERCISE 8—ORAL (BOOKS CLOSED): Answer the question. Begin your response with "Yes, I have never . . . ."

(*To the teacher: Write "Yes, I have never . . ." on the board.*)

Example: Your friend told a story. Was it funny?
Response: Yes, I have never heard a funnier story in my life.

1. You took an entrance exam. Was it difficult?
2. You were in an earthquake. Were you frightened?
3. You read a book that you liked very much. Was it a good book?
4. Someone said something bad to you. Were you angry?
5. You were sitting on a rock by a mountain stream. Was the place peaceful?
6. You have met many people in your lifetime, but one person is special. Is this person kind?
7. Is this person considerate?
8. Is this person generous?
9. You have had many experiences in your lifetime, but you remember one in particular. Was it an interesting experience?
10. Was it an embarrassing experience?

EXERCISE 9: Study the examples, then complete the sentences by using *more than* and *less than* with appropriate "quantity or number expressions."

(a) **More than two-thirds of** the earth's surface is covered by water.
(b) **More than fifty percent of** the people in the United States are women.
(c) That car costs **less than six thousand** dollars.
(d) It is **less than three hundred** miles from here to Houston.

1. She has been working for that company for ___more than twenty-five years.___

   ___less than two months.___

2. It took us _____ to drive to Washington, D.C.

   _____

3. I understood _____ of the instructor's lecture.

   _____

4. I studied _____ last night.

   _____

5. I met them _____ ago.

   _____

6. _____ of the people in that country are illiterate.

   _____

7. I'm rich! I have _____ in my pocket.

   I'm broke! I have _____ in my pocket.

8. I'm not sure how much it cost to build that new hospital, but my best guess

   would be that it cost _____ but _____ .

13-8 REPEATING A COMPARATIVE

(a) Because he was afraid, he walked **faster and faster**. (b) Life in the modern world is becoming **more and more complex**.	Repeating a comparative gives the idea that something becomes progressively greater; i.e., it increases in intensity, quality, or quantity.

EXERCISE 10: Using the words in the following list (or your own words), complete the sentences. Repeat the comparative.

angry	*good*
big	*long*
discouraged	*loud*
enthusiastic	

1. Her English is improving. It is getting ___better and better___ .

2. They just had their sixth child. Their family is getting _____.

3. The line of people waiting to get into the theater got _____.

4. As the soccer game progressed, the crowd became _____.

5. The weather is getting _____ with each passing day.

6. I've been looking for a job for a month and still haven't been able to find one. I'm getting _____.

7. As the ambulance came closer to us, the siren became _____.

8. She sat there quietly, but during all that time she was getting _____. _____. Finally she exploded.

13-9 USING DOUBLE COMPARATIVES

(a) **The harder** you study, **the more** you will learn. (b) **The older** he got, **the quieter** he became. (c) **The more** she studied, **the more** she learned. (d) **The warmer** the weather (is), **the better** I like it.	A double comparative is used to indicate that the two parts of the comparison increase in direct proportion to each other. The second part of the comparison is often the *result* of the first part. In (a): If you study harder, the result will be that you will learn more.
(e) A: Should we ask Jenny and Jim to the party too? 　　B: Why not? **The more, the merrier.** (f) A: When should we leave? 　　B: **The sooner, the better.**	*The more, the merrier* and *the sooner, the better* are two common expressions. In (e): It is good to have more people at the party. In (f): It is good if we leave as soon as we can.

EXERCISE 11: Combine the ideas given in italics into a double comparative.

1. *I became bored.*
   He talked.

   I met a man at a party last night. I tried to be interested in what he was saying, but __the more he talked, the more bored I became.__

2. *I waited long*
   I got angry.

   My friend told me that she would pick me up at the corner at seven o'clock. By seven-thirty, she still hadn't come. _____.
   _____.

3. *I became nervous.*
   She drove fast.

   Wilma offered to take me to the airport, and I was grateful. But we got a late start, so on the way she stepped on the accelerator. I got a little uncomfortable. _____

_____

4. *You understand more.*
   You are old.

There are many advantages to being young, but

_____

_____

5. *He thought about his*
   family.
   He became homesick.

He tried to concentrate on his studying, but his
mind would drift to his family and his home.

_____

6. *We ran fast to reach the*
   house.
   The sky grew dark.

A storm was threatening. _____

_____

7. *I became confused.*
   I thought about it.

At first I thought I understood what she said,

but _____

_____

8. *The air is polluted.*
   The chances of develop-
   ing respiratory diseases
   are great.

Pollution poses many threats. For example, ____

_____

_____

13–10   USING SUPERLATIVES

(a) Tokyo is one of **the largest** cities *in the world*. (b) This is **the most valuable** painting *in the museum*. (c) I have three books. These two are quite good, but this one is **the best** (book) *of all*. (d) Living in a refugee camp was **the worst** experience *I have ever had in my life*. (e) David is one of **the kindest** and **most generous** people *I have ever known*.	Superlatives (*most* or *-est*) are used when three or more things or people are being compared. In the examples, notice the typical completions when a superlative is used.
(f) I took four final exams. The final in accounting was **the least** difficult *of all*.	*Least* has the opposite meaning of *most*.
(g) China has **the most people** of any country in the world. (h) **Most people** need six to eight hours of sleep every night.	In (g): *Most* is used in a superlative sense, so *the* precedes it. In (h): *Most* has the meaning of "over fifty percent," so no *the* is used.

EXERCISE 12: Use the appropriate superlative form (***most*** or ***-est***) for the word in parentheses and complete the sentence.

1. The physics course I took last semester is (*difficult*) ___the most difficult___ course ___I have ever taken.___

2. Ms. Steinberg is one of (*fascinating*) _____ speakers _____

3. My hometown is (*friendly*) _____ place _____ _____

4. What is (*embarrassing*) _____ experience _____ _____

5. Who is (*important*) _____ political figure _____ _____

6. What is (*high*) _____ mountain _____

7. Margaret is one of (*lazy*) _____ people _____ _____

Use ***least*** in the following.

8. When I go shopping, I always look for (*expensive*) _____ items.

9. Ed is not lazy, but he is certainly one of (*ambitious*) _____ people _____

10. What is (*useful*) _____ or (*important*) _____ _____thing you own?

EXERCISE 13—ORAL (BOOKS CLOSED): Make sentences from the given words by using ***one of the*** and a superlative.

Example: good student.
Response: John is one of the best students in the class.

Example: interesting *person*
Response: One of the most interesting *people* I have ever met is my roommate's mother.

1. beautiful country
2. important person

3. bad experience
4. hard metal

5. generous person
6. dangerous experience
7. happy day
8. large city
9. easy class
10. friendly person

11. bad book
12. lucky day
13. handsome man
14. strange thing
15. long river
16. good experience

13-11   MAKING COMPARISONS WITH *AS . . . AS*

Mary is 21. John is 21. (a) Mary is **as old as** John (is). (b) Mary is **as old as** he is. (c) Mary is **as old as** him. (*very informal*)	In (a): *as + adjective + as*
(d) It rains **as frequently** here **as** (it does) in my country. (e) I'm working **as fast as** I can. He came **as quickly as** he could. (f) I plan to stay here **as long as** possible. Please come **as soon as** possible. I write to them **as often as** possible.	In (d): *as + adverb + as* In (e): *Can* and *could* are frequently used in the completion. In (f): *possible* is another typical completion.
(g) She makes **as much (money) as** I do. There are **as many (students)** in my class **as** there are in your class.	In (g): *much* *as +* or *+ (noun) + as* *many*
(h) I work **just as hard as** you do. It's **just as hot today as** it was yesterday. I have **just as many problems as** you do.	In (h): *Just* is often used with *as . . . as* to emphasize that the two parts of the comparison are exactly the same.
(i) He is **not as** old **as** he looks. (j) He is **not so** old **as** he looks.	Negative form: *not as . . . as* or *not so . . . as.* Examples (i) and (j) have the same meaning. (Note: *not so . . . as* is generally preferred in formal English.)

EXERCISE 14: The *as . . . as* structure is used in many common idiomatic phrases.* How many of these phrases are you familiar with? Find out in this and the following exercise.

Complete the sentences by using *as . . . as* and the given words.

---

*These idiomatic usages of *as . . . as* are generally more common and appropriate in spoken than in written English. Also, with these expressions, the first *as* is sometimes omitted: *I'm hungry as a bear.*

bat
√ bear
bird
bull, ox
cat

kitten
mouse
mule
pig
wet hen

1. When will dinner be ready? I'm _____ as _____ hungry as a bear _____ .

2. If you don't stop eating so much, you're going to get _____ fat

_____

3. I'm _____ blind _____
without my glasses on.

4. I promise I won't say a word. You won't even know I'm there. I'll be _____
_____ quiet _____

5. Did he really lift that heavy box all by himself? He must be _____

strong _____

6. It was a lovely summer day. School was out and there was nothing in particular
that I had to do. I felt _____ free _____

7. Stop pacing the floor! You're _____ nervous _____

_____

8. Was she angry? You'd better believe it! She was _____ mad ____

_____

9. He won't change his mind. He's _____ stubborn _____

_____

10. I don't know what's the matter with me. Maybe I'm getting a cold. I feel
_____ weak _____

EXERCISE 15: Same as the preceding exercise.

beet
cucumber
daisy
feather
the hills

kite
pancake
pin
rock
sheet

1. Even in the face of danger, she was calm. She was _____ cool

   _____

2. Of course I've heard that joke before! It's _____ old _____

   _____

3. He felt very embarrassed. He turned _____ red _____

   _____

4. Do you feel all right? You look _____ white _____

   _____

5. How can anyone expect me to sleep in this bed? It's _____ hard

   _____

6. Thanks, but I don't need any help carrying this. It's _____ light

   _____

7. I tend to be a little messy, but my roommate is _____ neat ___

   _____

8. When she received the good news, she felt _____ high _____

   _____

9. No, I'm not tired. In fact, I feel _____ fresh _____

10. There's not a hill in sight for miles and miles. The whole countryside is ____

    _____ flat _____

EXERCISE 16: Complete the sentences by using *as . . . as.* (Use either *not as . . . as* or *not so . . . as* in negative sentences.)

1. We can't go any farther. This is _____ as far as we can go. _____

2. That politician used to be popular, but now he's not ___as(so)___ _____

   popular as he used to be. _____

3. I can't work any faster. I'm working _____

4. I had expected the test to be difficult, and it was. The test was just _____

   _____

5. I can't tell you any more about it. I've already told you _____

6. You might think it is easy to do, but it's not _____

7. We had a lot of snow last winter. I hope we don't get _____

_____

8. There was nothing else I could do. I did _____

9. The Atlantic Ocean is not _____ the
Pacific.

10. You're only old if you feel old. You are _____ young

_____

11. An orange is not _____ a lemon.

12. It is important to use your English. You should practice speaking English

_____

13. This knife is _____ sharp _____

14. It takes an hour to drive to the airport. It takes an hour to fly to Chicago. It

takes _____

_____

EXERCISE 17: Supply appropriate forms of comparisons for the words in parentheses.

1. Steve is (*tall*) _____ taller _____ than I am.

2. I need more facts. I can't make my decision until I get (*information*) _____

_____ .

3. I have much (*little*) _____ free time now than I had
when I was in high school.

4. You'd better buy the tickets for the show soon. (*Long*) _____

you wait, (*difficult*) _____ it will be to get good seats.

5. This brand of aspirin is just (*effective*) _____ in reliev-
ing pain as that brand.

6. Riding a bicycle can be dangerous. (*People*) _____
were killed in bicycle accidents last year than have been killed in airplane accidents in the last four years.

7. You can trust her with your life. You will never meet a (*honest*) _____

_____ and (*dependable*) _____
person.

8. I don't think I have ever met a (*kind*) _____ and

(*generous*) _____ person.

9. That is by far (*bad*) _____ movie I have ever seen!

10. She is very rich. She spends (*money*) _____ in a day
than I make in a year.

11. (*Hard*) _____ I tried, (*impossible*) _____

_____ it seemed to solve that math problem.

12. Howard Anderson is one of (*delightful*) _____ people
I have ever met.

13. I feel (*safe*) _____ in a plane than I do in a car.

14. Why don't you take physics next semester? It's not (*hard to understand*)

_____ you might think.

15. We expected thirty people to come to the meeting, but only twenty showed

up. (*People*) _____ came than we had expected.

13-12   USING *THE SAME, SIMILAR, DIFFERENT, LIKE, ALIKE*

(a) John and Mary have **the same books.** (b) John and Mary have **similar books.** (c) John and Mary have **different books.** (d) Their books are **the same.** (e) Their books are **similar.** (f) Their books are **different.**	*The same, similar,* and *different* are used as adjectives. Notice: *the* always precedes *same.*

(g) This book is **the same as** that one.
(h) This book is **similar to** that one.
(i) This book is **different from** that one.
	Notice: *the same* is followed by *as;*
	          similar is followed by *to;*
	          different is followed by *from.* *

(j) She is **the same age as** my mother. My shoes are **the same size as** yours.	A noun may come between *the same* and *as,* as in (j).
(k) My pen **is like** your pen. (l) My pen and your pen **are alike.**	Notice in (k) and (l): *noun + be like + noun* *noun and noun + be alike*

*In informal speech, native speakers might use ***than*** instead of ***from*** after ***different. From*** is considered correct in formal English, unless the comparison is completed by a clause: *I have a different attitude now than I used to have.*

(m) She **looks like** her sister. It **looks like** rain. It **sounds like** thunder. This material **feels like** silk. That **smells like** gas. This chemical **tastes like** salt. Stop **acting like** a fool. He **seems like** a nice fellow.	In addition to following *be, like* also follows certain verbs, primarily those dealing with the senses. Notice the examples in (m).
(n) The twins **look alike**. We **think alike**. Most four-year-olds **act alike**. My sister and I **talk alike**. The little boys **are dressed alike**.	*Alike* may follow a few verbs other than *be*. Notice the examples in (n).

EXERCISE 18: Use *the same (as)*, *similar (to)*, *different (from)*, *like,* and *alike* in the following. There may be more than one possible response in some of the sentences. Use whatever response sounds best to you.

1. This city is _____ my hometown. Both are quiet and conservative.

2. Jennifer and Jack both come from Rapid City. They come from _____ _____ town.

3. In many respects, our new house is _____ our old house.

4. Sue and Ann live in _____ apartment building. Sue's apartment is directly above Ann's.

5. A male mosquito is not _____ size _____ _____ a female mosquito. The female is larger.

6. We don't agree. Your ideas are _____ mine.

7. He never wears _____ clothes two days in a row.

8. An ant colony is _____ a well-disciplined army.

9. In terms of shape, cabbage looks _____ lettuce. But cabbage and lettuce don't taste _____.

10. The pronunciation of "caught" is _____ the pronuciation of "cot."

11. There wasn't a breath of wind. The surface of the lake looked _____

_____ glass.

12. We must have ESP. Our minds were thinking exactly _____.

Both of us had _____ idea at _____
time.

13. Trying to get through school without studying is _____
trying to go swimming without getting wet.

14. I'm tired. I feel _____ going home and lying down for
a while.

15. My math course this term is easy because I took a _____
course in high school.

16. He is _____ an ostrich. Whenever there is trouble, he
sticks his head in the sand.

17. "Meat" and "meet" are homonyms: they have _____
pronunciation.

18. I'm used to strong coffee. I think the coffee Americans drink tastes _____

_____ dishwater!

13-13   USING PRONOUNS (*ONE, ONES, THAT, THOSE*)
IN THE SECOND PART OF A COMPARISON

(a) This book is **more** interesting **than the one** I read last week. (b) My piece of pie isn't as big **as the one** you gave Tom. (c) The zoo in St. Louis is **similar to the one** in Washington, D.C.	In (a): The noun *book* is not repeated in the second part of the comparison. Instead, the pronoun *one* is used. Usually *the one* is used for singular count nouns, as in (a), (b), and (c).
(d) The weather is this city is **similar to that** in my hometown. (e) The bread my mother makes is much **better than that** which you can buy at a store.	Usually *that* is used for noncount nouns, as in (d) and (e).
(f) The students in this class have to work harder **than those** in Mr. Lee's class. (g) The students in this class have to work harder **than the ones** in Mr. Lee's class.	For plural nouns, either *those* or *the ones* is used.*

*When the pronoun in the second part of the comparison is followed by a phrase beginning with *of*, usually *that* or *those* is used, not *one* or *ones*:

*The brain of a porpoise is larger than **that** of most other mammals.*

*Influenza is sometimes difficult to diagnose because its symptoms are similar to **those** of the common cold.*

EXERCISE 19: In completing the following sentences, use *the one, the ones, that,* or *those.*

1. The test we took yesterday was more difficult ___than the one we had___
   _____ last week.

2. The grocery store on Fifth Street has cheaper prices _____
   _____

3. I could understand the speech Ms. Kim gave better _____
   _____

4. The weather in my country is much warmer _____
   _____

5. The courses I am taking this semester are less difficult _____
   _____

6. The explanation in this book is not quite the same _____
   _____

7. The apartments in the suburbs are not quite so expensive _____
   _____

8. The mountains in the western part of the United States are much higher _____
   _____

9. I think the movie we went to last night was just as _____
   _____

10. The textbook I am using in my marketing course this semester is similar _____
    _____

EXERCISE 20—ORAL: Before you come to class, prepare statements of comparison and contrast on the following topics. Be inventive, original, and specific. Prepare at least three statements on each topic to share with the rest of the class.

TOPICS: (1) Language
           (2) Food
           (3) Seasons of the year
           (4) Children/adults
           (5) Sports

Study the following examples. Notice the various structures and words that may be used to make statements of comparison and contrast.

(a) *more (-er)*	I feel *more comfortable* speaking my native language *than* I do speaking English.
	The English alphabet has *fewer letters than* the Spanish alphabet.
	I think learning a second language is *more difficult than* studying mathematics.
	It is *easier* to write in one's native language *than* (it is to write) in a second language.
(b) *most (-est)*	My friend has studied many languages. He thinks Japanese is *the most difficult* of all the languages he has studied.
	I think English is one of *the most important* languages in the world today.
(c) *as . . . as*	Usually adults don't pick up a new language *as quickly as* a child does.
	I try to practice speaking English *as often as* I can.
(d) *the same*	Even though Mohammed and I come from different countries, we have become friends because we speak *the same language,* Arabic.
	Except for a few minor differences, American English and British English are *the same.*
(e) *different*	The English spoken in the United States is only slightly *different from* that spoken in England.
(f) *similar*	Chinese is *similar to* Japanese in certain respects.
(g) *like*	Portuguese is *like* Spanish in some respects.
(h) *however,*	English uses an alphabet. Chinese, *however,* uses characters.
but	English uses an alphabet, *but* Chinese uses characters.
(i) *whereas, while*	Arabic is written from right to left, *whereas* (*while*) English is written from left to right.
(j) *would rather*	I *would rather* learn Spanish than French.
(k) *prefer*	I *prefer* studying science *to* trying to learn a second language.
(l) "double comparative"	A universal language would be desirable in that *the better* people are able to communicate, *the greater* the chances are of achieving an enduring peace in the world.

EXERCISE 21—ORAL: Do you have sayings in your language that are similar to or the same as the following English proverbs?

1. Don't count your chickens before they're hatched.
2. The early bird gets the worm.
3. Too many cooks spoil the broth.
4. A bird in the hand is worth two in the bush.
5. A stitch in time saves nine.
6. When in Rome, do as the Romans do.
7. Birds of a feather flock together.
8. A rolling stone gathers no moss.

EXERCISE 22—WRITTEN: Following are topics for writing.

Compare and contrast:

(1) Being single and being married.
(2) Cities you have lived in or have visited.
(3) Different schools or universities you have attended.
(4) Your way of life before and after you became a parent.
(5) Yourself now to yourself ten years ago.
(6) Your country now to your country 100 years ago.

EXERCISE 23—PREPOSITIONS: Supply appropriate prepositions.

1. Max is known _____ his honesty.

2. Mr. and Mrs. Jones have always been faithful _____ each other.

3. The little girl is afraid _____ an imaginary bear that lives in her closet.

4. Do you promise to come? I'm counting _____ you to be there.

5. Trucks are prohibited _____ using residential streets.

6. Do you take good care _____ your health?

7. I'm worried _____ this problem.

8. I don't agree _____ you.

9. We decided _____ eight o'clock as the time we should meet.

10. Who did you vote _____ in the last election?

11. How many students were absent _____ class yesterday?

12. It is important to be polite _____ other people.

13. The farmers are hoping _____ rain.

14. He was late because he wasn't aware _____ the time.

15. We will fight _____ our rights.

Conditional Sentences

14-1 SUMMARY OF BASIC VERB FORM USAGE IN CONDITIONAL SENTENCES

MEANING OF THE "*IF* CLAUSE"	VERB FORM IN THE "*IF* CLAUSE"	VERB FORM IN THE "RESULT CLAUSE"	
True in the present/future	*simple present*	*simple present* *simple future*	(a) If I **have** enough time, I **write** to my parents every week. (b) If I **have** enough time tomorrow, I **will write** to my parents.
Untrue in the present/future	*simple past*	*would + simple form*	(c) If I **had** enough time now, I **would write** to my parents. (*In truth, I do not have enough time, so I will not write to them.*)
Untrue in the past	*past perfect*	*would have + past participle*	(d) If I **had had** enough time, I **would have written** to my parents yesterday. (*In truth, I did not have enough time, so I did not write to them.*)

14-2 TRUE IN THE PRESENT OR FUTURE

(e) If I **don't eat** breakfast, I always **get** hungry during class. (f) Water **freezes (will freeze)** if the temperature **goes** below 32°F.	In (e): The simple present is used in the result clause to express a habitual activity or situation. In (f): Either the simple present or the simple future is used in the result clause to express an established, predictable fact.

(g) If I **don't eat** breakfast tomorrow morning, I **will get** hungry during class.	In (g) and (h): The simple future is used in the result clause when the sentence concerns a particular activity or situation in the future.
(h) If the weather **is** nice tomorrow, we **will go** on a picnic.	Note: The simple present, not the simple future, is used in the "*if* clause."

14-3 UNTRUE (CONTRARY TO FACT) IN THE PRESENT/FUTURE

(i) If I **taught** this class, I **wouldn't give** tests.	In (i): In truth, I don't teach this class.
(j) If he **were** here right now, he **would help** us.	In (j): In truth, he is not here right now.
(k) If I **were** you, I **would accept** their invitation.	In (k): In truth, I am not you.
	Note: *Were* is used for both singular and plural subjects. *Was* (with *I, he, she, it*) is sometimes used in very informal speech but is not generally considered grammatically acceptable.

14-4 UNTRUE (CONTRARY TO FACT) IN THE PAST

(l) If you **had told** me about the problem, I **would have helped** you.	In (l): In truth, you did not tell me about it.
(m) If they **had studied**, they **would have passed** the exam.	In (m): In truth, they did not study. They failed the exam.
(n) If I **hadn't slipped** on the ice, I **wouldn't have broken** my arm.	In (n): In truth, I slipped on the ice. I broke my arm.
	Note: The auxiliary verbs are almost always contracted in speech. "If you'd told me, I would've helped you (*or*: I'd've helped you)."

EXERCISE 1: Supply the appropriate form for the verbs in parentheses.

1. If I (*have*) _____ enough money, I will go with you.

2. If I (*have*) _____ enough money, I would go with you.

3. If I (*have*) _____ enough money, I would have gone with you.

4. If the weather is nice tomorrow, we (*go*) _____ to the zoo.

5. If the weather were nice today, we (*go*) _____ to the zoo.

6. If the weather had been nice yesterday, we (*go*) _____ to the zoo.

7. I would change majors if I (*be*) _____ you.

8. It's too bad that Helen isn't here. If she (*be*) _____ here, she (*know*) _____ what to do.

9. Fred failed the test because he didn't study. However, if he (*study*) _____ _____ for the test, he (*pass*) _____ it.

10. You should tell him exactly what happened. If I (*be*) _____ you, I (*tell*) _____ him the truth as soon as possible.

11. I got wet because I didn't take my umbrella. However, I (*get, not*) _____ _____ wet if I (*remember*) _____ to take my umbrella with me yesterday.

12. I (*change*) _____ the present economic policy if I (*be*) _____ the President of the United States.

EXERCISE 2: Supply the appropriate auxiliary verb.

1. I don't have a pen, but if I _____ did _____, I would lend it to you.

2. He is busy right now, but if he _____ weren't _____, he would help us.

3. I didn't vote in the last election, but if I _____ had _____, I would have voted for Senator Anderson.

4. I don't have enough money, but if I _____, I would buy that book.

5. The weather is cold today, but if it _____, I would go swimming.

6. She didn't come, but if she _____, she would have met my brother.

7. I'm not a good cook, but if I _____, I would make all of my own meals.

8. I have to go to class this afternoon, but if I _____, I would go downtown with you.

9. My wife isn't here yet, but if she _____, I would invite you over for some delicious cooking.

10. He didn't go to a doctor, but if he _____, the cut on his hand wouldn't have gotten infected.

EXERCISE 3–ORAL (BOOKS CLOSED): Answer the question. Begin with "No, but . . . ."

Example: Do you have a dollar?
Response: No, but if I did (No, but if I had a dollar), I would lend it to you.

1. Are you rich?
2. Do you have a car?
3. Are you a bird?
4. Are you in (student's country/hometown)?
5. Do you live in an apartment? Dormitory? Hotel?
6. Are you the teacher of this class?
7. Do you have your own airplane?
8. Are you the President of the United States?
9. Are you tired?
10. Are you at home right now?
11. Are you married? Single?
12. Do you speak (another language)?
13. Is the weather hot/cold today?
14. Are you hungry?
15. Do you live in (New York City)?

EXERCISE 4—ORAL (BOOKS CLOSED):   Begin your response with "But if I had known . . . ."

> *Example:*   There was a test yesterday. You didn't know that, so you didn't study.
>
> *Response:*   But if I had known (that there was a test yesterday), I would have studied.

1. Your friend was in the hospital. You didn't know that, so you didn't visit her.
2. I've never met your friend. You didn't know that, so you didn't introduce me.
3. There was a party last night. You didn't know that, so you didn't go.
4. Your friend's parents are in town. You didn't know that, so you didn't invite them to dinner.
5. I wanted to go to the soccer game. You didn't know that, so you didn't buy another ticket.
6. I was at home last night. You didn't know that, so you didn't visit me.
7. Your sister wanted a gold necklace for her birthday. You didn't know that, so you didn't buy her one.
8. I had a problem. You didn't know that, so you didn't offer to help.

EXERCISE 5:   Change the following statements into conditional sentences.

1. I didn't buy it because I didn't have enough money. But . . . (*I would have bought it if I'd had enough money.*)

2. I won't buy it because I don't have enough money. But . . . .

3. You got into so much trouble because you didn't listen to me. But . . . .

4. The woman didn't die because she received immediate medical attention. But . . . .

5. Jack came, so I wasn't disappointed. But . . . .

6. Ann didn't pass the entrance examination, so she wasn't admitted to the university. But . . . .

7. There are so many bugs in the room because there isn't a screen on the window. But . . . .

8. We ran out of gas because we didn't stop at the service station. But . . . .

14-5 USING PROGRESSIVE VERB FORMS

(a)	TRUE:	It **is raining** right now, so **I will not go** for a walk.
	CONDITIONAL:	If it **were not raining** right now, **I would go** for a walk.
(b)	TRUE:	**I am not living** in Chile. **I am not working** at a bank.
	CONDITIONAL:	If I **were living** in Chile, **I would be working** at a bank.
(c)	TRUE:	It **was raining** yesterday afternoon, so **I did not go** for a walk.
	CONDITIONAL:	If it **had not been raining**, **I would have gone** for a walk.
(d)	TRUE:	**I was not living** in Chile last year. **I was not working** at a bank.
	CONDITIONAL:	If I **had been living** in Chile last year, **I would have been working** at a bank.

Note: Even in conditional sentences, progressive verb forms are used in progressive situations. (See 3–5 for a discussion of progressive verbs.)

14-6 USING "MIXED TIME" IN CONDITIONAL SENTENCES

(e)	TRUE:	**I did not eat** breakfast several hours ago, so **I am** hungry now.
	CONDITIONAL:	If I **had eaten** breakfast several hours ago, **I would not be** hungry now.
		(past) *(present)*

(f) TRUE:	He **is not** a good student. He **did not study** for the test yesterday.
CONDITIONAL:	If he **were** a good student, he **would have studied** for the test.
	(present) *(past)*

Note: Frequently the time in the "*if* clause" and the time in the "result clause" are different: one clause may be in the present and the other in the past.

EXERCISE 6: Change the following statements into conditional sentences.

1. It is snowing, so I won't go with you. But . . . .
2. I am hungry because I didn't eat dinner. But . . . .
3. The child is crying because his mother isn't here. But . . . .
4. Helen is sick because she didn't follow the doctor's orders. But . . . .
5. You weren't listening, so you didn't understand the directions. But . . . .
6. You are tired this morning because you didn't go to bed at a reasonable hour last night. But . . . .
7. I'm not you, so I didn't tell him the truth. But . . . .
8. Joe got a ticket because he was driving too fast. But . . . .

14-7 USING *COULD, MIGHT,* AND *SHOULD*

(a) If I were a bird, I **could fly** home.	In (a): *could fly = would be able to fly*
(b) If I **could sing** as well as you, I **would join** the opera.	In (b): *could sing = were able to sing*
(c) If I'**d had** enough money, I **could have gone** to Florida for vacation.	In (c): *could have gone = would have been able to go*
(d) If I **don't get** a scholarship, I **might get** a job instead of going to graduate school next fall.	In (d): *I might get = maybe I will get*
(e) If you **were** a better student, you **might get** better grades.	In (e): *you might get = maybe you would get*
(f) If you **had told** me about your problem, I **might have been** able to help you.	In (f): *I might have been = maybe I would have been*
(g) If John **should call, tell** him I'll be back around five.	In (g): *If John should call* indicates a little more uncertainty or doubt than *If John calls,* but the meaning of the two is basically the same.
(h) If there **should be** another world war, the continued existence of the human race **would be** in jeopardy.	In (h): *If there should be* indicates more uncertainty or doubt than *If there were.*

EXERCISE 7: Complete the following.

1. I could go _____ to Arizona over vacation if I had enough time. _____

2. I could buy _____

3. I would buy _____

4. I could have bought _____

5. I would have bought _____

6. If I could speak _____

7. You might have passed the test _____

8. If you should need to get in touch with me later _____

9. If it should rain tomorrow _____

10. I could have finished my work on time _____

14-8 OMITTING *IF*

(a) **Were I** you, I wouldn't do that.	With *were, had* (past perfect), and *should*,
(b) **Had I known** about it, I would have told you.	sometimes *if* is omitted and the subject and verb are inverted.
(c) **Should anyone call**, please take a message.	In (a): *Were I you = If I were you*
	In (b): *Had I known = If I had known*
	In (c): *Should anyone call = If anyone should call*

14-9 IMPLIED CONDITIONS

(d) **I would have gone** with you, but I had to study. (*Implied condition: . . . if I hadn't had to study*)	Often the "*if* clause" is implied, not stated. Conditional verbs are still used in the "result clause."
(e) I never **would have succeeded** without your help. (*Implied condition: . . . if you hadn't helped me*)	
(f) She ran; otherwise, she **would have missed** her bus.	Conditional verbs are frequently used following *otherwise.* In (f), the implied "*if* clause" is: *If she had not run . . . .*

EXERCISE 8: Give an appropriate form for the verb in parentheses. Some of the verbs are passive.

1. If I could speak Japanese, I (*spend*) _____ next year studying in Japan.

2. Had I known Mr. Jung was in the hospital, I (*send*) _____ him a note and some flowers.

3. We will move into our new house next month if it (*complete*) _____ by then.

4. How old (*be, you*) _____ now if you (*be*) _____ born in the year 1900?

5. It's too bad that it's snowing. If it (*snow, not*) _____, we could go for a drive.

6. I was very tired. Otherwise, I (*go*) _____ to the party with you last night.

7. I'm broke, but I (*have*) _____ plenty of money now if I (*spend, not*) _____ so much yesterday.

8. That child had a narrow escape. She (*hit*) _____ by a car if her father (*pull, not*) _____ her out of the street.

9. I'm glad I have so many friends and such a wonderful family. Life without any friends or family (*be*) _____ lonely for me.

10. My grandfather is no longer alive, but if he (*be*) _____, I'm sure he (*be*) _____ proud of me.

11. If you (*sleep, not*) _____ last night when we arrived, I would have asked you to go with us, but I didn't want to wake you up.

12. Bill has such a bad memory that he (*forget*) _____ his head if it (*be, not*) _____ attached to his body.

EXERCISE 9: Same as the preceding exercise.

1. A: What would you be doing right now if you (*be, not*) _____ in class?

   B: I (*sleep*) _____.

2. A: Why were you late for the meeting?

B: Well, I (*be*) _____ there on time, but I had a flat tire on the way.

3. A: How did you get to work this morning?

B: I drove. I (*take*) _____ the bus, but I overslept.

4. A: Did you know that Bob got 100% on the test?

B: Really? That surprises me. If I didn't know better, I (*think*) _____

_____ he cheated.

5. A: Boy, is it ever hot today!

B: You said it! If there (*be*) _____ only a breeze, it (*be, not*) _____ quite so unbearable.

6. A: Why isn't Peggy Adams in class today?

B: I don't know, but I'm sure she (*be, not*) _____ absent unless* she (*have*) _____ a good reason.

7. A: When did Mark graduate?

B: He didn't.

A: Oh?

B: He had to quit school because of some trouble at home. Otherwise, he (*graduate*) _____ last June.

8. A: Hi, sorry I'm late.

B: That's okay.

A: I (*be*) _____ here sooner, but I had car trouble.

9. A: Want to ride on the roller coaster?

---

*unless = if not (See 12–4)

B: No way! I (*ride, not*) _____ on the roller coaster even if you paid me a million dollars!

10. A: Hi, Pat. Come on in.

B: Oh, I didn't know you had company. I (*come, not*) _____

(*know, I*) _____ someone was here.

A: That's okay. Come on and let me introduce you to my friends.

11. A: How did you do on the test?

B: Not so well. I (*do*) _____ much better, but I misread the directions for the last section.

12. A: Do you really mean it?

B: Of course! I (*say, not*) _____ it unless I (*mean*) _____

_____ it.

13. A: Are you coming to the party?

B: I don't think so, but if I change my mind, I (*tell*) _____ you.

14. A: I hear Dorothy had an accident. Was it serious?

B: No. Luckily, she wasn't driving fast at the time of the accident. If she

(*drive*) _____ fast, I'm sure it (*be*) _____ a more serious accident.

EXERCISE 10:   Complete the following.

1. If it hadn't rained _____

2. If it weren't raining _____

3. You would have passed the test had _____

4. It's a good thing we took a map with us. Otherwise, _____

_____

5. Without electricity, modern life _____

6. If you hadn't reminded me about the meeting tonight, _____

_____

7. Should you need any help, _____

8. If I could choose any profession I wanted, _____

9. If I were at home right now, _____

10. Without your help yesterday, _____

EXERCISE 11—ORAL (BOOKS CLOSED):   Answer the questions.

> *Example:*   Suppose the student sitting next to you drops his/her pen. What would you do?
>
> *Response:*   I would pick it up for him/her.

1. Suppose (pretend) there is a fire in this building right now. What would you do?

2. Suppose there is a fire in your room or apartment or house. You have time to save only one thing. What would you save?

3. Suppose you go to the bank to cash a check for twenty dollars. The bank teller cashes your check and you leave, but when you count the money, you find she gave you thirty dollars instead of twenty. What would you do?

4. Same situation, but you find she gave you only fifteen dollars instead of twenty.

5. John was cheating during an examination. The teacher saw him. Suppose you were the teacher. What would you have done?

6. You go to a party. A man starts talking to you, but he is speaking so fast that you can't catch what he is saying. What would you do?

7. Late at night you're driving your car down a deserted street. You're all alone. In an attempt to avoid a dog in the road, you swerve to one side and hit a parked car. You know that no one saw you. What would you do?

8. Mary goes to a friend's house for dinner. Her friend serves a dish that Mary can't stand, doesn't like at all. What if you were Mary?

9. My friend John borrowed ten dollars from me and told me he would repay it in a couple of days, but it's been three weeks. I think he has forgotten about it. I really need the money, but I don't want to ask him for it. Give me some advice.

10. John was driving over the speed limit. A police car began to chase him, with red lights flashing. John stepped on the accelerator and tried to escape the police car. Put yourself in his position.

11. You are walking down the street and suddenly a large dog jumps in front of you. The dog doesn't look friendly. He is growling and moving toward you. If that happened . . . .

12. Suppose you are walking down the street at night all by yourself. A man suddenly appears in front of you. He has a gun. He says, "Give me your money." Would you try to take his gun away?

13. Suppose you go to (Chicago) to visit a friend. You have never been there before. Your friend said he would meet you at the airport, but he's not there. You wait for a long time, but he never shows up. You try to call him, but nobody answers the phone. Now what?

14. You are just falling asleep when you hear a burglar opening your bedroom window and climbing in. What would you do?

15. You ask a very special person to go to dinner with you. You like this person very much and want to make a good impression. You go to a fancy restaurant and have a wonderful meal. But when you reach for your wallet, you discover that it is not there. You have no money with you.

EXERCISE 12—WRITTEN: Following are topics for writing.

1. If, beginning tomorrow, you had a two-week holiday and unlimited funds, what would you do? Why?
2. If you had to teach your language to a person who knew nothing about your language at all, how would you begin? What would you do so that this person could learn your language as quickly and easily as possible?
3. If you were Philosopher-King of the world, how would you govern? What would you do? What changes would you make? (A "Philosopher-King" may be defined as a person who had ideal wisdom and unlimited power to shape the world as he/she wished.)
4. Suppose you had only one year to live. What would you do?
5. Describe your activities if you were in your own country at present. Describe your probable activities today, yesterday, and tomorrow. Include the activities of your family and friends.

14-10   VERB FORMS FOLLOWING *WISH*

	VERB FORM IN "TRUE" SENTENCE	**VERB FORM FOLLOWING *WISH***	
A wish about the future	(a) She **will not tell** me. (b) He **isn't going to be** here. (c) She **can't come** tomorrow.	I wish (that) she **would tell** me. I wish he **were going to be** here. I wish she **could come** tomorrow.	*Wish* is used when the speaker wants reality to be different, to be exactly the opposite. Verb forms similar to those in conditional sentences are used. Notice the examples.
A wish about the present	(d) I **don't know** French. (e) It **is raining** right now. (f) I **can't speak** Japanese.	I wish I **knew** French. I wish it **weren't raining** right now. I wish I **could speak** Japanese.	*Wish* is followed by a noun clause. The use of *that* is optional. Usually it is omitted in speaking.
A wish about the past	(g) John **didn't come**. (h) Mary **couldn't come**.	I wish John **had come**.* I wish Mary **could have come**.	

*Sometimes in very informal speaking: *I wish John would have come.*

EXERCISE 13:   Supply appropriate completions in the following.

1. Our classroom doesn't have any windows. I wish our classroom ____had____ windows.

2. The sun isn't shining. I wish the sun _____ right now.

3. I didn't go shopping. I wish I _____ shopping.

4. I don't know how to dance. I wish I _____ how to dance.

5. You didn't tell me about it. I wish you _____ me about it.

6. It's cold today. I'm not wearing a coat. I wish I _____ a coat.

7. I don't have enough money to buy that book. I wish I _____ enough money.

8. Martha is tired because she went to bed late last night. She wishes she _____ _____ to bed earlier last night.

9. I can't go with you. I wish I _____ with you tomorrow.

10. He won't lend me his car. I wish he _____ me his car for my date tomorrow night.

11. Patricia isn't coming to dinner with us tonight. I wish she _____ to dinner with us.

12. The teacher is going to give an exam tomorrow. I wish the teacher _____ _____ us an exam tomorrow.

13. You can't meet my parents. I wish you _____ them.

14. Jerry didn't come to the meeting. I wish he _____ to the meeting.

15. I am not lying on a beach in Hawaii. I wish I _____ on a beach in Hawaii.

EXERCISE 14:   Supply an appropriate auxiliary in the following.

1. I'm not at home, but I wish I ____were____ .

2. I don't know her, but I wish I ____did____ .

3. I can't sing well, but I wish I ____could____ .

4. I didn't go, but I wish I ____had____ .

5. He won't talk about it, but I wish he ____would____ .

6. I didn't read that book, but I wish I _____ .

7. I want to go, but I can't. I wish I _____ .

8. I don't have a bicycle, but I wish I _____ .

9. He didn't buy a ticket to the game, but he wishes he _____ .

10. She can't speak English, but she wishes she _____ .

11. It probably won't happen, but I wish it _____ .

12. He isn't old enough to drive a car, but he wishes he _____ .

13. They didn't go to the movie, but they wish they _____ .

14. I don't have a driver's license, but I wish I _____ .

15. I'm not living in an apartment, but I wish I _____ .

14-11 USING *WOULD* TO MAKE WISHES ABOUT THE FUTURE

(a) It is raining. I wish it **would stop**. (*I want it to stop raining.*) (b) I'm expecting a call. I wish the phone **would ring**. (*I want the phone to ring.*)	*Would* is usually used to indicate that the speaker *wants* something to happen in the future. The wish may or may not come true (be realized).
(c) It's going to be a good party. I wish you **would come**. (*I want you to come.*) (d) We're going to be late. I wish you **would hurry**. (*I want you to hurry.*)	In (c) and (d): *I wish you would . . .* is often used to make a request.

EXERCISE 15: Give the appropriate form of the verbs in parentheses to make wishes about the future.

1. Are you sure you won't be able to come with us? I wish you (*change*) _____ _____ your mind.

2. Bob's mother doesn't like his beard. She wishes he (*shave*) _____ _____ it off.

3. He needs some money. He wishes his parents (*send*) _____ him some.

4. The newspaper strike has been going on for two weeks. I wish it (*end*)_____ _____ .

5. My roommate is very messy. I wish she (*pick*) _____ up after herself more often.

EXERCISE 16: Supply an appropriate form.

1. We need some help. I wish Alfred (*be*) _____ here now.

   If he (*be*) _____, we could finish this work very quickly.

2. We had a good time in Houston over vacation. I wish you (*come*) _____

   _____ with us. If you (*come*) _____

   _____ with us, you (*have*) _____

   a good time.

3. I wish it (*be, not*) _____ so cold today. If it (*be, not*)

   _____ so cold, I (*go*) _____

   swimming.

4. I missed part of the lecture because I was daydreaming, and now my notes are

   incomplete. I wish I (*pay*) _____ more attention to the lecturer.

5. A: Do you have enough money to buy that antique lamp?

   B: No, but I certainly wish I _____.

6. A: Did you study for the test?

   B: No, but now I wish I _____ because I flunked it.

7. A: Is the noise from the record player in the next apartment bothering you?

   B: Yes. I'm trying to study. I wish he (*turn*) _____ it down.

8. A: What a beautiful day! I wish I (*lie*) _____ in the sun by a swimming pool instead of sitting in a classroom.

   B: I wish I (*be*) _____ anywhere but here!

9. A: I can't go to the game with you this afternoon.

   B: Really? That's too bad. But I wish you (*tell*) _____ me sooner so that I could have found someone else to go with.

10. A: How long have you been sick?

    B: For over a week.

    A: I wish you (*go*) _____ to see a doctor today. You should find out what's wrong with you.

    B: Maybe I'll go tomorrow.

11. A: I wish we (*have, not*) _____ to go to class today.

    B: So do I. I wish it (*be*) _____ Saturday.

12. A: He couldn't have said that! That's impossible. You must have misunder-
stood him.

   B: I only wish I _____, but I'm sure I heard him
correctly.

EXERCISE 17—ORAL (BOOKS CLOSED):   Answer the questions. Use *wish*.

1. Where do you wish you were right now? What do you wish you were doing?
2. Are you pleased with the weather today, or do you wish it were different?
3. Look around this room. What do you wish were different?
4. Is there anything you wish were different about the place you are living?
5. What do you wish were different about this city/town?
6. What do you wish were different about your country or the United States?
7. What do you wish were different about a student's life?
8. Just for fun, what do you wish were or could be different in the world? What about animals being able to speak? People being able to fly? There being only one language in the world? Being able to take vacations on the moon? Speed of transportation?
9. Where do you wish you could go on your next vacation?
10. Your friend gave you his phone number, but you didn't write it down because you thought you would remember it. Now you have forgotten the number. What do you wish?
11. John kept all of his money in his wallet instead of putting it in the bank. Then he lost his wallet. What does he probably wish?
12. You didn't eat breakfast/lunch/dinner before you came to class. Now you are hungry. What do you wish?
13. Mary stayed up very late last night. Today she is tired and sleepy. What does she probably wish?
14. Is there anything in your past life that you would change? What do you wish you had or had not done?

14-12   USING *AS IF/AS THOUGH*

(a) It looks **like** rain.	Notice in (a): *like* is followed by a noun object.
(b) It looks **as if** it is going to rain.	Notice in (b) and (c): *as if* and *as though* are followed by a clause.
(c) It looks **as though** it is going to rain.	
(d) It looks **like** it is going to rain. *(informal)*	Notice in (d): *like* is followed by a clause. This use of *like* is common in informal English but is not generally considered appropriate in formal English. *As if* or *as though* is preferred.
	(a), (b), (c), and (d) all have the same meaning.

"TRUE" STATEMENT	VERB FORM AFTER *AS IF/AS THOUGH*	
(e) **He is not** a child. (f) **She did not take** a shower with her clothes on. (g) **He has met** her. (h) **She will be** here.	She talked to him **as if he were** a child. When she came in from the rainstorm, she looked **as if she had taken** a shower with her clothes on. He acted **as though he had never met** her. She spoke **as if she wouldn't be** here.	Usually the idea following *as if/as though* is "untrue." In this case, verb usage is similar to that in conditional sentences. Notice the examples.

EXERCISE 18: Using the idea given in parentheses, complete each sentence with *as if/as though.*

1. (*I wasn't run over by a ten-ton truck.*)

    I feel terrible. I feel _____ as if (as though) I had been run over by a ten-ton

    _____ truck.

2. (*English is not her native tongue.*)

    She speaks English _____

3. (*His animals aren't people.*)

    I know a farmer who talks to his animals _____

4. (*You didn't see a ghost.*)

    What's the matter? You look _____

5. (*His father is not a general in the army.*)

    Sometimes his father gives orders _____

6. (*I didn't climb Mt. Everest.*)

    When I reached the fourth floor, I was winded. I felt _____

    _____ instead of just three flights of

    stairs.

7. (*He does have a brain in his head.*)

    Sometimes he acts _____

8. (*We haven't known each other all of our lives.*)

We became good friends almost immediately. After talking to each other for

only a short time, we felt _____

9. (*A giant bulldozer didn't drive down Main Street.*)

After the tornado, the town looked _____

10. (*I don't have wings and can't fly.*)

I was so happy that I felt _____

11. (*The child won't burst.*)

The child was so excited that he looked _____

12. *Note:* The following sentiments were expressed by Helen Keller, a woman who was both blind and deaf but who learned to speak and to read (Braille).

Use your eyes as if tomorrow you _____ become blind.

Hear the music of voices, the song of a bird, as if you _____ become deaf tomorrow. Touch each object as if tomorrow you _____ never be able to feel anything again. Smell the perfume of flowers and taste

with true enjoyment each bite of food as if tomorrow you _____ never be able to smell and taste again.

EXERCISE 19: General review of verb forms.

1. Some of the students (*speak, never*) _____ English before they came here last fall.

2. I wish I (*come, not*) _____ here last year.

3. It is essential that you (*be*) _____ here tomorrow.

4. Had I known he wouldn't be here, I (*come, not*) _____.

5. My passport (*stamp*) _____ at the airport when I arrived.

6. My seventy-year-old grandfather, who owns his own business, (*continue, probably*) _____ to work as long as he (*live*) _____

_____ .

7. I arrived here in September 1979. By September 1989, I (*be*) _____

_____ here for ten years.

8. Before (*go*) _____ to bed, I have to finish my homework.

9. (*Hear*) _____ that story many times before, I got bored when Jim began to tell it again.

10. Do you know that man (*sit*) _____ in the brown leather chair?

11. Many of the goods which (*produce*) _____ since the beginning of the twentieth century are totally machine-made.

12. The instructor said that she (*give*) _____ an exam next Friday.

13. I (*know*) _____ Beth for six years. When I (*meet*) _____ her, she (*work*) _____ in a law office.

14. If you (*be*) _____ here yesterday, you (*meet*) _____ my father and mother.

15. This evening the surface of the lake is completely still. It looks as if it (*make*) _____ of glass.

16. I don't know why the food service has to be so slow. We (*stand*) _____ here in the cafeteria line for over half an hour and there (*be*) _____ still a lot of people in front of us.

17. Sue says she can't come on the picnic with us. I wish she (*change*) _____ her mind and (*decide*) _____ to come with us.

18. My dog turned her head toward me and looked at me quizzically, almost as if she (*understand*) _____ what I said.

19. (*Be*) _____ an excellent researcher, Dr. Barnes (*respect*) _____ by the entire faculty.

20. Without the sun, life as we know it (*exist, not*) _____ .

EXERCISE 20: Same as the preceding exercise.

1. Since (*come*) _____ to the United States six months ago, she (*learn*) _____ a lot of English.

2. Mrs. McKay (*give, already*) _____ birth to the child by the time her husband arrived at the hospital.

3. I recommended that he (*apply*) _____ to at least three universities.

4. Thank you for your help. I never (*be*) _____ able to finish this work without it.

5. Peggy told me she (*be*) _____ here at six tomorrow.

6. (*Sit*) _____ on a park bench and (*watch*) _____ _____ the brightly colored leaves fall gently to the ground, he felt at peace with the world.

7. Why didn't you tell me about this before? I certainly wish I (*inform*) _____ _____ earlier.

8. The large dormitory (*destroy, completely*) _____ by fire last week. Since all of the students (*go*) _____ home for the holidays, there was no loss of life.

9. He blushed when his friend asked him an (*embarrass*) _____ question.

10. She is grown up now. You shouldn't speak to her as if she (*be*) _____ _____ a child.

11. I asked all of the people (*invite*) _____ to the party to RSVP.

12. When the (*puzzle*) _____ student could not figure out the answer to the (*puzzle*) _____ problem, she demanded that I (*give*) _____ her the correct answer, but I insisted that she (*figure*) _____ it out for herself.

13. Ever since I can remember, mathematics (*be*) _____ my favorite subject.

14. The people (*work*) _____ to solve the problems of urban poverty are hopeful that many of these problems (*solve*) _____ _____ within the next ten years.

15. It's a funny story. I'll tell you the details when I (*call*) _____ you tomorrow.

EXERCISE 21–PREPOSITIONS: Supply appropriate prepositions.

1. I am grateful _____ you _____ your assistance.

2. The criminal escaped _____ prison.

3. She is not content _____ the progress she is making.

4. His comments were not relevant _____ the topic under discussion.

5. Have you decided _____ a date for your wedding yet?

6. My boots are made _____ leather.

7. I'm depending _____ you to finish this work for me.

8. She applied _____ admission _____ the university.

9. He dreamed _____ some of his childhood friends last night.

10. He dreams _____ owning his own business someday.

11. The accused woman was innocent _____ the crime with which she was charged.

12. She is friendly _____ everyone.

13. He was proud _____ himself for winning the prize.

14. The secretary provided me _____ a great deal of information.

15. He compared the wedding customs in his country _____ those in the United States.

15

Gerunds and Infinitives - II

EXERCISE 1–PRETEST: In the following, supply an appropriate form, gerund or infinitive, of the verbs in parentheses.

1. She decided (*come*) _____ with us.

2. I enjoy (*talk*) _____ to him.

3. We prepared (*leave*) _____ .

4. Please remind me (*take*) _____ this letter to the post office.

5. I couldn't persuade him (*come*) _____ with us.

6. I wouldn't mind (*be*) _____ a politician.

7. I have no intention of (*change*) _____ my mind.

8. Do you want (*come*) _____ with us?

9. She refused (*talk*) _____ about her problems.

10. I am considering (*go*) _____ to Mexico on my vacation.

11. The teacher encouraged me (*be*) _____ more careful when I write.

12. She keeps (*promise*) _____ to visit us, but she never does.

13. He expects (*graduate*) _____ next June.

14. She put off (*do*) _____ her homework.

15. She seems (*be*) _____ quite intelligent.

16. He begged me (*help*) _____ him.

17. I appreciate your (*take*) _____ the time to help me.

18. I can't afford (*buy*) _____ a new car.

19. He managed (*change*) _____ my mind.

20. I can't help (*wonder*) _____ if I did the right thing.

21. I think he deserves (*have*) _____ another chance.

22. She offered (*lend*) _____ me her umbrella.

23. Carol suggested (*go*) _____ out for dinner.

24. My uncle advised me not (*buy*) _____ a car.

25. My uncle advised not (*buy*) _____ a car.

26. The little boy's mother warned him not (*eat*) _____ dirt.

27. The children are excited about (*go*) _____ swimming.

28. My parents never allowed me (*stay*) _____ out past midnight.

29. He doesn't appear (*be*) _____ more than fourteen or fifteen.

30. Finally she admitted (*be*) _____ responsible for the error.

31. You should practice (*speak*) _____ English at every opportunity.

32. She claims (*be*) _____ twenty-one, but I doubt if she's even eighteen.

33. I don't recall ever (*hear*) _____ you mention his name before.

34. Do you promise not (*tell*) _____ anyone my secret?

35. Finally she completed (*write*) _____ her report.

15-1 REFERENCE LIST OF VERBS FOLLOWED BY GERUNDS

1. *admit*	He **admitted stealing** the money.
2. *advise*	She **advised waiting** until tomorrow.
3. *anticipate*	I **anticipate having** a good time on vacation.
4. *appreciate*	I **appreciate hearing** from them.
5. *avoid*	He **avoided answering** my question.
6. *complete*	I finally **completed writing** my term paper.

7. *consider*	I will **consider going** with you.
8. *delay*	He **delayed leaving** for school.
9. *deny*	She **denied knowing** anything about it.
10. *discuss*	They **discussed opening** a new business.
11. *enjoy*	We **enjoyed visiting** them.
12. *finish*	She **finished studying** about ten.
13. *can't help*	I **can't help worrying** about it.
14. *keep*	I **keep hoping** he will come.
15. *mention*	She **mentioned going** to a movie.
16. *mind*	Would you **mind helping** me with this?
17. *miss*	I **miss being** with my family.
18. *postpone*	Let's **postpone leaving** until tomorrow.
19. *practice*	The athlete **practiced throwing** the ball.
20. *quit*	He **quit trying** to solve the problem.
21. *recall*	I don't **recall meeting** him before.
22. *recommend*	She **recommended seeing** that show.
23. *regret*	I **regret telling** him my secret.
24. *remember*	I can **remember meeting** him when I was a child.
25. *resent*	I **resent her interfering** in my business.
26. *resist*	I couldn't **resist eating** the dessert.
27. *risk*	She **risks losing** all her money.
28. *stop*	She **stopped going** to classes.
29. *suggest*	She **suggested going** to a movie.
30. *tolerate*	She won't **tolerate cheating** during an examination.
31. *understand*	I don't **understand his leaving** school.

15–2 REFERENCE LIST OF VERBS FOLLOWED BY INFINITIVES

A. VERBS FOLLOWED IMMEDIATELY BY AN INFINITIVE

1. *afford*	I can't **afford to buy** it.
2. *agree*	They **agreed to help** us.
3. *appear*	She **appears to be** tired.
4. *arrange*	I'll **arrange to meet** you at the airport.
5. *ask*	He **asked to come** with us.
6. *beg*	He **begged to come** with us.
7. *care*	I don't **care to see** that show.
8. *claim*	She **claims to be** a descendent of George Washington.
9. *consent*	She finally **consented to marry** him.
10. *decide*	I have **decided to leave** on Monday.
11. *demand*	I **demand to know** who is responsible.
12. *deserve*	She **deserves to win** the prize.
13. *expect*	I **expect to enter** graduate school in the fall.

14. *fail*	She **failed to return** the book to the library on time.
15. *forget*	I **forgot to mail** the letter.
16. *hesitate*	Don't **hesitate to ask** for my help.
17. *hope*	Jack **hopes to arrive** next week.
18. *learn*	He **learned to play** the piano.
19. *manage*	She **managed to finish** her work early.
20. *mean*	I didn't **mean to hurt** your feelings.
21. *need*	I **need to have** your opinion.
22. *offer*	They **offered to help** us.
23. *plan*	I am **planning to have** a party.
24. *prepare*	We **prepared to welcome** them.
25. *pretend*	He **pretends not to understand.**
26. *promise*	I **promise not to be** late.
27. *refuse*	I **refuse to believe** his story.
28. *regret*	I **regret to tell** you that you failed.
29. *remember*	I **remembered to lock** the door.
30. *seem*	That cat **seems to be** friendly.
31. *struggle*	I **struggled to stay** awake.
32. *swear*	She **swore to tell** the truth.
33. *threaten*	She **threatened to tell** my parents.
34. *volunteer*	He **volunteered to help** us.
35. *wait*	I will **wait to hear** from you.
36. *want*	I **want to tell** you something.
37. *wish*	She **wishes to come** with us.

B. VERBS FOLLOWED BY A (PRO)NOUN + AN INFINITIVE

38. *advise*	She **advised me to wait** until tomorrow.
39. *allow*	She **allowed me to use** her car.
40. *ask*	I **asked John to help** us.
41. *beg*	They **begged us to come.**
42. *cause*	Her laziness **caused her to fail.**
43. *challenge*	She **challenged me to race** her to the corner.
44. *convince*	I couldn't **convince him to accept** our help.
45. *dare*	He **dared me to do** better than he had done.
46. *encourage*	He **encouraged me to try** again.
47. *expect*	I **expect you to be** on time.
48. *forbid*	I **forbid you to tell** him.
49. *force*	They **forced him to tell** the truth.
50. *hire*	She **hired a boy to mow** the lawn.
51. *instruct*	He **instructed them to be** careful.
52. *invite*	Harry **invited the Johnsons to come** to his party.
53. *need*	We **needed Chris to help** us figure out the solution.
54. *order*	The judge **ordered me to pay** a fine.
55. *permit*	He **permitted the children to stay** up late.

56. *persuade*		**I persuaded him to come** for a visit.
57. *remind*		She **reminded me to lock** the door.
58. *require*		Our teacher **requires us to be** on time.
59. *teach*		My brother **taught me to swim**.
60. *tell*		The doctor **told me to take** these pills.
61. *urge*		**I urged her to apply** for the job.
62. *want*		**I want you to be** happy.
63. *warn*		**I warned you not to drive** too fast.

EXERCISE 2–ORAL (BOOKS CLOSED): Complete the sentence with *doing it* or *to do it*.

> *Example:* I promise . . . .
> *Response:* . . . to do it.

1. I enjoyed . . . .
2. I can't afford . . . .
3. She didn't allow me . . . .
4. We plan . . . .
5. Please remind me . . . .
6. I am considering . . . .
7. They postponed . . . .
8. He persuaded me . . . .
9. I don't mind . . . .
10. He avoided . . . .
11. I refused . . . .
12. I hope . . . .
13. She convinced me . . . .
14. He mentioned . . . .
15. I expect . . . .
16. I encouraged him . . . .
17. I warned him not . . . .
18. We prepared . . . .
19. I don't recall . . . .
20. We decided . . . .
21. They offered . . . .
22. When will you finish . . . .
23. Did you practice . . . .
24. She agreed . . . .
25. Keep . . . .
26. Stop . . . .
27. I didn't force him . . . .
28. I couldn't resist . . . .
29. How did he manage . . . .
30. He admitted . . . .
31. He denied . . . .
32. I didn't mean . . . .
33. She swore . . . .
34. I volunteered . . . .
35. He suggested . . . .
36. He advised me . . . .
37. I struggled . . . .
38. I don't want to risk . . . .
39. He recommended . . . .
40. I miss . . . .

(*To the teacher: Repeat the exercise by having the students complete the sentences with their own words.*)

368

EXERCISE 3: In addition to following certain verbs, infinitives follow certain adjectives, passive verbs, nouns, and pronouns. Notice the examples and then complete the sentences. Use an infinitive in each completion.

(a) He **is lucky to be** alive after the accident.

(b) I was **sorry to hear** the bad news.

(c) I was **surprised to see** him at the party.

(d) She **was ashamed to admit** her mistake.

(e) She has the **ability to make** friends easily.

(f) I asked for **permission to use** the phone.

(g) I have **nothing to say**.

(h) He doesn't have **anyone to help** him.

1. Sam doesn't know how to swim, so he was afraid _____

2. The semester will be over in one more week. I'm anxious_____

3. It was a complicated recipe, so he was careful _____

4. The children are eager _____

5. The weather is likely_____

6. When will you be ready _____

7. Thank you for your kind invitation. I would be pleased_____

8. I was surprised _____ to _____ hear _____ that John was in the hospital.

9. My friend was disappointed _____ learn that she _____

_____

10. The students were relieved _____ find out that _____

_____

11. I have an appointment _____

12. I don't need your permission _____

13. Mexico would be a nice place _____

14. The weekend is the best time _____

15. There are many things_____

16. Do you have a minute? I have something _____

17. He is very lonely. He has no one _____

18. Are you sure you can handle that by yourself? Don't you need someone _____

_____

EXERCISE 4: Complete the following by using infinitives.

1. He's not old enough _____

2. She went to the store _____

3. It is interesting _____

4. I was told not _____

5. It is impolite _____

6. I had to wait in line _____

7. It is advisable for you _____

8. She turned on the television set _____

9. I understood his question, but I was too surprised by it _____

10. It was foolish of you _____

15-3 PASSIVE AND PERFECT FORMS OF INFINITIVES AND GERUNDS

PASSIVE INFINITIVE (*to be + -ed**)	(a) I didn't expect **to be invited** to his party.	In (a): *to be invited* is passive. The understood "*by phrase*" is *by him: I didn't expect to be invited **by him** to his party.*
PASSIVE GERUND (*being + -ed*)	(b) I appreciated **being invited** to your home.	In (b): *being invited* is passive. The understood "*by* phrase" is *by you: I appreciated being invited **by you** to your home.*
		The event expressed by a perfect infinitive or a perfect gerund happened before the time of the main verb.
PERFECT INFINITIVE (*to have + -ed*)	(c) The rain seems **to have stopped.**	In (c): *The rain seems **now** to have stopped **a few minutes ago.***
	(d) The rain seemed **to have stopped.**	In (d): *The rain seemed **at six p.m.** to have stopped **before six p.m.***
PERFECT GERUND (*having + -ed*)	(e) I appreciate **having had** the opportunity to meet the king.	In (e): I met the king yesterday. *I appreciate **now** having had the opportunity to meet the king **yesterday.***
	(f) I appreciated **having had** the opportunity to meet the king.	In (f): I met the king in 1978. *I appreciated **in 1979** having had the opportunity to meet the king **in 1978.***

*-ed = past participle

PERFECT-PASSIVE INFINITIVE *(to have been + -ed)*	(g) Jane is fortunate **to have been given** a scholarship.	In (g): Jane was given a scholarship last month by her government. She is fortunate. *Jane is fortunate now to have been given a scholarship last month by her government.*
PERFECT-PASSIVE GERUND *(having been + -ed)*	(h) I appreciate **having been told** the news.	In (h): I was told the news yesterday by someone. I appreciate that. *I appreciate now having been told the news yesterday by someone.*

EXERCISE 5: Supply an appropriate form for each verb in parentheses.

1. I don't enjoy (*laugh*) ___being laughed___ at by other people.

2. I'm angry at him for (*tell, not*) _____not telling (OR: not having told*)_____ me the truth.

3. It is easy (*fool*) ___to be fooled___ by his lies.

4. Jack had a narrow escape. He was almost hit by a car. He barely avoided (*hit*)

   _____ by the speeding automobile.

5. Sharon wants us to tell her the news as soon as we hear anything. If we find

   out anything about the problem, she wants (*tell*) _____
   about it immediately.

6. Yesterday Anna wrote a check for fifty dollars, but when she wrote it she
   knew she didn't have enough money in the bank to cover it. Today she is very

   worried about (*write*) _____ that check. She has to find a way
   to put some money in her account right away.

7. A: What's the difference between "burn up" and "burn down"?

   B: Hmmm. That's an interesting question. I don't recall ever (*ask*) _____

   _____ that question before.

8. Living in a foreign country has been a good experience for me. I am glad that

   my company sent me here to study. I am very pleased (*give*) _____
   the opportunity to learn about another culture.

9. You must tell me the truth. I insist on (*tell*) _____ the truth.

----

*The perfect gerund is used to emphasize that the action of the gerund took place *before* that of the main verb. However, often there is little difference in meaning between a simple gerund and a perfect gerund.

10. Don't all of us want (*love*) _____ and (*need*) _____
    by other people?

11. I enjoy (*watch*) _____ television in the evenings.

12. Dear Jim,

    I feel guilty about (*write, not*) _____
    to you sooner, but I've been swamped with work lately.

EXERCISE 6: Same as the preceding exercise.

1. Martha doesn't like to have her picture taken. She avoids (*photograph*) _____

   _____ .

2. Tim was in the army during the war. He was caught by the enemy but he

   managed to escape. He is lucky (*escape*) _____ with his
   life.

3. A: It's been nice talking to you. I really have enjoyed our conversation, but I

      have to leave now. I'm very happy (*have*) _____
      this opportunity to meet you and talk with you. Let's try to get together
      again soon.

   B: I'd like that.

4. A: Is Ted a transfer student?

   B: Yes.

   A: Where did he go to school before he came here?

   B: I'm not sure, but I think he mentioned something about (*go*) _____

      _____ to UCLA or USC.

5. A: You know Jim Frankenstein, don't you?

   B: Jim Frankenstein? I don't think so. I don't recall ever (*meet*) _____

      _____ him.

6. A: This letter needs (*send*) _____ immediately. Will
      you take care of it?

   B: Right away.

7. Sally is very quick. You have to tell her how to do something only once. She

   doesn't need (*tell*) _____ twice.

8. A: I thought Sam was sick.

   B: So did I. But he seems (*recover*) _____ very

      quickly. He certainly doesn't seem (*be*) _____ sick
      now.

9. Last year I studied abroad. I appreciate (*have*) _____ the opportunity to live and study in a foreign country.

10. This year I am studying abroad. I appreciate (*have*) _____ this opportunity to live and study in a foreign country.

15-4   USING GERUNDS OR PASSIVE INFINITIVES FOLLOWING *NEED*

(a) I **need to borrow** some money. (b) John **needs to be told** the truth.	Usually an infinitive follows *need,* as in (a) and (b).
(c) The house **needs painting.** (d) The house **needs to be painted.**	In certain situations, a gerund may follow *need.* In this case, the gerund carries a passive meaning. Usually the situations involve fixing or improving something. (c) and (d) have the same meaning.

EXERCISE 7:   Supply an appropriate form for the verbs in parentheses:

1. The chair is broken. I need (*fix*) _____ it. The chair needs (*fix*) _____ .

2. What a mess! This room needs (*clean*) _____ up. We need (*clean*) _____ it up before the company arrives.

3. The baby's diaper needs (*change*) _____ . It's wet.

4. My shirt is wrinkled. It needs (*iron*) _____ .

5. There is a hole in our roof. The roof needs (*repair*) _____ .

6. I have books and papers all over my desk. I need (*take*) _____ some time to straighten up my desk. It needs (*straighten*) _____ up.

7. The apples on the tree are ripe. They need (*pick*) _____ .

8. The dog needs (*wash*) _____ . He's been digging in the mud.

15-5   USING A POSSESSIVE TO MODIFY A GERUND

(a) We are excited about **the fact that Mary is coming to visit us.** (*noun clause*) (b) We are excited about **Mary's coming to visit us.** (*gerund phrase*)	The noun clause in (a) and the gerund phrase in (b) have the same meaning.* A possessive noun or pronoun is used to modify a gerund. In (b): *Mary's* is possessive.

*See Chapter 9 for a discussion of noun clauses.

EXERCISE 8: In the following, change the noun clauses to gerund phrases. Use possessive nouns or pronouns to modify the gerunds.

1. I appreciate the fact that you asked me to help on the research project.

   I appreciate __your_____

2. The fact that he didn't want to go surprised me.

   _____ surprised me.

3. The fact that Ann borrowed my book without telling me made me angry.

   _____ made me angry.

4. I can't understand the fact that he wasn't given a scholarship.

   I can't understand _____

5. The fact that they got married shocked everyone.

   _____ shocked everyone.

6. The fact that the dog was barking alerted me.

   _____ alerted me.

EXERCISE 9: Supply an appropriate form for each verb in parentheses.*

1. Alice didn't expect (*ask*) _____ to Bill's party.

2. I'm not accustomed to (*drink*) _____ coffee with my meals.

3. I'll help you as soon as I finish (*wash*) _____ the dishes.

4. She took a deep breath (*relax*) _____ herself before getting up to give her speech.

5. He left without (*tell*) _____ anyone.

6. It's useless. Give up. Don't keep (*beat*) _____ your head against a brick wall.

7. His (*be, not*) _____ able to come is disappointing.

_____

*This exercise includes verb forms discussed in both Chapter 7 (Gerunds and Infinitives—I) and this chapter.

8. I have considered (*get*) _____ a part-time job (*help*)

   _____ pay for my school expenses.

9. I hope (*award*) _____ a scholarship for the coming
   semester.

10. Please forgive me for (*be, not*) _____ here to help you
    yesterday.

11. (*Help*) _____ the disadvantaged children learn how

    (*read*) _____ was a rewarding experience.

12. We have fifty pages (*read*) _____ for class tomorrow.

13. He wants (*like*) _____ and (*trust*) _____

    _____ by everyone.

14. I can't help (*wonder*) _____ why he did such a foolish
    thing.

15. He is very lucky (*choose*) _____ by the committee as
    their respresentative to the meeting in Paris.

16. (*Live*) _____ in a city has certain advantages.

17. I'm used to (*go*) _____ to bed early.

18. Keep on (*do*) _____ whatever you were doing. I didn't

    mean (*interrupt*) _____ you.

19. It is very kind of you (*take*) _____ care of that problem for me.

20. She opened the window (*let*) _____ in some fresh air.

21. They agreed (*cooperate*) _____ with us to the fullest
    extent.

22. Did you remember (*turn*) _____ in your assignment?

23. I don't remember ever (*hear*) _____ that story before.

24. Do you regret (*leave*) _____ home and (*come*) _____

    _____ to a foreign country (*study*) _____

    _____?*

Regret may be followed by either a gerund or an infinitive, but the intended meaning is different. If followed by a gerund, *regret* indicates that the speaker is sorry about something that happened in the past. If followed by an infinitive, *regret* indicates that the speaker is sorry about something that occurs or occurred at the same moment.

25. I regret (*say*) _____ that I can't come to your party. I wish I could come, but I've already made other plans.

EXERCISE 10: Same as the preceding exercise.

1. He wouldn't let them (*take*) _____ his picture.

2. I couldn't understand what the passage said, so I had my friend (*translate*) _____ it for me.

3. No, that's not what I meant (*say*) _____. How can I make you (*understand*) _____?

4. I have finally assembled enough information (*begin*) _____ writing my thesis.

5. It's a serious problem. Something needs (*do*) _____ about it soon.

6. I was terribly disappointed (*discover*) _____ that he had lied to me.

7. I had the operator (*put*) _____ the call through for me.

8. No one could make him (*feel*) _____ afraid. He refused (*intimidate*) _____ by anyone.

9. I don't see how she can possibly avoid (*fail*) _____ the course.

10. Do something! Don't just sit there (*twiddle*) _____ your thumbs.

11. She stopped her car (*let*) _____ a black cat (*run*) _____ across the street.

12. He's a terrific soccer player! Did you see him (*make*) _____ that last goal?

13. We spent the entire class period (*talk*) _____ about the revolution.

14. She got along very well in France despite not (*be*) _____ able to speak French.

15. Mary Beth suggested (*go*) _____ on a picnic.

16. I don't like (*force*) _____ (*leave*) _____ the room (*study*) _____

whenever my roommate feels like (*have*) _____ a party.

17. He's at an awkward age. He's old enough (*have*) _____ adult problems but too young (*know*) _____ how (*handle*) _____ them.

18. (*Look*) _____ at the car after the accident made him (*realize*) _____ that he was indeed lucky (*be*) _____ _____ alive.

19. We sat in his kitchen (*sip*) _____ very hot, strong tea and (*eat*) _____ chunks of hard cheese.

20. I admit (*be*) _____ a little nervous about the job interview. I don't know what (*expect*) _____ .

21. I'm tired. I wouldn't mind just (*stay*) _____ home tonight and (*get*) _____ to bed early.

22. It is the ancient task of the best artists among us (*force*) _____ _____ us (*use*) _____ our ability (*feel*) _____ and (*share*) _____ emotions.

23. Please speak softly. My roommate is in the other room (*sleep*) _____ _____ .

24. I don't anticipate (*have*) _____ any difficulties (*adjust*) _____ to a different culture when I go abroad.

25. She expected (*admit*) _____ to the university, but she wasn't.

EXERCISE 11: Verb form review. The following is based on compositions written by students who were members of a multicultural class.

Next week, when I _____ _____
  (finish) *(take)*

my final examinations, I _____ one of the best experiences I
  (finish, also)

_____ in my lifetime. In the last four months, I _____
  (have, ever)

_____ more about foreign cultures than I _____
  (learn) *(anticipate)*

before _____ to the United States. _____
  (come) *(Live)*

in a foreign country and _____ to school with people from
  (go)

various parts of the world _____ me the opportunity _____
  (give)

_____ and _____ with people from
  (encounter) *(interact)*

different cultures. I _____ to share some of my experiences
  (like)

and thoughts with you.

When I first _____, I _____ no
  (arrive) *(know)*

one and I _____ all of my fingers _____
  (need) *(communicate)*

what I was trying to say in English. All of the foreign students were in the same

situation. When we _____ the right word, we _____
  (can find, not)

_____ strange movements and gestures _____
  (use) *(communicate)*

our meaning. _____ some common phrases, such as "How
  (Know)

are you?" "Fine, thank you, and you?" and "What country are you from?",

_____ enough in the beginning for us _____
  (be) *(make)*

friends with each other. The TV room in the dormitory _____
(become)

our meeting place every evening after dinner. _____
(Hope)

_____ our English, many of us tried to watch television
(improve)

and _____ what the people _____
(understand)   (appear)

on the screen _____, but for the most part their words
(say)

were just a strange mumble to us. After a while, _____
(bore)

and a little sad, we slowly began to disappear to our rooms. I _____
(think)

that all of us _____ some homesickness. However, despite
(experience)

my loneliness, I had a good feeling within myself because I _____
(do)

what I _____ to do for many years: _____
(want)   (live)

and _____ in a foreign country.
(study)

After a few days, classes _____ and we _____
(begin)

_____ another meeting place: the classroom.
(have)

_____ quite what _____ the first
(Know, not)   (expect)

day of class, I was a bit nervous, but also _____. After
(excite)

_____ the right building and the right room, I walked in
(find)

and _____ an empty seat. I _____
(choose)   (introduce)

myself to the person _____ next to me, and we sat

(*sit*)

_____ for a few minutes. Since we _____

(*talk*)   (*be*)

from different countries, we _____ in English. At first, I

(*speak*)

was afraid that the other student _____ what I

(*understand, not*)

_____ , but I _____ when she

(*say*)   (*surprise, pleasantly*)

_____ to my questions easily. Together we _____

(*respond*)   (*take*)

the first steps toward _____ a friendship.

(*build*)

As the semester _____ , I _____

(*progress*)   (*find*)

out more and more about my fellow students. Students from some countries were

reticent and shy in class. They almost never _____ questions

(*ask*)

and _____ very softly. Others of different nationalities

(*speak*)

_____ just the opposite: they spoke in booming voices and

(*be*)

never _____ _____ questions—and

(*hesitate*)   (*ask*)

sometimes they _____ the teacher. I _____

(*interrupt, even*)   (*be, never*)

in a classroom with such a mixture of cultures before. I learned _____

(*surprise, not*)

by anything my classmates might say or do. The time we spent _____

(*share*)

our ideas with each other and _____ about each other's

(*learn*)

customs and beliefs _____ valuable and fun. As we pro-

(*be*)

gressed in our English, we slowly learned about each other, too.

Now, several months after my arrival in the United States, I _____

(be)

able to understand not only some English but also something about different cul-

tures. If I _____ here, I _____ able

        (come, not)   *(be, not)*

to attain these insights into other cultures. I wish everyone in the world

_____ the same experience. Perhaps if all the people in the

        (have)

world _____ more about cultures different from their own

        (know)

and _____ the opportunity _____

        (have)   *(make)*

friends with people from different countries, peace _____

                                        (be)

secure.

EXERCISE 12–WRITTEN: Following are composition topics.

1. Summarize the major events that have occurred in your country and/or in the world in the past three or four months.

2. *For students who have been using this text in a multicultural class:*
   This class has given you the opportunity to meet and interact with students from countries other than your own. Describe your experiences and discuss any insights you might have made into other cultures.

3. What advice would you give to a person who wants to learn English as a second language?

Basic Grammar Terminology

0-1 SUBJECTS, VERBS, AND OBJECTS

S   V (a)   **Birds** **fly**.   (*noun*) (*verb*)

S   V
(a)   **Birds** **fly**.
    (*noun*) (*verb*)

    S   V
(b) The **baby** **cried**.
     (*noun*) (*verb*)

      S   V   O
(c) The **student needs** a **pen.**
     (*noun*) (*verb*) (*noun*)

     S   V   O
(d) My **friend enjoyed** the **party.**
    (*noun*) (*verb*)   (*noun*)

Almost all English sentences contain a subject (S) and a verb (V). The verb may or may not be followed by an object (O).

VERBS: Verbs that are not followed by an object are called *intransitive verbs*. (In a dictionary, these verbs are noted as *v.i.*) The verbs in (a) and (b) are intransitive.

Verbs that are followed by an object are called *transitive verbs* (*v.t.* in a dictionary). The verbs in (c) and (d) are transitive.

Some verbs are either intransitive or transitive:

   intransitive: A student studies.
   transitive: A student studies books.

Examples of verbs: *walk, talk, see, go, laugh, contain, decide, want, arrive*

SUBJECTS AND OBJECTS: The subjects and objects of verbs are nouns (or pronouns—see 0-6).

Examples of nouns: *person, place, thing, pen, door, John, information, appearance, amusement*

0-2 PREPOSITIONS AND PREPOSITIONAL PHRASES

Common prepositions:			
about	beside	like	till
above	between	near	to
across	beyond	of	toward
after	by	off	under
along	despite	on	until
among	down	out	up
around	during	over	upon
before	for	since	with
behind	from	through	within
below	in	throughout	without
beneath	into		

	S V PREP O of PREP
	(a) The student studies **in** **the library.**
	                              (*noun*)
	         S V O PREP O of PREP
	(b) My brother enjoyed the party **at** **your house.**
	                                  (*noun*)
		An important element of English sentences is the prepositional phrase. It consists of a preposition (PREP) and its object (O). The object of a preposition is a noun or pronoun. In (a): *in the library* is a prepositional phrase.

(c) We went **to the zoo** **in the afternoon.** (*place*) (*time*)	In (c): In most English sentences, *place* comes before *time*.
(d) In the afternoon, we went to the zoo.	In (d): Sometimes a prepositional phrase comes at the beginning of a sentence.

0-3 ADJECTIVES

(a) Mary is an **intelligent** **student.**
           (*adjective*) (*noun*)
(b) We are enjoying the **nice**   **weather.**
                 (*adjective*) (*noun*)
	Adjectives describe nouns. In grammar, we say that adjectives *modify* nouns. The word *modify* means "change a little." Adjectives give a little different meaning to a noun: *intelligent student, lazy student, good student.*
	Examples of adjectives: *young, old, rich, poor, beautiful, simple*

0-4 ADVERBS

(a) He walks **quickly**.
      (*adverb*)
(b) They talked to each other **quietly**.
                     (*adverb*)
	Adverbs modify verbs. Often they answer the question *"How?"* In (a): *How does he walk?* Answer: *Quickly.* Adverbs are often formed by adding *-ly* to an adjective.
	adjective: quick
	adverb: quickly

(c) **Quickly** he walked to the door. (d) He **quickly** walked to the door. (e) He walked to the door **quickly**.	Adverbs may be found in various places in a sentence.
(f) I am **extremely happy** about the good news. (*adverb*) (*adjective*)	Adverbs are also used to modify adjectives, i.e., to give information about adjectives.
(g) The children **often** go to the zoo. (*adverb*)	Adverbs are also used to express time or frequency. Examples: *today, yesterday, tomorrow, soon, never, usually, always, seldom*

0-5 THE VERB *BE*

(a) John **is a student**.
         (*noun*)
(b) John **is intelligent**.
         (*adjective*)
(c) John **is at the library**.
         (*prep. phrase*)
	A sentence with *be* as the main verb has three basic patterns:
	In (a): *be + a noun*
	In (b): *be + an adjective*
	In (c): *be + a prepositional phrase*

(d) Mary **is writing** a letter. (e) They **were listening** to some music.	*Be* is also used as an auxiliary verb (i.e., a helping verb) in certain verb tenses. In (d): *is = auxiliary verb* *writing = main verb*

TENSE FORMS OF *BE*

Simple Present	*Simple Past*	*Present Perfect*
I am	I was	I have been
you are	you were	you have been
he, she, it is	he, she, it was	he, she, it has been
we, you, they are	we, you, they were	we, you, they have been

0-6 PERSONAL PRONOUNS

	SINGULAR	PLURAL	A pronoun is used in place of a noun. It refers to a noun which comes before it. The noun it refers to is called the *antecedent*.
SUBJECT PRONOUNS	I	we	
	you	you	Example: I read the *book*. *It* was good. The noun *book* is the antecedent for *it*.
	he, she, it	they	
OBJECT PRONOUNS	me	us	Examples of possessive pronoun usage:
	you	you	*It is my book. It is mine.*
	him, her, it	them	*This is your coat. This is yours.*
POSSESSIVE PRONOUNS	my, mine	our, ours	
	your, yours	your, yours	Examples of reflexive pronoun usage:
	his, her–hers, its	their, theirs	*I look at myself in the mirror.*
REFLEXIVE PRONOUNS	myself	ourselves	*He helps himself.*
	yourself	yourselves	
	himself, herself, itself	themselves	

0-7 ARTICLES: *A, AN,* AND *THE*

(a) I bought **a book** yesterday.	*A* is an article. It is used in front of singular nouns that you can count: one book, two books, three books, etc. This kind of noun is called a *count noun.*
(b) Bob saw **an elephant.**	*An* is used, instead of *a,* in front of count nouns that begin with a vowel (*a, e, i, o,* or *u*) or vowel sound.
(c) I would like **some water.**	*A* is not used in front of nouns that you cannot count. This kind of noun is called a *noncount noun.* In (c): *water* is a noncount noun. *Some* is frequently used in front of a noncount noun.
(d) I bought **some books** yesterday.	*Some* is also used with plural count nouns, as in (d).
(e) **The sun** is bright today.	*The* is also an article. There are many different situations in which *the* is used, but generally *the* is used when both the speaker and listener have a specific thing or person in mind; they are both thinking about the same thing or person. In (e): The speaker and listener are both thinking about the same sun.

(f) Please close **the door**.	In (f): Both the speaker and listener are thinking about the same door: the door in this room, the door that is open.
(g) Yesterday I saw **a dog**. **The dog** was running after **a cat**. **The cat** was running after **a mouse**. **The mouse** ran into **a hole**. **The hole** was very small.	*The* is used the second time a speaker mentions a noun. In (g): *the dog* = the dog that the speaker was talking about in the first sentence, the dog that the speaker saw yesterday.
(h) **A student** came into the room. I looked at **the student**. (i) **Some students** came into the room. I looked at **the students**. (j) I drank **some water**. **The water** was very cold.	*The* may be used with any noun: In (h): *the student* = singular count noun In (i): *the students* = plural count noun In (j): *the water* = noncount noun

Preposition Combinations

0-8 TWO-WORD VERBS

The term *two-word verb* refers to a verb and preposition which together have a special meaning. Two-word verbs are especially common in informal English. Following is a list of common two-word verbs and their usual meanings. (This list contains only those two-word verbs which are used in the exercises in the text.)*

A   ask out . . . . *ask someone to go on a date*

B   bring about, bring on . . . . *cause*

      bring up . . . . *(1) rear children; (2) mention or introduce a topic*

---

*The two-word verbs marked with an asterisk are *nonseparable*.

(1) *Separable two-word verbs:*

With a separable two-word verb, a noun may come either between the verb and the preposition or after the preposition. A pronoun comes between the verb and the preposition.

Example: *I handed my paper in.*   *I handed in my paper.*   *I handed it in.*

(2) *Nonseparable two-word verbs:*

With a nonseparable two-word verb, a noun or pronoun must follow the preposition.

Example: *I ran into an old friend yesterday.*   *I ran into her yesterday.*

C call back . . . . *return a telephone call*

call in . . . . *ask to come to an official place for a specific purpose*

call off . . . . *cancel*

*call on . . . . (1) *ask to speak in class;* (2) *visit*

call up . . . . *call on the telephone*

*catch up (with) . . . . *reach the same position or level*

*check in, check into . . . . . . *register at a hotel*

*check into . . . . *investigate*

check out . . . .(1) *take a book from the library;* (2) *investigate*

*check out (of) . . . . *leave a hotel*

cheer up . . . . *make (someone) feel happier*

clean up . . . . *make clean and orderly*

*come across . . . . *meet by chance*

cross out . . . . *draw a line through*

cut out . . . . *stop an annoying activity*

D do over . . . . *do again*

*drop by, drop in (on) . . . . . . *visit informally*

drop off . . . . *leave something/someone at a place*

*drop out (of) . . . . *stop going to school, to a class, to a club, etc.*

F figure out . . . . *find the answer by reasoning*

fill out . . . . *write the completions of a questionnaire or official form*

find out . . . . *discover information*

G *get along (with) . . . . *exist satisfactorily*

get back (from) . . . . (1) *return from a place;* (2) *receive again*

*get in, get into . . . . (1) *enter a car;* (2) *arrive*

*get off . . . . *leave an airplane, a bus, a train, a subway, a bicycle*

*get on . . . . *enter an airplane, a bus, a train, a subway, a bicycle*

*get out of . . . . (1) *leave a car;* (2) *avoid work or an unpleasant activity* *get over . . . . *recover from an illness*

*get through . . . . *finish*

*get up . . . . *arise from bed, a chair*

give back . . . . *return an item to someone*

give up . . . . *stop trying*

*go over . . . . *review or check carefully*

*grow up (in) . . . . *become an adult*

H   hand in . . . . *submit an assignment*

hang up . . . . *(1) conclude a telephone conversation; (2) put clothes on a hanger or a hook*

have on . . . . *wear*

K   keep out (of) . . . . *not enter*

*keep up (with) . . . . *stay at the same position or level*

kick out (of) . . . . *force (someone) to leave*

L   *look after . . . . *take care of*

*look into . . . . *investigate*

*look out (for) . . . . *be careful*

look over . . . . *review or check carefully*

look up . . . . *look for information in a reference book*

M   make up . . . . *(1) invent; (2) do past work*

N   name after, name for . . . . *give a baby the name of someone else*

P   *pass away . . . . *die*

pass out . . . . *(1) distribute; (2) lose consciousness*

pick out . . . . *select*

pick up . . . . *(1) go to get someone (e.g., in a car); (2) take in one's hand*

point out . . . . *call attention to*

put away . . . . *remove to a proper place*

put back . . . . *return to original place*

put off . . . . *postpone*

put on . . . . *put clothes on one's body*

put out . . . . *extinguish a cigarette or cigar*

*put up with . . . . *tolerate*

R   *run into, *run across . . . . *meet by chance*

    run out (of) . . . . finish a supply of something

S   *show up . . . . *appear, come*

    shut off . . . . *stop a machine, light, faucet*

T   *take after . . . . *resemble*

    take off . . . . *(1) remove clothing; (2) leave on a trip*

    take out . . . . *(1) take someone on a date; (2) remove*

    take over . . . . *take control*

    take up . . . . *begin a new activity or topic*

    tear down . . . . *demolish; reduce to nothing*

    tear up . . . . *tear into many little pieces*

    think over . . . . *consider carefully*

    throw away, throw out . . . . . *discard; get rid of*

    throw up . . . . *vomit; regurgitate food*

    try on . . . . *put on clothing to see if it fits*

    turn down . . . . *decrease volume or intensity*

    turn in . . . . *(1) submit an assignment; (2) go to bed*

    turn off . . . . *stop a machine, light, faucet*

    turn on . . . . *begin a machine, light, faucet*

    turn out . . . . *extinguish a light*

    turn up . . . . *increase volume or intensity*

0-9   PREPOSITION COMBINATIONS WITH ADJECTIVES AND VERBS†

A   *be* absent from
    accuse of
  be accustomed to
  be acquainted with
  be afraid of
    agree with
  be angry at, with
    apologize for
    apply to, for
    approve of
    argue with
    arrive in, at

  be aware of

B   believe in
    blame for

C   *be* capable of
    care about, for
  be committed to
    compare to, with
    complain about
  be composed of
    consist of

†This list contains only those preposition combinations used in the exercises in the text.

be content with
contribute to
count (up)on
cover with

D decide (up)on
be dedicated to
depend (up)on
be devoted to
be disappointed in, with
distinguish from
be divorced from
be done with
dream of, about
be dressed in

E *be* engaged to
be envious of
escape from
excel in
be excited about
excuse for

F *be* faithful to
be familiar with
fight for
be finished with
be fond of
forgive for
be friendly to, with

G *be* grateful to, for
be guilty of

H hide from
hope for

I *be* innocent of
insist (up)on
be interested in

J *be* jealous of

K *be* known for

L look forward to

M *be* made of, from
be married to

O object to
be opposed to

P participate in
be patient with
be polite to
pray for
prevent from
prohibit from
protect from
be proud of
provide with

R recover from
be related to
be relevant to
rely (up)on
rescue from
respond to
be responsible for

S *be* satisfied with
be scared of
stare at
stop from
subscribe to
substitute for
succeed in

T take advantage of
take care of
be terrified of
thank for
be tired of, from

V vote for

W *be* worried about

Guide for Correcting Compositions

To the student: Each number represents an area of usage. Your teacher will use these numbers when marking your writing to indicate that you have made an error. Refer to this list to find out what kind of error you have made and then make the necessary correction.

1	SINGULAR-PLURAL	He have been here for six month. (①...①) *He has been here for six months.*
2	WORD FORM	I saw a beauty picture. (②) *I saw a beautiful picture.*
3	WORD CHOICE	She got on the taxi. (③) *She got into the taxi.*
4	VERB TENSE	He is here since June. (④) *He has been here since June.*
5+	ADD A WORD	I want ∧ go to the zoo. (⑤+) *I want to go to the zoo.*
5-	OMIT A WORD	She entered to the university. (⑤-) *She entered the university.*

6   WORD ORDER

⑥

I saw five times that movie.
I saw that movie five times.

7   INCOMPLETE SENTENCE

⑦

I went to bed. Because I was tired.
I went to bed because I was tired.

8   SPELLING

⑧

An accident occured.
An accident occurred.

9   PUNCTUATION

⑨

What did he say.
What did he say?

10   CAPITALIZATION

⑩

I am studying english.
I am studying English.

11   ARTICLE

⑪

I had a accident.
I had an accident.

12?   MEANING NOT CLEAR

⑫?

He borrowed some smoke.
(? ? ?)

13   RUN-ON SENTENCE*

⑬

My roommate was sleeping, we didn't want to wake her up.
My roommate was sleeping. We didn't want to wake her up.

---

*A run-on sentence occurs when two sentences are incorrectly connected: the end of one sentence and the beginning of the next sentence are not properly marked by a period and a capital letter or by a semicolon. (See 10–3 and 11–9.)

Index

*Information given in footnotes to charts or exercises is noted by the page number plus *fn.*:
e.g., 46*fn.*